TEMPLES OF INDIA

TEMPLES OF INDIA

Editor-in-Chief
Swami Chidatman Jee Maharaj

ANMOL PUBLICATIONS PVT. LTD.
NEW DELHI - 110 002 (INDIA)

ANMOL PUBLICATIONS PVT. LTD.
H.O.: 4374/4B, Ansari Road, Daryaganj,
New Delhi-110 002 (India)
Ph.: 23278000, 23261597
B.O.: No. 1015, Ist Main Road, BSK IIIrd Stage
IIIrd Phase, IIIrd Block,
Bangalore - 560 085 (India)
Visit us at: www.anmolpublications.com

Temples of India

First Published, 2009
ISBN 978-81-261-3604-9

PRINTED IN INDIA

Printed at Mehra Offset Press, Delhi.

Contents

Preface

India colourful and vibrant, a land as diverse as its people. A mosaic of faiths, cultures, customs and languages that blend harmoniously to form a composite whole. One of the world's oldest living civilizations—which gave to the world—the concept of zero, the primordial sound Aum..., Yoga and Buddhism.

She is old. She is young. The two diametrically opposite, different yet unique and dynamic faces of India coexist even at this turn of the millennium. With a history of heritage, learning and civilisation dating back to almost 5000 years or perhaps even more, the modern India presents itself as an ideal country. From snow clad mountains to breezy sparkling blue sea side. From arid deserts with shifting sand dunes to lush green country sides. From ancient relics and architectural ruins dating back into antiquity to modern cities, India has it all.

To the north it is bordered by the world's highest mountain chain, where foothill valleys cover the northernmost of the country's maximum states. Further south, plateaus, tropical rain forests and sandy deserts are bordered by palm fringed beaches. Its southernmost tip is the meeting point of three Oceans.

India is a land of staggering contrast with a mingling of the tradition and modernity that is an unique experience to be in India. One will forever remember the stay in this wonderful Homeland-a land truly of mystery and enchantment. Only India can offer such an astonishing variety of contrasts.

She has given birth to numerous spiritual leaders and founders of some of the popular religions of the present day world. India probably has the most religious diversity in any country. It's the birthplace of Hinduism, Buddhism, Sikhism and Jainism and is among the few places to have a resident

Zoroastrian population. India with her veritable treasure trove of culture, mysticism, philosophy, art, music and architecture to name a few. Much of India's classical music is devotional and the North Indian Hindustani and South Indian Carnatic streams are distinct and both have a complex 'raga' framework. The legacy of dance in India is tremendous. The classical dances of India are numerous such as Kathakali of Kerala, Bharatnatyam of Tamil Nadu, Kuchipudi of Andhra Pradesh, Manipuri and Odissi from Orissa are the prominent dance forms in this country that sways to an altogether novel beat. The Yakshagana, nautanki and puppetry are ancient folk forms that live on till date. The earliest specimens of Indian painting are the ones on the walls of the Ajanta Caves dating back to 2nd century BC. The Mughals had a huge impact on Indian art. The influence of Persian art brought placid garden scenes, illustrations from myths, legends and history into Indian art. Word craft, handicrafts, architecture and sculpture all contribute to this rich and varied domain. Indian literature, both in English and in the vernacular, is ever more popular around the world.

The book aims at presenting perspectives of different aspects of Indian culture. It has topics on Indian classical music and dance, painting, ayurveda and yoga which are traditional and indigenous system of physical and mental wellbeing, language, philosophy and excellence achievements by Indian in the different branches of science and social sciences. It also includes our ancient religious and classic literature.

It is hoped that this book will be welcomed by the general readers as also scholars who are interested in the Indian heritage.

—Editors

1

Hindu Temples in Andhra Pradesh

Ahobilam

Ahobilam or Ahobalam is a major centre of pilgrimage in south India. According to the legend, this is where Lord Narasimha blessed Prahlada and killed the demon Hiranyakashipa. It is an important place of worship for Vaishnavas. It is one of the 108 Divya desam.

Ahobilam is located in the Nandyal Taluka of Kurnool district in Andhra Pradesh, India. It is located at a distance of 40 km from Nandyal, and is conveniently accessibly by bus from Nandyal, Kurnool and Hyderabad. *Ahobilam* is not connected by rail; the closest railway stations are Nandyal (on the Bangalore-Vizag (Vishakapatnam) route) and Cuddapah (on the Mumbai-Chennai route).

The Temple

There are nine temples around the Nallamala Forest range. Few temples can be reached through trekking. Some temples are inside the cave. Some temples are very difficult to trek. However, this is disputed by other historical data, which indicates that Multan in Pakistan was formerly Mulastan, which used to have a large Narasimha worshipping Vaishnava community.

The temples were later destroyed by Islamic invaders, and the residents killed or forcibly converted to Islam. The holy shrines of Ahobilam (all the Nava are Nine Nrusimhars) are eulogized by Thirumangai Mannan. Hence Ahobilam is one of the 106 Divya Desams. The hereditary powers of the temple rest with the Pontiff HH Azhagiyasingar of Ahobila Mutt. Currently the 45th Jeer of this lineage is the reigning Pontiff. The Azhagiyasingars have the unique privilege of being Aradhakars to a Divya Desam (a distinction no other Pontiff enjoys). Occasionally when HH Jeer performs Mangalasasanam (pays respects at the temple) at Ahobilam, the Serthi Utsavam is performed (the Moolavar of Malola Nrusimhar and the Utsavar) are united.

This place was visited by Lord Chaitanya Mahaprabhu and it is located in remote place far away from main roads. The Nallamala hills are personified as Adisesha with his head at Tirumala, middle at Ahobilam and the tail at Srisailam.

Legend

According to legend it is believed that when the Devas saw the manifestation of Lord Vishnu as half lion half man they shouted "Ahobala" (great strength) as well as "Ahobila" (great cave in which the current sanctum is). Hence this place could be called "Ahobalam" or "Ahobilam". Another Legend talks about that Lord Garuda did penance to see Lord Vishnu in Lord Narasimha form. Hence, Lord Narasimha took nine different forms in this hill. Lord Narasimha in nine forms are

Varaha Narasimhar

Malola Narasimhar

Yogananda Narasimhar

Pavana Narasimhar

Karaancha Narasimhar

Chatra Vata Narasimhar

Bhargava Narasimhar

Jwala Narasimhar

Ahobila Narasimhar

Legend also states that Goddess Mahalakshmi was took birth as a tribe named Chenchu Lakshmi and married Lord Narasimha after the death of Hiranyakashpa.

Sri Ahobilam Mahatyam

The Lord Narasimha is a vara prasaddhi (boon giver). He is the Lord who had taken a special Lion Man form in order to save his devotee. He is there in different form as Ugra Murthi, Shanta Murthy, Yoga Murthy and Kalyana Murthy with his consort Sri Mahalakshmi.

Prasadam

Temples which is present in cave does not have any specific prasadam. Pilgrims offer some fruits for the Lord inside the cave. The temple which is accessible has the Vaishanava traditional prasadams. The local tribes used to offer their traditional offerings to Lord Narasimha.

Amararama

Amararama is one of the Pancharama Kshetras which is located at Amaravati town near Guntur City in Andhra Pradesh in South India. Lord Shiva is known as Amareswara Swamy or Amaralingeswara Swamy here. The temple is situated on the southern bank of Krishna River. The consort of Lord Amareswara Swamy is Bala Chamundika. The Shivalinga at this place is installed and established by Lord Indra.

Vasireddy Venkatadri Naidu, King of Chintapalli and later Dharanikota, was a great devotee of Amaralingeswara. He expanded and renovated the temple. The popular legend has it that once during the course of putting down a rebellion in his land the King had to have recourse to a massacre of the Chenchus, whereupon he lost his mental peace, which he regained only when he came to Amaravati. He shifted his place from Chintapalli to Amaravati in 1796, and devoted his entire life, time and revenues to building temples to Lord Shiva.

He renovated the Amareswaraswamy temple here, got nine learned archakas to be brought for the daily archana of the Lord, and provided them with all the needs of livelihood, including 12 acres of land to each. The temple as it stands owes much to him.

Amaravati temple has also a wealth of inscriptions on its walls like those of the Kota chiefs of Amaravati and of Sri

Krishandevaraya, the great Vijayanagara emperor. On a pillar in the Mukhamantapa the wife of Proli Nayudu, a Kota king, has left an inscription.

The main festivals in the temple are the Mahashivaratri, which comes in the Magha Bahula Dasami and the Navaratri and the Kalyana Utsavas. Amaravati is thus an important Kshetra situated at a particularly sacred spot of the holy river Krishna and is a consecrated place of worship, of importance to both Buddhism and Hinduism.

Arasavalli

Arasavalli is an ancient Hindu temple dedicted to the Sun god Surya, located near Srikakulam town of Andhra Pradesh, India. It has Suryanarayana Swamy (Sun God) as the presiding deity. Ratha Saptami is the most important festival which is celebrated in this temple.

People suffering with eye and skin diseases are believed to be cured by the god at this temple. The temple is believed to have been built in the 7th Century AD by the Kalinga rulers Devendra Varma of Orissa..

Basar—Saraswathi Temple

The Saraswathy Temple in Basar is located in Adilabad Dist of Andhra Pradesh, India. It is about 200 km from Hyderabad and 50 km from Nizamabad. Also Basar Station from Mumbai is about 600 km by Train on the new Secunderabad-Mumbai Devagiri Express.

The Saraswathy Temple in Ananthasagar is located inMedak Dist of Andhra Pradesh, India. It is about 120 km from Hyderabad and 20km from Siddipet. it is solely built by Ashtavadhani Sri Astakala Narasimha Rama Sharma here saraswathi is in standing Posture and unique of its kind in the world.

Bhattiprolu

Bhattiprolu is a small village in Guntur District of Andhra Pradesh State in Southern India.

History

The original name of Bhattiprolu was Pratipalapura a flourishing Buddhist town in the ancient Sala kingdom that predated Andhra Satavahanas. From available inscriptional evidence, King Kubera was ruling over Bhattiprolu around 230 BCE. Bhattiprolu is well known for its Buddha stupa (Chinna Lanja dibba and Vikramarka kota dibba) built about 3rd-2nd century BCE. During excavations at Bhattiprolu there has been found linguistic evidence of a South Indian language that belongs to 3rd Century BCE, and the progenitor of Brahmi script, well known as Bhattiprolu script to historians. Merchants took the script to Southeast Asia where it parented the scripts of Mon, Burmese, Thai, Khmer, Javanese and Balinese languages. Their similarities to Telugu script can be discerned even today.

The Stupa

Three mounds were discovered in Bhattiprolu in 1870. In 1892 when excavations were undertaken by Alexander Rea, three inscribed stone relic caskets containing crystal caskets, relics of Buddha and jewels were found. The stupa was found to be 40 meters in diameter with an additional basement of 2.4 meters wide running all around. The most significant discovery is the crystal relic casket of sarira dhatu of the Buddha from the central mass of the stupas. The Mahachaitya (great stupa) remains of a large pillared hall, a large group of ruined votive stupas with several images of Buddha, a stone receptacle containing copper vessel, which in turn, contained two more, a silver casket and with in it, a gold casket enclosing beads of bone and crystal were found.

The Script

The earliest evidence of Brahmi script in South India comes from Bhattiprolu. The script was written on an urn containing Buddha's relics. Historians surmise that this script gave rise to the Telugu and Tamil scripts. Bhattiprolu had been a great centre of Buddhism since pre-Mauryan times (4th century BCE). From there Buddhism spread to east Asia, giving rise to the modern Thai, Burmese, Javanese and Balinese scripts which bear a strong resemblance to the Telugu script. The script also spread to the Rayalaseema region.

Chilkur Balaji

Chilkur Balaji Temple is located at Chilkur in Moinabad mandal in the Rangareddi district, Andhra Pradesh, India.

This temple is also popularly known as Visa Temple because many devotees come here with the wish of going abroad.

It's customary to go around the temple (known as Pradakshina) eleven times and pray to god for a specific wish. Once this wish comes true, the recipient has to go again and take 108 Pradakshinas.

This is one of the few temples in India which does not accept monetary donations.

Chilkur balaji temple is one of the most famous temples in Hyderabad area. The nice concept that is implemented in darshan of the lord balaji, is that all people must stand in queue with utmost discipline. There are no VIP passes and there is no Hundi for donations. When people ask for wish from the god here, they have to do 11 pradakshinas and ask their wish with the witness of Lord Anjaneya. When the wish gets fulfiled, they need to do 108 pradakshinas. The 11 pradakshinas have a significant meaning according to the temple priests. When people wish anything from god, mind has to think about only god and one's self i.e 11(1-1) signifies that god takes care of everybody and everybody should understand that.

History

Twenty Five kilometres from Hyderabad off the Vikarabad road and on the banks of Osmansagar is the picturesque village of Chikur with its ancient temple dedicated to Sri Balaji Venkateshwara. From the style, structure and appearance, it can be inferred that the temple was built half a millennium ago. Set in sylvan surroundings, the temple attracts thousands of pilgrims every year and is an ideal place for sequestered retreat and meditation. It enjoyed in the past, great days of pomp and glory.

The temple is one of the oldest in Telengana, having been built during the time of Akkanna and Madanna, the uncles of Bhakta Ramdas. According to tradition, a devotee who used to visit Tirupati every year could not do so on one occasion owing to serious ill-health. Lord Venkateshwara appeared in his dream and said, "I am right here in the jungle nearby. You don't have to worry." The devotee at once moved to the place indicated by the Lord in the dream and saw a molehill there, which he dug up. Accidentally, the axe struck Lord Balaji's idol covered by the molehill below the chin and on the chest, and surprisingly blood started flowing profusely from the "wounds", flooding the ground and turning it scarlet.

The devotee could not believe his eyes when he saw this. Suddenly he could not believe his ears also when he heard a voice from the air which said, "Flood the molehill with cow's milk. "When the devotee did so, a Swayambhu idol of Lord Balaji accompanied by Sridevi and Bhoodevi (a rare combination) was found, and this idol was installed with the due rites and a temple built for it.

Sri Balaji venkateshwara, the Pratyaksha Daiva in kaliyuga, is thus available at Chilkur to shower blessings on His devotees who for any reason are unable to go to Tirupati. Many devout worshippers flock to the temple, to receive the blessings of the Lord and his consorts throughout the year particularly during the Poolangi, Annakota and Brahmothsavams.

With the earnest desire to revive the former glory and importance of the temple, the idol of Ammavaru was installed in 1963 the year following the Chinese aggression, and when the aggression was unilaterally vacated, Ammavaru was given the name of Rajya Lakshmi, signifying this welcome event. The unique feature of this idol is that lotus flowers are held in three hands and the fourth hand is in such a position towards the lotus feet which signifies the doctrine of Saranagathi.

The temple has been visited by great Acharyas from time to time. A visit to the temple is a must for the Jeer of Sri Ahobila Mutt every time he visits the twin cities, and in the temple is installed the idol of the first Jeer. The Tilakayaths of Sri Vallabhacharya Sampradaya have been regularly visiting the shrine. Jagadguru Sri Sankaracharya of Sringeri Mutt and his disciple graced the efforts of the trustees in improving the temple.

Recent Governments were trying to take Chilkur Balaji Temple. The endowments department is hell bent and is trying to keep hundi in temple to mint money as the foot falls to the temple are very high. The only temple in India where every man is equal, irrespective of religion, caste and creed. We request you to support us in fighting against the governments to protect chilkur balaji temple. In India it is the only temple temple which is effectively managed with out taking single paisa.

Dakkili

Dakkili is a mandal in the Nellore District in the state of Andhra Pradesh in India. In recent years it has been the site of Communist Party of India activities; in addition Maoist guerillas have begun hiding in the forests of the area.

Temples

Two temples are located here. One temple, the Venkayaiah swamy temple, is near Mopuru Road. Another one is Velampalli Eswaraiah swami temple.

Devipuram

Devipuram is a Hindu temple complex located near Visakapatnam, Andhra Pradesh, India. Belonging primarily to the Shakta school of Hinduism, it is dedicated to the goddess Sahasrakshi ("she who has a thousand [infinite] eyes"; a form of Lalita Tripurasundari or Parvati); and her consort Kameshwara (Shiva).

Overview

Devipuram's primary focus is the Sahasrakshi Meru Temple, a unique three-story structure built in the shape of a Sri Meru Yantra; *i.e.*, a three-dimensional projection of the sacred Hindu diagram known as Sri Chakra, which is central to Srividya upasana (an ancient and intricate form of Tantric Shakta worship). Measuring 108 feet square at its base and rising 54 feet high, the temple has become an increasingly popular pilgrimage destination over the past decade. Two other shrines, the Kamakhya Peetham and Shivalayam, are located on hills adjacent to the main temple.

The sanctum sanctorum of the Sahasrakshi Meru Temple is reached by circumambulating inward and upward, past more than 100 life-sized murthis of various *shaktis* or *yoginis* (deities expressing essential aspects of the Devi) who are, in Srividya cosmology, said to inhabit and energize the Sri Chakra. Their exact locations are "mapped" in an elaborate ritual called the *Navavarana Puja* ("Worship of the Nine Enclosures"), which in turn has been condensed into an important mantric composition called the *Sri Devi Khadgamala Stotram* ("Hymn to the Auspicious Goddess's Garland of Swords"), forming the basis of the temple's layout.

This temple is unconventional in its practice of allowing devotees to perform puja to the Devi themselves, without regard to caste, creed or gender. The fact that many of the temple's murthis are portrayed as "sky-clad," or nude, has also, over the years, gained Devipuram considerable attention and a certain amount of notoriety.

History

Construction of the Sahasrakshi Meru Temple in Devipuram began in 1985, and its completion and consecration (*kumbha-abhishekam*) took place in 1994. In accordance with Hindu tradition, the temple was re-consecrated for its twelfth anniversary in February 2007.

The founder of Devipuram is Dr. N. Prahalada Sastry (1934-), a former university professor and nuclear physicist who left an illustrious 23-year career with the Tata Institute of Fundamental Research in Mumbai to begin work on the Devipuram temple in 1983. Now a noted spiritual guru, better known as Sri Amritananda Natha Saraswati (and generally addressed as "Guruji"), Sastry reports that his creation of Devipuram was based on several visions of the Divine Mother, in which she specified both the design and mission of the temple complex. Each of the many murthis within the Sahasrakshi Meru Temple was individually sculpted to Sastry's specifications, physically manifesting his meditative visions of these deities.

According to Devipuram's official history: "In 1983, during Devi Yajna, Guruji was approached by the brothers of the Putrevu family with a request to build a temple for the Divine Mother. In addition to the three acres of land that they had donated, Guruji bought the adjoining ten acres and it was registered as land for the Devi temple.

"Having acquired the land, Guruji was looking for divine guidance, a sign of approval to commence construction of the temple. In the vicinity of the donated land, there was a small hillock where Guruji would often spend time in meditation. On the slopes of the hillock, he noticed a formation [*i.e.*, a cleft rock forming a natural yoni] very similar to that of the Kamakhya Peetam in Assam. One day while in meditation he experienced himself lying on the *peetam* [holy site], while four others performed a homa, with flames emanating from his body. And during *purnahuthi* [the final round of ritual offerings], he felt a heavy object being placed on his heart. Awakening from his meditative state, Guruji was prompted to dig that site. Unearthed from that very spot, he found a Sri Chakra Maha Meru made of panchaloha. It was later discovered that a huge yajna had been performed in that area more than 250 years earlier.

"Guruji had visions of the Devi as a 16-year-old girl. With her blessings, he built the Kamakhya Peetam on the hillock and a Shiva temple on the peak in 1984. Construction of the Sahasrakshi Meru Temple in Devipuram was started in 1985." A recent Devipuram publication reflected, "Even a fleeting glance at what has been accomplished around what used to be a no-man's land is enough to astound anyone."

Draksharama

Draksharama is one of the Pancharama Kshetras which is located at Draksharamam town near Kakinada city in East

Godavari District of Andhra Pradesh in South India. The Shiva deity is known as *Bhimesvara Swamy*. The temple is situated on the eastern bank of Godavari River. The consort of Lord Bhimesvara is Manikyamba. According to local belief the Shiva linga at the temple was installed and established by the god, Surya. Maha Shivaratri, Devi Navaratrulu, Karthika Masam, Dhanurmasam are the main festivals celebrated at this temple.

According to local legend, the temple was built by angels in one night. The construction of the perimeter wall could not be completed before sunrise and still stands incomplete. Several attempts have been made to construct the uncompleted part of the wall but all those efforts have failed with the constructed wall collapsing within a few months.

Kalahasti Temple

Sri Kalahasthi is a temple town in the state of Andhra Pradesh. Located here is one of the famous Shiva temples in South India, and is said to be the site where Kannappa, one of the 63 Shaivite Nayanars, was ready to offer his last remaining eye to cover blood flowing from the Shiva linga before the Lord Shiva stopped him and granted mukti. Sri Kalahasti temple, situated 36 km away from Tirupati is famous for its Vayu deva temple, which is the only shrine of the god of wind in India. Constructed in the 12th century by the Chola king, Rajendra Chola, Vayu is incarnated as Lord Shiva and worshipped as Kalahasteeswara.

The temple is also associated with Rahu and Kethu (of the nine grahams or celestial bodies in the Indian astrological scheme). The river Suvarnamukhi takes the northerly course at Sri Kalahasthi almost washing the west wall of the famous Sri Kalahasthi temple in the Chittor district of Andhra Pradesh. Inside this very large temple situated between two steep hills-Sripuram and Mummidi-cholapuram-is the Shivalinga set to represent the element of Vayu (air or wind), whose presence is evident by a continuous flame which flickers though there is no loophole for air to enter the temple.

Sri Kalahasthi Temple is in fact considered as the Kailash of the south or Dakshin Kailash. The protector of devotees, the granter of boons, the merciful Lord Shiva, the Three-eyed, manifested in the form of Vayu linga in the Bilwaka grove on the banks of river Suvarnamukhi. Lord Shiva, manifest in the form of Vayu linga, is known to the devotees as Sri Kalahastheeswara. Worship of lord shiva was there in India even before Christian era. Saiva saints of first century sang about this temple.

The initial structure of this temple was constructed by the great Pallava dynasty. Tamil Chola kings and the Vijayanagara kings also gave great help for the temple development. Like other great temples, the construction period of Srikalahasthi lasted centuries. Near about tenth century, the Chola kings renovated the temple and constructed the main structure. The outer walls and the four gopurams were constructed in the period of Sri Veera Narasimharayar in twelfth century. The 120 feet high main gopuram and the 100 pillar mandapam were constructed by Krishnadeva Raya, the great Vijayanagara king in 1516. Nattukkotta Chettiyar of Devakkotta, developed the structure what we see today by spending on million dollar in 1912.

This ancient temple dedicated to Lord Shiva is one of the panchabhootha stalams (temples celebrating Lord Shiva as the embodiment of the primary elements), air being the element in case here, the other five temples being Tiruvannamalai (fire), Chidambaram (space), Thiruvanikkaval (water) and Kanchipuram (earth) respectively.

In another story, the temple is said to be the place where an elephant and a snake were fighting over their offerings to the Shiva linga. The elephant had poured water over the Shiva Linga while the snake offered jewels. A fight ensued between them over the nature of their offerings to the Lord. Shiva, pleased with the their worship, stopped both of them and granted mukti or salvation to both.

It seems that the animals retained evidence of their past lives as humans or intelligent beings in order for them to be steadfast in their devotion to the Lord.

Kalahasti is one of the Panchabhoota Stalams signifying the 5 elements, 1) wind (Kalahasti), 2) water (Thiruvanaikaval),

3) fire (Tiruvannamalai), 4) earth (Kanchipuram) and 5) space (Chidambaram) that Shiva embodies.

This is an important temple dedicated to Lord Shiva. This temple has one of the elemental lingas, the vayu (air) linga. There is a lamp inside the inner sanctum that is constantly flickering despite the lack of air movement inside. The air-linga can be observed to move even when the pujaris close off the entrance to the main deity room, which does not have any windows. One can see the flames on several ghee lamps flicker as if blown by moving air. The linga is white and is considered Swayambhu, or self-manifested.

Kalahasti is surrounded by two sacred hills. The Durgamba temple is on the northern hill. On the south hill there is the shrine of Kannabeswara, in memory of the Sage Kannappa, who offered an eye to the Lord. When he tried to offer his other eye as well, the Lord mercifully stopped him. There is also a temple dedicated to Subramanya on one of the surrounding hills.

The main linga is untouched by human hands, even by the priest. Abhisheka (bathing) is done by pouring a mixture of water, milk, camphor, and panchamrita. Sandal paste, flowers and the sacred thread are offered to the utsava-murti, not the main linga.

This temple is one of the most impressive Shiva temples in India. It features an enormous, ancient gopuram (tower) over the main gate. The tower is 36.5m (120 feet) high. The entire temple is carved out of the side of a huge stone hill. It was built in 1516 by King Krishnadeva Raya.

The temple is run by neatly dressed Shaivite Brahmins, who conduct the worship of the various deities inside. Inside the temple you will find the tremendously ornate and splendid architecture that South India is famous for. Elaborately designed pillars, altars, and paraphernalia abound.

As the legend goes, the town got its name because of the temple named after Sri (spider) Kala (serpent) hasti (elephant) after the three animals, who were ardent devotees of Lord

Shiva. These three animals attained divinity through worshipping Lord Shiva. The spider was Vishwakarma's (architect of the deva ganas) son Oornanabha. He was replicating Brahma-the creator's job and an annoyed Brahma cursed him to become a spider.

The snake was once cursed by Shiva himself.

The elephant was a gana (Hasti) cursed by Shiva's wife, Parvathi, when he intruded their privacy!

The Shiva linga at Srikalahasti is an amalgamation of the three animals.

Kalahasti is one of the Panchabhoota Stalams signifying the 5 elements, 1) wind (Kalahasti), 2) water (Tiruvanaikka), 3) fire (Tiruvannamalai), 4) earth (Kanchipuram) and 5) space (Chidambaram) that Shiva embodies.

According to Swami Shivananda's book, Sixty-Three Nayanar Saints, some Shaivite traditions believe that Kannapa was the reincarnation of Arjuna. Arjuna, worshipped Shiva for seeking the Pasupatha Astra and failed to recognize Him in the form of a hunter. Thus, according to this tradition, Arjuna had to be born as a hunter and adore the Lord before attaining final liberation. This belief is not adopted by all Hindus.

Kalva Srirampur

Kalva Srirampur is the mandal head quarter in Karimnagar District and is of 30 miles away from Karimnagar. There is a beautiful temple of Sri Sri Sri Veera Bhrahmendra Swami near Pandavula Gutta (Hill of Great Pandavas) and a Veda Patashala too. They teach classes through out the year.

Kanaka Durga Temple

Kanaka Durga Temple is a famous temple in Andhra Pradesh, India. It is located on the Indrakeeladri hill in the city of Vijayawada on the banks of Krishna River.

Legend of Goddess

According to a legend, the now verdant Vijayawada was once a rocky region strewn with hillocks that were obstructing the flow of River Krishna. The land was thus rendered unfit for habitation or cultivation. Invocation to Lord Shiva led to His directing the hills to give way to river Krishna. And lo! the river started flowing unimpeded with all its might, through the tunnels or "Bejjam" bored into the hills by Lord Shiva. That is how the place got its name Bezawada.

One of the many mythologies associated with this place is that Arjuna prayed to Lord Shiva on top of Indrakeela hill to win His blessings and the city derived its name "Vijayawada" after this victory. Yet another popular legend is about the triumph of goddess Kanakadurga over the demon king Mahishasura.

It is said that once upon a time, the growing menace of demons became unendurable for the natives living in this region. Sage Indrakila, took to severe penance and when the goddess appeared, the sage begged Her to reside on his head and keep vigil on the wicked demons.

As per his wishes, after killing the demons, goddess Durga made Indrakila Her permanent abode. Later She also slayed the demon king Mahishasura freeing the people of Vijayawada from the evil clutches of the demon.

At the Kanakadurga temple, the enchanting four-foot high icon of the deity bedecked in glittering ornaments and bright flowers, with eight powerful weapons in eight hands is in a standing posture over the demon Mahishashura and piercing him with her trident. The goddess is the epitome of beauty.

Adjacent to the Kanakadurga temple is the shrine of Malleswara Swamy on the Indrakiladri. By ascending the steps on the hill, one comes across little images of different deities, prominent among them being Kali, Shiva and Krishna.

Ksheerarama

Ksheerarama is one of the Pancharama Kshetras which is located in Palakollu near Narsapuram in West Godavari District of Andhra Pradesh in South India. Lord Shiva is known as Ksheera Ramalingeswara Swamy here. The Shivalinga at this place is installed and established by Lord Vishnu.

Kumararama

Kumararama is one of the Pancharama Kshetras that is located in Samarlakota in East Godavari District of Andhra Pradesh in South India.

Lord Shiva is known as Kumara Bhimeswara Swamy here. The consort of Lord Kumara Bhimeswara Swamy is Bala Tripurasundari. The Shivalinga at this place is installed and established by Lord Kumaraswamy. Maha Shivaratri, Karthika Masam and Sarannavarathri are the main festivals celebrated at this temple.

Lepakshi

Lepakshi is a small village located in the Anantapur District, in Andhra Pradesh, India. It is 15 km east of Hindupur and about 100 km north of Bangalore.

Lepakshi is very important historically and archaeologically. There are three shrines dedicated to Shiva, Vishnu and Virabhadra.

The famous Veerabhadra temple, dedicated to Veerabhadra, is located here. The temple is a notable example of the Vijayanagar architectural style. It is famous for its sculptures, which were created by the artisans of Vijayanagara empire. A huge Nandi bull made out of a single granite stone is one of the attractions in Lepakshi.

Pancharama Kshetras

Pancharama Kshetras are five ancient Hindu temples of Lord Shiva situated in Andhra Pradesh. The Shivalingas at these temples are made from a single Shivalinga.

As per the legend, this Shivalinga was owned by the Rakshasa King Tarakasura. Nobody could win over him due to the power of this Shivalinga. Finally Lord Kumaraswamy broke this Shivalinga into five pieces and killed Tarakasura. The five pieces of Shivalinga fallen at five different places on earth.

These five pieces are installed as Shivalingas at five different Temples by Indra, Surya, Chandra, Vishnu and Kumaraswamy at the respective places. These places (or Aaramas) are as follows:

Amaravathi Amararama

Draksharamam Draksharama

Ramachandrapuram Somarama

Palakollu Ksheerarama

Smarlakota Kumararama.

Pithapuram

Pithapuram railway station is on the Chennai-Howrah Railway line. Pithapuram is famous for its Ancient Hindu temples. Pithapuram was previously known as Puruhothika puram and later known as Pithikapuram. Pithapuram is also known as Dakshina Kasi.

Raikal

Raikal is the mandal (sub-district) headquarters and a small town in Karimnagar District, Andhra Pradesh, India.

Raikal is about 65 km from the district headquarters Karimnagar. This small town has historical significance for two things. The first is the ancient temple of Kesavanatha Swamy which was built in the 13th century A.D. by the Kakatiya dynasty. This temple's idol is Panchamukhalingeswara Swamy (Lord Shiva with five faces) which is believed to be one of the only two existing, the other being at Varanasi.

The second attraction is the annual Bhimanna Jatara (Hindu festival) held for 3 days during January-March. Dussera is celebrated in a big way with many people gathering at the Jambi near the shivaji statue. Agriculture is the main occupation of the people. Rice, corn, turmaric, Chilli is grown. Dairy, poultary and sheep farming are the upcomming industries. Though there are other business such as weaving and sawmill as well. Many people live on rolling the Bedies. Many people are migrating to bigger cities and countries to earn there living. A newly constructed Ayyappa temple is attracting lots of devoties. The Ayyappa temple resembles that of the the Shabirimala. Also there is a Saibaba Temple very close to

Raikal. Education is given lots of importance and many people from this small town are doctors, engineers and in various important administrative departments holding important positions.

Ramappa Temple

Ramappa Temple also known as the Ramalingeswara temple, is located 77 km from Warangal, the ancient capital of the Kakatiya dynasty, 157 km from Hyderabad in the state of Andhra Pradesh in southern India. It lies in a valley at Palampet village of Venkatapur Mandal, in erstwhile Mulug Taluq of Warangal district, a tiny village long past its days of glory in the 13th and 14th centuries. An inscription in the temple dates it to the year 1213 and said to have been built by a General Recherla Rudra, during the period of the Kakatiya ruler Ganapati Deva.

Ramatheertham

Ramatheertham is a village panchayat in Nellimarla mandal of Vizianagaram district in Andhra Pradesh in South India.

This place is about 12 kilometres from Vizianagaram city.

The Rama Temple

The famous ancient temple of Ramachandra Swamy can be found over here. The beautiful idols of Lord Ramachandra Swamy, Sita Devi and Lakshmana in Silver *kavachas* can be seen at this temple. There is a beautiful lake in vicinity of the temple. One has to visit this temple for its serenity. The festivals of Sri Ramanavami and Vaikunta Ekadasi are celebrated with pomp and fervour here. You can see many tortoises with Vishnu Namams on their backs, roaming around in the temple. There is also a Rama Stambham installed by Pedda Jeeyar.

Near to this temple, there is a black hill on which you can find the ruins of some Buddhist and Jain structures.

Ryali

Ryali is a small village in East Godavari district of Andhra Pradesh in South India. It is very famous for the temple of Lord

Jagan Mohini Kesava Swamy. The beauty of the idol of Jagan Mohini Kesava Swamy has to be seen to be believed. The idol is in the form of Kesava Swamy when seen from the front and it is in the form of Jagan Mohini when seen from the back. The priests at the temple show the idol in the light of burning camphor and explain the idol of the god in detail. There is temple of Lord Shiva in front of Lord Jagan Mohini Kesava Swamy temple. Lord Shiva is known as Sri Uma Kamandalesara Swamy here. The Legend of these two temples relates to Samudra manthan.

Simhachalam

Simhachalam temple is an Hindu temple located in Andhra Pradesh, a south Indian state.

Origin of the Name

SIMHA: Lion

Achala: hill

Atop the hill is a famous temple said to be the abode of narasimha swami, and hence the hill itself is called (nara) simhachalam.

Sanghi Temple

The Sanghi Temple located at Sanghi Nagar in the city of Hyderabad in India is located about 35 km from the heart of city. The sacred Raja Gopuram can be seen from several kilometres away which is very tall.

This beautiful temple complex is located on the top of hill Paramanand Giri, which attracts a number of devotees who seek gods blessings. The beauty of the slope around the temple is simply breath taking and beckoning ordent visitors. As you approach the Paramanand Giri, the gateway or Maha Dwaram welcomes the visitors.

As you further proceed, the stone elephant is seen at the stairway. There are three Gopurams seen at the foot of the hillock which are so tall and seen as if touching the heavens. On the top of the temple complex one can see the shrine of Lord

Anjaneya, the son of Anjana devi, and the son of wind God, who is believed to shower his blessings to his devotees.

This is a beautiful temple constructed in he South Indian style of temple architecture and hosts all important Hindu God idols. It is a favourite getaway point for the Hyderabadis as well as a popular tourist spot. Sanghi Temple 35 km away from Hyderabad. The idol of Venkateshwara inside the sanctum sanctorum is 9-½ ft tall.

There are small temples inside the complex dedicated to Padmavati, Shiva, Rama, Anjaneya, Ganesha, Navagrahas, Goddess Ashtalakshimi, Durga and Kartikeya. There is also a Pavitra Vanam or a holy garden in the temple complex where special leaves and flowers are grown for performing poojas. The temple opens early in the morning at 5.00 am. For one hour, Suprabhatam is recited, followed by Archana to the deities from 6 am to 8 am. General darshan for the devotees is allowed from 8.30 am to 10.30 am and again from 4 pm to 6 pm. Poojas and Sevas are held between 6 pm to 8 pm. The temple remains closed between 12 am to 4 pm and after 8 pm. Weekly Abhishekam is performed to the deities between 8 am and 9 am, Sri Ramalingeshwara (Mondays) Sri Hanuman (Tuesdays), Sri Venkateshwara, Ashtalakshmi, Parvathi, Padmavathi and Rama (Fridays)

Somarama

Somarama is one of the Pancharama Kshetras which is located in Ramachandrapuram Taluk in East Godavari District of Andhra Pradesh in South India. Lord Shiva is known as Someswara Swamy here. The temple is situated on the bank of Godavari River. The consort of Lord Someswara is Sri Rajarajeswari Ammavaru. The Shivalinga at this place is installed and established by Lord Chandra. Maha Shivaratri and Sarannavarathri are the main festivals celebrated at this temple.

Sri Raja Rajeshwara Temple

Sri Raja Rajeshwara Kshetram (holy place) is one of the most sacred spots in the southern part of the India. There are many evidences of inscriptions on stone to provide information of historical, political, religious, cultural and greatness of this holy place. The greatness of this sacred place came with the very existence of Sri Raja Rajeshwara swamy Suyambulingam, which is ancient than the Vemulawada village.

Once upon a time god Indra went to many holy places after he killed Vrithasura and still could not purify his life. Then he took the advice from the guru of gods, Bruhaspathi to visit Sri Raja Rajeshwara kshetram. There he took the holy dip in dharma-gundam and took the blessings of lord Sri Raja Rajeshwara and ruled a golden age of the history. By this ancient story, history gives us the evidence of existence of lord Sri Raja Rajeshwara in Krita yuga.

Another historical story about how the dharma-gundam was built. Once upon a time a king named Sri Raja Raja Narendra came to this place while hunting wild animals. But accidentally he killed a Brahmin boy with an arrow while the boy was drinking water from a pond. Then with the curse of Brahma hatya he got an incurable disease and went on pilgrimage to many holy places and returned back to this place. One day he drank the holy water from the dharma gundam and slept the night praying the lord Sri Raja Rajeshwara Swamy. In his dreams lord shiva asked him, that to take lord's existence, the lingam from the dharma-gundam and put in a temple.

When the king woke up in the morning he found that his incurable disease got cured. Then he built steps to the dharma gundam and cleaned lord Sri Raja Rajeshwara swamy lingam and built a temple on the hill to keep the lingam inside the temple. But while he was sleeping in the night holy sidhas came and established the gods idol inside the temple. When king was worried about missing the chance to establish the shiva linga, god came in to this dreams and promised that kings name will be associated with the place forever.

It is been said in many mythologies that Sri Raja Rajeshwara Swamy lingam existed in Krita Yuga, Treta Yuga and Dwapara Yuga. And this holy place was visited and praised by many holy persons in Indian ancient history and got never ending importance in holy pilgrimage. Even though the main deity is

Lord Shiva at this place, Sri Kodanda Rama Swamy Aalayam, Sri Ananta Padma Nabha Swamy Aalayam are also have the importance from long time for many pilgrims. Because of that reason this place is also called as "Hari Hara Khestram".

Sri Ranganathaswamy Temple (Nellore)

The Sri Ranganthaswami Temple in Nellore, Andhra Pradesh, India is a Hindu temple dedicated to Lord Ranganatha a resting form of Lord Vishnu. This temple, also called Talpagiri Ranganathaswami temple or Ranganayakulu is one of the oldest temples in Nellore. It is located on the banks of the Penna River and is believed to have been constructed in the 12th century. Just before the main entrance of the temple is a huge tower, called *Gaaligopuram*, which literally means "wind tower". This tower is approximately 70 feet high and has 10 feet of gold plated vessels on top of it, called *kalisams*. Every year during the month of march-april (varies according to Indian calendar) grand festival is celebrated these are called Brahmotsavam.

Undavalli Caves

The Undavalli Caves, and example of Indian rock-cut architecture are located in the village of Undavalli in Guntur District, in the state of Andhra Pradesh, India. The caves are 6km south west of Vijayawada, 22km north west of Guntur City and about 280 km from Hyderabad, Andhra Pradesh.

Ujjaini Mahakali Temple

"Sri Ujjaini Mahakali" temple in Telangana region at Secunderabad is 191 years old. Devotees offer prayers to the goddess every day. In particular, Lakhs of devotees in Ashada Jathara pray on principal days, which fall on Sunday and Monday.

Veerabhadra Temple (Lepakshi)

Veerabhadra temple in Lepakshi is located near Anantapur which is 15 km east of Hindupur in the Anantapur district in the state of Andhra Pradesh in southeastern India. Bangalore is the nearest large city.

Ventrapragada

Ventrapragada is a village in Krishna District in the Indian state of Andhra Pradesh. Ventrapragada is situated 30 km from Vijayawada and 9 km from Gudivada.

The neighbouring villages are Kalavapamula, Mudunuru, Vanapamula, Cheruvukommu and Nandamuru.

The famous ancient temple of Sri Nameswara Swamy (Lord Shiva) is here. Nowhere else in the world is Lord Shiva called with this name or has a temple with this name. The shivalingam in this temple has Namam (which is uncommon for shiva) and hence the name. It is told that the lingam is so long and deep-rooted that the end has not been found, but there is a well in the temple, the depth of which is said to be a measure of how deep the lingam was seen when it was first discovered.

For many generations there has been a strong belief that couples or women who pray for children get their wish fulfiled – they then name the child Nameswara rao, Nameshwari, Namesh etc. There is a strong belief that those who want to have children or get married or wish for anything, do 108 pradakshinas around the temple in a period of 1-3 months or 108 days.

In the temple there are idols of a veerabhadra swami and his wife; he is believed to be guardian of the village.

The festivals of Shivaratri, Srirama navami, Dussera, and Sankranthi fill the temple with pilgrims. Sankranthi is celebrated at harvest time, and it is traditional to decorate the village with rangolis.

This village also has an ancient famous temple of Shirdi Sai Baba.

The village has a bus station and an old railway station. Villagers here grow rice, wheat, sugar cane, and many vegetable crops. The village has a stream of the Krishna River flowing through it, which is mainly used for agricultural purposes; the stream fertilises around a 1000 acres (4 km^2).

2

Hindu Temples in Assam

Bhairabi Temple

The Bhairabi Temple is located on the outskirts Tezpur in Assam, India.

The Goddess Durga is worshipped here. The backdrop of the temple is a view looking towards the Kolia Bhomora Setu across the Brahmaputra River. The temple site is also locally known as *Maithan* and *Bhairabi Devalaya*. Legend has it that Usha (daughter of mighty Asura King Banasura) regularly came here for the worshipping of the Goddess. About a couple of kilometres away lie the Bamuni Hills where one can view the ruins of the palace that stood many centuries ago. The art work on stone carvings that were used within the structure are from the 9th century.

The temple is now managed by the Government through the office of the District Deputy Commissioner. There are sacrificial offerings of goats and bulls that still occurs regularly here.

The entrance to the temple is through a very long staircase that leads up from the approach road to the temple itself. There are numerous facilities for the purchase of ghee lamps, incense sticks, sweets and fruits etc. that are offered during prayers for blessings.

Da Parbatia

Da Parbatia is an ancient architectural site of a Hindu temple in the 4th Century AD. There is a door well which has survived the exposure to the natural elements for all these centuries. It is a protected site under the auspices of the Archaeological Survey of India.

Kamakhya Temple

The Kamakhya Temple is a *shakti* temple situated on the Nilachal Hill in western part of Guwahati city in Assam, India. It is the main temple in a complex of individual temples dedicated to different forms of the mother goddess that include *Bhubaneshwari*, *Bagalamukhi*, *Chinnamasta*, *Tara*, etc. It is an important pilgrimage destination for general Hindu and Tantric worshippers.

Description

The current temple structure was constructed in 1565 by Chilarai of the Koch dynasty in the style of medieval temples. The form of the earlier structure, destroyed by the Kala Pahar, is unknown. The current structure has a beehive-like shikhara with delightful sculptured panels and images of Ganesha and other Hindu gods and goddesses on the outside. The temple consists of three major chambers. The western chamber is large and rectangular and is not used by the general pilgrims for worship. The middle chamber is a square, with a small idol of the Goddess, a later addition.

The walls of this chamber contain sculpted images of Naranarayana, related inscriptions and other gods. The middle chamber leads to the sanctum sanctorum of the temple in the form of a cave, which consists of no image but a natural underground spring. The spring emanates from a fissure in a large rock that symbolizes a yoni. In summertime the water runs red with iron oxide resembling menstrual fluid, an occasion for the Ambubasi festival. Though the temple is aligned facing east like most Hindu temples, the worship of the yoni is performed facing north.

However, its origins are much older. It is likely that it is an ancient Khasi sacrificial site, and worshipping here still includes sacrifices. Devotees come every morning with goats to offer to Shakti.

The Kalika Purana, an ancient work in Sanskrit describes Kamakhya as the yielder of all desires, the young bride of Shiva, and the giver of salvation. Shakti is known as Kamakhya.

Worship

The Kamakhya Temple in Assam symbolizes the "fusion of faiths and practices" of Aryan and non-Aryan elements in Assam. The different names associated with the goddess are names of local Aryan and non-Aryan goddesses (Kakati 1989, p38). The Yogini Tantra mentions that the religion of the Yogini Pitha is of Kirata origin. According to Banikanta Kakati, there existed a tradition among the priests established by Naranarayana that the Garos, a matrilineal people, offered worship at the Kamakhya site by sacrificing pigs (Kakati 1989, p37).

The goddess is worshipped according to both the Vamachara (Left-Hand Path) as well as the Dakshinachara (Right-Hand Path) modes of worship (Kakati, 1989 p45). Offerings to the goddess are usually flowers, but might include animal sacrifices. In general female animals are exempt from sacrifice, a rule that is relaxed during mass sacrifices (Kakati 1989, p65).

Legends

According to the Kalika Purana, Kamakhya Temple denotes the spot where Sati used to retire in secret to satisfy her amour with Shiva, and it was also the place where her yoni fell after Shiva danced with the corpse of Sati (Kakati 1989, p34). This is not corroborated in the Devi Bhagavata, which lists 108 places associated with Sati's body, though Kamakhya finds a mention in a supplementary list (Kakati, 1989, p42). The Yogini Tantra, a latter work, ignores the origin of Kamakhya given in Kalika Purana and associates Kamakhya with the goddess Kali and emphasizes the creative symbolism of the yoni (Kakati, 1989 p35).

Kamakhya during Ahom era

According to a legend the Koch Bihar royal family was banned by Devi herself from offering puja at the temple. In fear of this curse, to this day no descendants of that family dares to even look upward towards the Kamakhya hill while passing by. Without the support of the Koch royal family the temple faced lot of hardship. By the end of 1658, the Ahoms under king Jayadhvaj Singha had conquered the Lower Assam and their interests in the temple grew. In the decades that followed the Ahom kings, all who were either devout Shaivite or Shakta continued to support the temple by rebuilding and rennovating it.

Rudra Singha (reign 1696 to 1714) was a devout Hindu and as he grew older he decided to formally embrace the religion and become an orthodox Hindu by being initiated or taking sharan of a Guru, who would teach him the mantras and become his spiritual guide. But, he could not bear the thought of humbling himself in front a Brahmin who is his subject. He therefore sent envoys to Bengal and summoned Krishnaram Bhattacharyya, a famous mahant of Shakta sect who lived in Malipota, near Santipur in Nadia district. The mahant was unwilling to come, but consented on being promised to be given the care of the Kamakhya temple to him. Though the king did not take sharan, he satisfied the mahant by ordering his sons and the Brahmins in his entourage to accept him as their spiritual guru.

When Rudra Singha died, his eldest son Siba Singha (reign 1714 to 1744), who became the king, gave the management of the Kamakhya temple and along with it large areas of land (Debottar land) to Mahant Krishnaram Bhattacharyya. The Mahant and his successors came to be known as Parbatiya Gosains, as they resided on top of the Nilachal hill. Many Kamakhya priests and modern Saktas of Assam are either disciples or descendants of the Parbatiya Gosains, or of the Nati and Na Gosains.

Ketakeshwar Dewal

Ketakeshwar Dewal (shrine) is a holy site in the Ketakibari area of Tezpur in Assam. It is reputed to have one of the largest Shiva lingas in the world.

The actual site has two parts-one part where the actual linga is located and another part a few metres away where the original base of the linga is located. Legend has it that during a severe earthquake in the past the linga was uprooted from its base and deposited where it currently stands.

This shrine is open to visitors and there is a local committee which oversees the development of the area around the site. Originally it was in the middle of bamboo groves with a small pathway for people to approach on foot. Recently there is a full shelter that has been built on the site for the protection of the holy area from the natural elements as well as fopr the devotees to assemble and offer their prayers.

Lankeshwar Temple

Lankeswar Temple is an ancient Shiva temple on top of a hillock in the western part of the Guwahati city near Gauhati University campus.

Mahabhairav Temple

The ancient temple of Mahabhairav is located in Tezpur town, Assam. This temple is believed to have been established by king Bana in the pre-historical times. This Shiva temple was originally built of stone but the present one was renovated and built with concrete. During the Ahom rule, the kings especially of the Tungkhungiya dynasty donated large area of Devottar land to the Temple and pujaris and Paiks were appointed to look after the temple. The responsibility of management was in the hands of a Borthakur. The temple is now managed by the Government through a managing committee headed by the District Deputy Commissioner. Shivaratri is celebrated in the temple with big festivity and people from all over the country visit it.

Navagraha Temple in Assam

The Navagraha Temple is found on the top of Chitrasal Hill (or Navagraha Hill), in Guwahati city, Assam. Enshrined in this temple are nine Shivalingams, representing the nine Celestial bodies, each covered with a coloured garment symbolic of each of the celestial bodies, with a Shivaligam in the centre symbolising the Sun. The Navagraha temple was built by the Ahom king Rajeswar Singha (1751-1769), son of Rudra Singha or Sukhrungphaa in late 18th century. It had been renovated in the modern times in the late 70's and 80's.

Rangnath Dol

Ahom king Swargadeo Rudra Singha dug the Joysagar tank the world largest man made tank covering comprising an area of 318 acres of land including its four banks in memory of his mother Sati Joymati. On its bank in 1703 he built the Rangnath Dol, a (Shiva) temple near the Borduar or main gate way on way from the Joysagar tank to the Talatal Ghar to offer prayer to Lord Shiva. Large number of devotees continue to visit and offer puja in this temple.

Rudreswar Temple

The Rudreswar Devaloy (Temple) was built by Ahom King Pramatta Singha (reign 1744 to 1751) in honour of his father Rudra Singha who died in August, 1714. It is located in North Guwahati in Mani Karneswar area on the northern bank of River Brahmaputra. The temple is located at the site where Rudra Singha was cremated as per Hindu last rites.

Shivadol

The Shivadol stands on the bank of Borpukhuri tank in the heart of Shivasagar, Assam. It was built in 1734 by Bar Raja Ambika, queen of Ahom king Swargadeo Siba Singha. The Shivadol (*dol* means temple in Assamese) is believed to be the tallest Shiva temple in India. Its height is 104 feet and the perimeter is 195 ft. at the base. It is capped by an eight feet high golden-dome. Each year during the Shivaratri, a huge mela (fair) is organised in the temple ground and pilgrims from all over India arrives here to offer puja.

Sukreswar Temple

The Sukreswar Temple is an important Shiva temple in the state of Assam in India and was constructed by Ahom King

Pramatta Singha (1744-1751). It is located on the Sukreswar or Itakhuli hill on the south bank of river Brahmaputra in the Panbazar locality of Guwahati city. Leading down from the temple compound is a long flight of steps to the river. Sitting on the steps of Sukreswar ghat one can enjoy the scenery of sun setting on the river, boats moving across the river, people performing puja in honour of their relatives who have left this world, children and older people bathing, far removed from the din and noise of the city.

Ugro Tara Temple

A temple dedicated to Tara (Devi) located in the western side of Jor Pukhury tanks in the heart of Guwahati city in the Lotaxil (Latasil) locality.

Uma Nanda Temple

Umananda Devaloi is a Shiva Temple is located at the Peacock island in middle of river Brahmaputra just opposite the office of the Deputy Commissioner of Kamrup or the Kachari Ghat in Guwahati. It was built by the Ahom King Gadadhar Singha (1681-1696) who was a devout Shaivaite.

Hajo

Hajo is an ancient pilgrimage centre for three religions: Hindus, Buddhists, and Muslims. It lies on the banks of the Brahmaputra River, 24 km from the city of Guwahati in the Kamrup district of Assam, India. The area is dotted with a number of ancient temples as well as other sacred artifacts. The Hayagriva Madhava Mandir is the most famous temple of Hajo. Lesser known temples of Hajo like that of Ganesha was constructed during the reign of Ahom King Pramatta Singha in 1744 AD. The Kedareswara Temple, a Shiva temple, has inscription on the temple showing that it is of Rajeswar Singha period.

Hayagriva Madhava Mandir is situated on the Monikut hill. The present temple structure was constructed by the King Raghudeva Narayan in 1583. According to some historians the

King of Pala dynasty constructed it in 6th century. It is a stone temple and it enshrines an image of Hayagriva Madhava. Some Buddhists believe that the Hayagriva Mahhava temple, best known in the group of Hindu temples, is where the Buddha attained Nirvana. At this imposing temple, the presiding deity is worshipped as the Man Lion incarnation of Vishnu by the Hindus. Sayani, the first wife of Kalia Bhomora Barphukan donated a family of paiks and also a plot of land for their maintenance to the Hayagriva Madhava temple during the days of Purnananda Burhagohain.

3

Hindu Temples in Goa

Mahalasa

Mahalasa is the Mohini avatar of Lord Vishnu. She is also known as Mhalshi and Mhalasa. In Goa and elsewhere, Mahalasa is considered as the Mohini form of Lord Vishnu and hence she is referred to as "Mahalasa Narayani". The deity, it may particularly be noted, also wears the holy thread, which is its unique feature. This holy thread is only worn by Brahmin men and also the male gods. No other goddess in the Hindu Pantheon wears this kind of thread except goddess Mahalasa. Mahalasa is the Kuldevi (family goddess) of many Goud Saraswat Brahmins.

According another tradition, Mhalsa is believed to be a combined avatara of Mohini and Parvati and the first wife of Khandoba (A warrior god in Maharashtra and believed to be an Avatar of Shiva). She is worshipped with Khandoba in all centres of his worship, including Jejuri.

The temple of Mhalsa lies in Mardol, Ponda, Goa, India. It was shifted here from the Velha conquistas (Saxty/salcette), Goa to avoid destruction during the forcible Christianization of Salcette, Goa, India.

Legend

When the Amrut was obtained by churning of the ocean by the Devas and Danavas, a fight broke between them to claim it. In order to help the gods, Lord Vishnu took the Mohini avatar (form of an enchantress). As a beautiful Damsel, Lord

Vishnu took hold of the Jar of Amrut and served it to the devas. This Mohini form of Lord Vishnu is worshipped by the Hindus as the Goddess Mahalasa Narayani.

According to another legend linking her to Khandoba, Mhalsa is believed to be a combined avatara of Mohini and Parvati. Mhalsa was born as the daughter of a rich merchant in Newase called Timshet. On the dinine orders of Khandoba in a dream to Timshet, she was married to Khandoba on Pausha Pournima (the full moon day of Hindu calendar month of Paush) in Pali (Pembar). Two shivlingas appeared on this occasion. An annual festival marking this event is celebrated in Pali every Paush Pournima.

Mahalasa Temple

Some believe that the main temple of Goddess was originally located in Nepal during the Kaliyuga. She was moved to Aurangabad in Maharashtra.

During the Mughal domination, Aurangabad fell under the Muslim rule and the idol was moved to a secret location in Goa. Later, a small temple was built at Verna. Roughly, a few hundred years later, the Portuguese conquered Goa, and the temple was moved to Mardol.

The temple complex also has smaller temples of Santeri and Laxmi-Narayan who are worshipped daily with Mahalasa. The five main ganas of the Goddess namely Grampurush, Bhagwati, Dadh, Simha Purush and Mhal Purush are also located within the same temple premises and daily worship of all these deities is carried out before worshipping the main goddess.

The temple is famous in Goa for its huge brass bell. The bell does not have a ringer. The ringer was attached only when somebody wanted to testify. It was believed that the goddess will punish the person who lied while ringing the bell. The belief was so strong that during the Portuguese rule the testimony in the temple was considered acceptable in the court of law.

The temple is also famous for its Brass Samai (oil lamp).

Mangueshi Temple

Shri Mangueshi temple is located at Mangueshim in Priol-Ponda Taluka,1 kilometre from Mardol close to Nagueshi, 22 kms from Panaji the capital of Goa and 26 kms from Margao.

This temple is one of the largest, most enchanting, serene and most frequently visited temples in Goa.

Deity

The temple is dedicated to Lord [[Mangueshi], an incarnation of Shiva. He is a kuldevta of many Hindus in Goa including the Saraswat Brahmins. He is also referred to as *Saib* (The Lord of Goa) by Hindus.

The Mangesh Linga is said to have been consecrated on the mountain of Mangireesh (Mongir) on the banks of river Bhagirathi by Lord Brahma, from where the Saraswat Brahmins brought it to Trihotrapuri in Bihar. They carried the linga to Gomantaka and settled at Mathagrama, the present-day Madgoa, establishing their most sacred and ancient temple of Mangesh on the banks of the river Gomati or Zuari as it is called today. Lord Mangesh is worshipped here in the shape of a Shiva linga. According to the legends Lord Shiva had manifested in to a tiger to scare Parvati. Paravati who was paranoid at the sight of the tiger went in search of Lord Shiva. Parvati was supposed to say “Trahiman Gireesh” but instead out of nervousness she said: “Trahimangeesh”.

History

This temple actually had its origins in Kushasthali Cortalim, a village in *Saxty* (Salcette) which fell to the invading Portuguese in 1543. In the year 1560, the Portuguese started Christian conversions in Salsette taluka, the Saraswats of Vatsa Gotra felt insecure and shifted the Mangesh Linga from the original site at the Kushasthali or Cortalim on the banks of river Agranashini (Zuari) to its present location at Mangeshim in Priol village of Atrunja Taluka, on May 1st, 1560 A.D. (according to Hindu calendar-1482 sakha) then ruled by the Hindu kings of Sonde of Antruz mahal (Ponda), to prevent certain destruction. After remaining in the house of a temple priest for sometime,

Sri Mangesh deity was finally installed in its present site at Priol. The original site was a very simple structure, and the current structure was only built under Maratha rule, some 150 years after it had been moved. The Peshwas donated the village of Mangeshi to the temple in 1739 on the suggestion of their Sardar, Shri Ramchandra Malhar Sukhtankar, who was a staunt follower of Shri Mangesh. Ironically, just a few years after it was built, this area too fell into Portuguese hand in 1764, but by now, the Portuguese had lost their initial religious zeal and had become quite tolerant of other religions, and so, this structure remained untouched.

Temple Complex

The 400-year-old Shri Mangesh temple dedicated to Shiva stands out with its simple and yet exquisitely elegant structure. The temple is noted for the pillars which are considered to be the most beautiful among the temples in Goa. There is a prominent Nandi Bull which is considered to be the Vahana (Vehicle) of Shiva A beautiful seven-storeyed deepstambha (lamp tower), stands at the gates in the temple complex. The temple also has a magnificent water tank, which is believe to be the oldest part of the temple.

The Sabha Griha is a spacious hall which accommodates over 500. The decor includes the chandeliers of the nineteenth century. The central part of the Sabha Griha leads to the Garbha Griha where image of Mangesh resides. The temple has shrines of Parvati and Ganesha. The other deities in the temple are Nandikeshvar, Gajana, Bhagavati and the Gramapurusha Deva Sharma of the Vatsa gotra. Other features to see here are the ancient stone devatas housed in the subsidiary shrines to the rear of the main building are Mulakeshwsar, Virabhadra, Lakshminarayana, Shanta Durga and Kala Bhairav.

Ramnathi

The temple of Ramnathi is located in Ramnathim, Bandivade in Goa. Ramnath was the form of Lord Shiva that Lord Rama prayed to before he crossed the ocean to Lanka to bring back his wife Sita. Therefore the name Ram-Nath=Lord of *shree* Rama. The temple also has the Idols of the Goddess Santeri (Shantadurga) from Rivona and the Goddess Kamakshi. There is also an Idol of *Shree* Lakshmi Narayan *Shree* Siddhanath (Ganesh) and *Shree* Betal. This completes the Ramnathi *Panchayatna.*

The original temple of Ramnathi in Goa, was located in Loutolim in salcette, Goa. The Idol of Ramnathi was shifted to the present site in the 16th century to prevent its destruction by the then Portuguese authorities. The Ramnathim temple is one of the first goud saraswat brahmin (GSB) Temples to build an *agrashala* for pilgrims. The *kulavis (associated* families) had migrated out of Salsette (Sasahasti)/(Saxti) due to religious persecution and now dwell all along the western coast of India. A large number of the Saraswats *kulavis* live in Mumbai, South Canara, Kerala and abroad. The tradition of coming to the temple after a major family event continues. At the site of the original Ramnathi temple at Loutolim, Salcette, a proposed church was never built. The land has now been reclaimed by Hindus and a new temple of Ramnathi has been recently built at Loutolim. The *kulavis* come from the Vatsa and the Kaundinya Gotras.

Saptakoteshwar

The Saptakoteshwar temple at Narve is considered to be one of the six great sites of temples of Lord Shiva in the Konkan area. The village of Narve is located about 35 kms from Panaji and can be reached via an interesting route which requires a ferryboat from the island of Divar.

This is also an ancient temple, Saptakoteshwar having been the deity of the Kings of the Kadamba dynasty around the twelfth century. Coins found from this era mention the name of the deity along with that of the King Jayakeshi.

In 1352, when the Kadamba kingdom was conquered by the Bahamani Sultan Allauddin Hasan Gangu and Goa was under the rule of the Sultan for about fourteen years. A number of temples were destroyed during this period and the linga (symbol of Lord Shiva) at the Saptakoteshwar temple was also dug up by the troops.

In 1367, the army of Vijayanagar King Harihararaya defeated the Bahamani Sultan's troops in Goa and managed to restore most of the temples to their former glory including that of Saptakoteshwar.

When the temple was demolished in 1560 by the Portuguese, (and a chapel dedicated to Nossa Senhora De Candelaria was erected in its place) the linga was used as a well shaft until some Hindus managed to rescue it. The idol was then smuggled across the river to Bicholim where it was installed in a brand new temple and revamped in 1668 by the Maratha Chatrapati Shivaji Maharaj.

With its shallow Moghul dome mounted on an octagonal drum sloping tiled roofs, European style mandapa, or assembly hall and tall lamp tower or deepastamba, the temple is situated in an archaeologically important area. The surroundings of the temple are tinged with several Brahminical laterite and stone caves. In the vicinity of it existed a Jain Math, the ruins of which are still visible. It was probably an important Jain temple patronised by the Kadamba rulers prior to their shifting loyalty to Sri Saptakoteshwar. In front of the temple towards the right side of the Deepastamba is a shrine of Kalbhairav and outside it are seen the padukas of Dattatraya carved on the stone. Little ahead of the Deepastamba are seen two huge laterite pillar like structures buried deep. Probably they maybe stone henges. Behind the temple are seen carved stone walls with niches. It may have been an ancient Agrashala. Similarly, close to the temple there is a man-made tunnel like structure which is presently silted. Near the temple site there is a sacred tank known as Panchaganga Tirtha which is used for ablutions by the devotees during the birth day of Lord Shiva.

Shanta Durga Temple

Shree Shantadurga: Shantadurga temple is a large temple complex 33 kms from Panajim at the foothill of Kavalem in Ponda Taluka, Goa, India.

Deity

The temple is dedicated to Shantadurga, the Goddess who mediates between Vishnu and Shiva. The deity is also called 'Santeri' colloquially.

Local legends tell of a battle between Shiva and Vishnu The battle was so fierce that Lord Brahma prayed to Parvati to intervene, which she did in the form of Shantadurga. Shantadurga placed Vishnu on her right hand and Shiva on her left hand and settled the fight. The deity of Shantadurga is shown as holding two serpents, one in each hand, representing Vishnu and Shiva. She is then said have gone to Shankleswari a village in Ponda Taluka (goa in which she went to Gothana (a small place in Shankleswari) to kill the demons that were harassing the Brahmins. As a reward, she was given the name of Vijaya where she is now called Shri Vijayadurga. Shri Vijayadurga shrine was located in Shankleshwari along with Shri Shantadurga and Shri Lakshmi Narsimha but was later shifted to a place called Kerim in Ponda Taluka during the Portuguese invasions..

Temple Complex

The original temple at Cavellossim (Quelshim) in Salsette was destroyed by the Portuguese in 1564. The *devi* was shifted to Kavlem and worship was continued there. The site on which the original temple of Shree Shantadurga stood at Cavellossim is known as "Deoolbhata" and it is in the possession of the temple trust.

The current temple was constructed during the reign of Maratha ruler *Chatrapati* Shahu Raje of Satara about 1738 A.D. *Shri* Naroram Mantri (Naroram Shenvi Rege) originally from Kochar village in the Vengurla region was a *Mantri* (minister) in the *Chatrapati* Shahu's Court around 1723 A.D. He obtained finances to construct the new temple for the Devi from the *Chatrapati*. The temple construction started around 1730 A.D. and with the help from other mahajans, the present beautiful temple was completed. Due to his efforts the village Kavalem was bequeathed to the temple authorities by Shahu Maharaja in the year 1739 A.D.

The temple complex is on the slope of the foothills of a mountain chain, surrounded by lush vegetation. There is a main temple and three smaller temples of other deities which have been built on three sides of the temple. The temple consists of a collection of pyramidal roofs with an interesting dome. The pillars and floorings are made of Kashmir stone. The temple has a huge tank, a *Dipa* Stambha and *agrashalas* (guest houses).

Many renovations have been completed over the years to the main temple and the temples of the other deities as well as to the *agrashala*.

4

Hindu Temples in Gujarat

Akshardham (Gandhinagar)

Akshardham Gandhinagar is one of the largest temples in the Indian state of Gujarat. The temple complex combines devotions, art, architecture, education, exhibitions and research at one place. The temple came to international attention when two heavily armed terrorists attacked it in September 2002, one year after the '9/11' attack.

Akshardham Gandhinagar is a predecessor to the Akshardham at Delhi, built by the same religious organisation, *Bochasanwasi Akshar-Purushottam Swaminarayan Sanstha* (BAPS) led by Pramukh Swami Maharaj. It was inaugurated by him on Monday, November 2, 1992 CE, during the centenary celebrations of Yogiji Maharaj. The complex is very popular among tourists visiting Gujarat.

Ambaji

Ambaji is a census town in Banaskantha district in the state of Gujarat, India. Ambaji is an important temple town with millions of devotees visiting the Ambaji temple every year. It is one of the 51 Shaktipeeths.

Ambaji mata temple is a major Shakti Peeth of India. It is situated at a distance of approximately 65 kilometres from Palanpur and 45 kilometres from Mount Abu and 20 kilometres from Abu Road near the Gujarat and Rajasthan border.

The original seat of Ambaji mata is on gabbar hilltop in the town. A large number of devotees visit the temple every year specially on Purnima days. A large mela on Bhadarvi poornima (full moon day) is held.

Ambaji town is known for possessing mines which produce fine quality marble and granite.

Bahuchara Mata

Bahuchara Mata is a Hindu goddess, patroness of—and worshipped by—the hijra community in India. Her followers believe in non-violence and consider killing of all animals and creatures a sin.

Camp Hanuman Temple

Camp Hanuman Temple is one of the biggest Hanuman temples of India. It is situated in Ahmedabad Cantonment area in Shahibaug, Ahmedabad, Gujarat. This temple was established by Pandit Gajanan Prasad around 100 years ago. From that time this temple has gained immense popularity. Former Prime Ministers of India Mr. Atal Bihari Vajpayee & Smt. Indira Gandhi have made visits to this temple.

Dakor

Dakor is a city and a municipality in Kheda district in the state of Gujarat, India. It is prominent for its grand temple of Shree Krishna in the entire province of Gujarat.

History

This story is as told by the people there in 1957. One devotee (Bholanath) could not go to Dwaraka for praying there due to his old age. Then God told him that he would come himself to his place. When he was being removed by some devotees the local people objected his removal and fought with them. God told them to throw him into the water. Then local people searched for the God under water by piercing sticks. Thus the God got hurt all over his body with wounds as seen when he was removed. God told the devotees to give the local people gold equal to his weight to satisfy them. Only gold they could find was the nose ring of the above devotee which she reluctantly gave. When it was weighed against God, God made the nose ring very heavy. Thus the local people actually got only very small quantity of gold and they had to get satisfied. This idol of Lord Krishna was installed at Dakor. This shows how God always helps his devotees.

Jalaram

Shree Jalaram Bapa was born in Virpur, Rajkot district, Gujarat, India in 1799, on the seventh day of the Kaartika month.

Saint Jalaram was a devotee of Lord Ram.

Biography

Jalaram Bapa was however not willing to live household life and to continue to do business of his father. He was mostly engaged in serving Pilgrims, sadhus and saints. He separated himself from his father's business and his uncle, Valjibhai asked Jalaram Bapa and Virbaima to stay in his house.

It was obvious that Jalaram Bapa was inclined to completely withdraw from marital life. Fortunately his wife, Virbaima decided to follow the path of Jalaram. So, when Jalaram decided to go for a pilgrimage for holy places like Ayodhya, Kasi, Badrinath and several other sacred places. Virbaima followed him. At the age of 18, Jalaram Bapa accepted Shree Bhojalram from Fatehpur as guru and was given a "Guru Malaa and Mantra" in the name of Shree Ram. With blessings of his guru, he started "Sadavrat" a feeding centre, a place where all sadhus and saints as well as the needy could have food any time during 24 hours. Nobody returned from that place without having food. All this he did single handed with Virbaima assisting him. Soon his fame spread as an incarnation of the divine. Whoever come to Virpur, whether Hindu, Muslim or any Religion was fed by Bapa.

This tradition of feeding the people continues even today in Jalaram Main temple in Virpur, Gujarat.

Jalaram Jayanti

Even today Jalaram's birthday (the seventh day of Kartik month) is celebrated as Jalaram Jayanti. On this day various groups of Jalaram devotees feed the food as prasad. This happens at a lot of Jalaram temples in Mumbai. Jalaram Jayanti also happens to fall on the seventh day after Diwali.

Nageshwar Temple, Dwarka

Nageshwar Temple or Nagnath Temple is a famous Hindu temple dedicated to Lord Shiva located in the holy town of Dwarka in Gujarat, India. It is one of the 12 Jyotirlingas, the sacred abodes of Lord Shiva and according to Hindu mythology the Nageshwar (meaning, the Lord of Snakes in Sanskrit) symbolizes the removal of poison (evil activities) by Lord Shiva. In the Rudra Samhita this deity is referred as Daarukaavane Naagesham.

Santram Mandir

Santram Mandir is a famous temple situated in Nadiad, Gujarat, India. It is home to Santram Maharaj who is a holy figure in Gujarat. It is very famous for other social activities for the needy too. The Santram mandir trust runs a physiotherapy centre, an eye clinic as well as various other charitable organizations. It also carries out various cultural activities. There are other "santram mandir's" located in vadodara, karamsad and other places.

Many people offer fast on Thursdays in reverence to Santram Maharaj.

These are the places where Santram Mandirs' are located in Gujarat

Umreth, Karamsad, Nadiad, Koyli, Vadodra, Rhadhu, Pachegam, Padra

Shamlaji

Shamlaji is one of the largest pilgrim temples of the Sabarkantha district in India. It is more commonly known among locals as "Dhodi Dhwaja Vada" because it always has a white silk flag flittering on top of temple. Its unique designs on the outer part of temple is one of its greatest attractions; the image becomes more interesting with the mountains in the background. The temple has a beautiful sculpture of Lord Krishna as Shamdiya bhagwan, with a piece of real diamond embossed on his chin.

Somnath

The Somnath Temple located in the *Prabhas Kshetra* near Veraval in Saurashtra, on the western coast of Gujarat, India is one of the twelve Jyotirlings (lingas of light) symbols of the God Shiva. It is mentioned in the Rig Veda. Somnath means "The Protector of Moon God". The Somnath Temple is known as 'the Shrine Eternal', as although the temple has been destroyed six times it has been rebuilt every single time.

Folklore

It has been said that The Moon God Chandra, being arrogant about his beauty, was cursed by his father-in-law Daksha to wane. The Moon then prayed to Lord Shiva at the Prabhas tirth who then removed the curse partially, thus causing the periodic waning of moon.

It's been said that Somnath Temple was first built with gold by Moon God, with silver by Ravana, with sandalwood by Lord Krishna, and with stone by Bhimdeva (Solanki Ruler of Gujarat)

History

The present temple is the seventh temple reconstructed on the original site. The first temple of Somnath is said to have existed before the beginning of the Christian era. The second temple, built by the Maitraka kings of Vallabhi in Gujarat, replaced the first one on the same site around 649.

In 725 Junayad, the Arab governor of Sind, sent his armies to destroy the second temple. The Pratihara King Nagabhata II constructed the third temple in 815, a large structure of red sandstone.

In 1024, Mahmud Ghazni raided the temple from across the Thar Desert. During his campaign, Mahmud was challenged by Ghogha Rana, who at the ripe age of 90, sacrificed his own clan fighting against this iconoclast. The temple and citadel were ransacked, and more than 50,000 defenders were massacred; Mahmud personally hammered the temple's gilded lingam to pieces and the stone fragments were carted back to Ghazni, where they were incorporated into the steps of the city's new Jamiah Masjid (Friday mosque).

The fourth temple was built by the Paramara King Bhoj of Malwa and the Solanki king Bhima of Gujarat (Anhilwara) between 1026 and 1042. The wooden structure was replaced by Kumarpal who built the temple of stone.

The temple was razed in 1297 when the Sultanate of Delhi conquered Gujarat, and again in 1394. The Mughal Emperor Aurangzeb destroyed the temple again in 1706.

Sardar Vallabhbhai Patel, then Home Minister & the first Deputy Prime Minister of India took a pledge on November 13, 1947 for its reconstruction for the seventh time. A mosque present at that site was shifted few miles away. It was completed on December 1, 1995 and President of India, Dr. Shankar Dayal Sharma dedicated it in the service of the nation. The present temple was built by the Shree Somnath Trust which looks after the entire complex of Shree Somnath and its environs.

Sun Temple, Modhera

The Sun Temple, Modhera (Gujarat) was built in 1026 AD by King Bhimdev of the Solanki dynasty and is dedicated to Lord Surya, the Sun God of Hinduism. It is akin to the Konark Temple of Orissa. One more sun temple is Martand of Jammu and Kashmir.

The Modhera sun temple is situated on the bank of the river Pushpavati, 25 kms from Mehsana and 102 kms from Ahmedabad.

History

According to the Skanda Purana and Brahma Purana, the areas near Modhera were known during ancient days as Dharmaranya (literally meaning the forest of righteousness). According to these Puranas, after defeating Ravana, Lord Rama asked sage Vasistha to show him a place of pilgrimage where he could go and purify himself from the sin of Brahma-hatya (the sin of killing a Brahmin, because ravan was a Brahmin by birth). sage Vasistha showed him Dharmaranya, which was near the modern town of Modhera. In the Dharmaranya, he settled at a village Modherak and performed a yagna there. Thereafter he established a village and named it Sitapur. This village is about 8 km from Becharaji Modherak village and it subsequently came to be known as Modhera.

The Sun Temple was built by Raja Bhimdev I of Solanki Dynasty in AD 1026. This was the time when Somnath and the adjoining area was plundered by Mahmud Ghazni and reeled under the effects of his invasion. The Solankis, however, regained much of their lost power and splendour. Anahilvad Patan, the Solanki capital, was restored to glory. Royalty and traders jointly contributed to build grand temples.

Solankis were considered to be Suryavanshis, or descendants of Sun god. The temple was so designed that the first rays of the sun fell on the image of Surya, the Sun God, at the time equinoxes.

The temple is partially in ruins after it was also finally destroyed by the Mahmud of Ghazni.

However, enough has reamined of the temple to convey its grandeur.

Shri Swaminarayan Mandir, Ahmedabad

Headquarters of the Shri NarNarayan Dev Gaadi. This is the world's first Swaminarayan Temple and was built in Ahmedabad by the instructions of Bhagwan Swaminarayan.

About this Mandir

The land for construction of this first shrine of Swaminarayan Sampraday, was gifted by the British Government.The tremendous task of constructing this great pilgrimage place was entrusted personally by Shri Hari to S.G. Ananandand Swami.

S.G. Ananadanand Swami has arranged to have this first temple of the Shri Swaminarayan Sampraday constructed as per scriptural norms with intricate carving in pure burma-teak and has had the temple constructed with eye catching sculptural art by depicting deities episodes, auspicious symbols and religious icons representing axiomatic religion and Indian culture. The temple at present is a most valuable cultural heritage in the socio-religious history of Gujarat and India.

The installation ceremony of the idols in the temple was celebrated in the presence of thousands of people from all over India, with great spendour and auspicity.

Lord Shriji Maharaj Himself had embraced the idols of Lord Narnarayan dev and had helped Gods to take a seat in the heart of this first temple of the Sampraday. While standing at the threshold, opposite the majestic seat of Lord Narnarayan dev, He had pronounced that Lord Narnarayan dev was the Supreme Emperor of Bharat Khanda and was now residing there in the temple with all his divine majesty and divine presence. He will help and guide his devotee-follower and fulfil the wishes of the people doing a hearty darshan of him.

Besides the Gods in the main temple, Lord Shri Hari in various divine images sits in the prasadi places too. Lord Balswaroop Ghanshyam Maharaj graces Akshar Bhavan, where prasadi items of Shriji Maharaj have been displayed for darshan by the visitors and devotees. Lord Ghanshyam Maharaj graces Rang Mahol of the temple where Shriji Maharaj stayed during his Ahmedabad visits.

The idol is carved in sacred wood. Shriji Maharaj had personally enlightened His devotee artist about His worldly form for the actualisation of the idol. That fortunate Margosa tree, under the shade of which, Shriji Maharaj had conducted soul stirring sessions of the spiritual discourses for his saints and devotees, presently sanctifies the devotees doing darshan of it and touching its trunk.

The Haveli of the temple is the most cherished place, as it had been the official residence of H.H. Acharya Maharaj of the Uttar Desh. Now, the ground floor of the front side, houses the offices and the inner portion accommodates the residency of the Samkhya Yogi women. There in the inner temple, Her

Holiness Shri Gadiwalla (H H Acharya Maharajshri's wife & spiritual leader of the females in the Swaminarayan Sampraday) holds religious assemblies solely for the spiritual benefit of the females. Lord Ghanshyam Maharaj resides in this temple and is served by the Sankhya Yogi female devotees.

Shri Swaminarayan Mandir, Vadtal

Headquarters of the Shri LaxmiNarayan Dev Gaadi.

About the Mandir

The town of Vadtal is also known as Vadtal Swaminarayan. The temple here is in the shape of a lotus, with nine domes in the inner temple. The land for this great shrine was donated by Joban Pagi, a dacoit converted into a faithful devotee by Lord Shriji Maharaj. The temple was constructed under the supervision of S.G. Brahmanand Swami.

The devotees from Vadtal had come to Lord Shriji Maharaj on the most sacred day of Nirjala Ekadashi to do darshan of Lord Shri Hari in Gadhada. On the next day-the twelfth day of the bright half of Jyestha-they, with folded hands, prayed to Shriji Maharaj to construct a Shri Krishna Mandir in Vadtal. Lord Shriji Maharaj commanded his dearest disciple Brahmanand Swami to temporarily leave the construction of the Muli temple and proceed with a team of saints to plan and supervise the construction of a splendid temple to strengthen the devotional fervour of the residents of Vadtal region.

The construction of this great temple was completed within 15 months and the majestic idols of Lord Shri Lakshminarayan dev were installed by Shriji Maharaj himself on the twelfth day in the bright half of Kartika in V.S. 1881, amidst chants of vedic hymns and great devotional fervour of installation ceremony. In the middle of the temple, He installed the idols of Lord Lakshminarayan dev and Ranchhodji.

On the north, there are the idols of Dharmdev and Bhaktimata and His own form Harikrishna. And on the south, Shriji Maharaj installed the idols of Radhakrishna Harikrishna Maharaj to give devotional pleasure to His devotees.

Besides the Gods sitting in the central temple, in the south of the middle temple, were installed the divine form of Dakshinavart Shankh (Southern-sea conch) and Shaligrama (icon of Lord Vishnu). In the inner dome, there are the stone-idols of the ten incarnations of Supreme Lord, besides the idols of Lord Vishnu resting on the majestic seat of Sheshnaag (heavenly snake).

The temple is the highest seat of the Acharya and preceptor of the dakshin desh. On the south end of the main temple, there is the Akshar Bhavan. Its first floor has standing idols of Ghanshyam Maharaj. On the second floor, there is the idol of Lord Ghanshyam Maharaj in sitting posture. Objects of personal prasadi are kept here. On the west there is the Hari Mandap where Shri Hari wrote the 'Shikshapatri.'

The town of Vadtal is a prasadi place of Shri Hari. In the east of the town, there is a mango garden where Shriji Maharaj ignited Holi and played with colours. A canopy has been constructed at this place. On the south side of this place, Shriji Hari had swung on a swing of twelve doors. A marble seat has been constructed at that prasadi place. The Gomati lake which was dug by Shri Hari is in the north of the town. In the middle of the lake is a shelter and a canopy is built on the west of it. Shriji Maharaj used to sit there at the place of the present canopy when the lake was being excavated. Shriji Maharaj had preached Vachanamrit under the mango tree near the lake.

Shri Swaminarayan Mandir, Junagadh

This Mandir was built by Lord Swaminarayan himself.

About this Mandir

The city of Junagadh is nestled in the lap of Mt Girnar. The temple here has five magnificent domes and beautiful sculptures. The construction of this temple was supervised by S.G. Brahmanand Swami. The land for this majestic shrine was gifted by Darbar Jhinabhai of Panchala state, and the memories of this great devotee have been maintained well by the Sampraday here.

Lord Shriji Maharaj graced this pilgrim place on an invitation from his senior followers Shri Anupsinh (younger brother of King Hematsinh) and others from Junagadh. Invocation ceremony of the Gods lasted for two full days in great festivities of the auspicious events. On the auspicious 2nd day of the dark half of Vaishakha in Vikram Samvat 1884, Shriji Maharaj himself installed Lord Ranchhodrai and Trikamrai in the seat of the principal Gods of the temple.

In the eastern temple he installed Lord Radharaman dev and Harikrishna Maharaj and in the western side he installed Lord Siddheswar Mahadev, Parvatiji, Ganapatiji and Nandishwar. The Mughal Subba Bahadurkhan paid a personal visit to the place and Lord Shriji Maharaj. Shriji Maharaj blessed the provincial head of the Mughal empire and honoured the king Hemantsinh for his generous gift of the land for the temple.

Shri Swaminarayan Mandir, Bhuj

This Mandir was built by Lord Swaminarayan himself.

About this Mandir

This mandir falls in uttar desh. Senior devotees Shri Gangarambhai, Sundarjibhai and others from the Bhuj region of Kutch had come to Gadhada as Shriji Maharaj was gracing Gadhada to give blissful pleasure of Fuldol festival to his devotees. There in that festival, the faithful devotees of Bhuj, submitted their hearty prayer to Shriji Maharaj and requested him to construct a splendid temple in Bhuj to give to the devotees the blissful pleasure of serving him and the pleasure of doing His darshan everyday.

Lord Shriji Maharaj, conceding to the plea from His devotees, asked S.G. Vaishnavananand Swami to proceed with a team of the saints to Bhuj and construct a splendid temple to give devotional pleasure to the devotees. S.G. Vaishnavanand Swami and the accompanying saints came to Bhuj in the sacred month of Chaitra in V.S. 1878, camped at the place neighbouring the land of temple drew plans of the temple, complex, executed the plans with minute details and within a short span of one year, they built a splendid temple abode of Lord Narnarayan dev. Satsang in Kutch-region is deep rooted and firm in devotional dedication.

This model Satsang was nursed by Late Guru Ramanand Swami by his constant visits to Bhuj and other places in Kutch. Satsangis of Kutch have transmitted the spirit of Satsang in the remotest destinations of the earth through their spirited efforts and rock-steady faith in Lord Narnarayan dev Gadi. Lord Shriji Maharaj too, had great godly love for the devotees of this region and had sanctified this religious land with his personal touch.

Lord Shriji Maharaj, had graced this splendid temple in the western belt of India and had Himself installed the idols of Lord Narnarayan dev and His own form-Harikrishna Maharaj in central sanctum sanctorum of the temple.

Besides these divine manifestations of God at the central dome there under the eastern dome, are seated Lord Shri Radhakrishna Harikrishna Maharaj and in the western dome Lord Ghanshyam Maharaj-along with the seat of divine pleasure. Roop Chowki-the main square of the inner temple-houses the images of Lord Ganapati and Lord Hanuman.

There are many prasadi places besides this temple in the ancient city of Bhuj. There are many prasadi places, which Shriji Maharaj had graced. The house of Sunderjibhai had the glorious memories of Guru Ramanand Swami and Shriji Maharaj, both.

A devotee, visiting this place realises tranquility and divine bliss. Besides this place, the house of Gangaram Mall, cottage of Ladhibai, and the temple of Jansari are the prasadi places where Shriji Maharaj stayed.

Akshar Bhavan treasures priceless prasadi items of Shriji Maharaj.

Shri Swaminarayan Mandir, Dholera

This Mandir was built by Lord Swaminarayan himself. It is one of the only six Mandirs built by him.

About the Mandir

This great temple with three majestic domes was supervised and planned by S.G. Shri Nishkulanand Swami, Brai Atmanand Swami Akshardanand Swami and Dharmprasad Swami. Dholera itself is an ancient port-city, 30 k.m. away from Dhandhuka of Ahmedabad district. The temple work was inspected time and again by S.G. Niskhulanand Muni, Bhai Atmanand Swami, Akhandanand Swami and Dharmprasada-nand Swami.

The land for this earthly abode of Gods, was gifted by Darbar Punjabhai. Lord Shriji Maharaj, camping in Kamiala to give devotional pleasure to his devotees, was requested by the devotees Shri Punjabhai and others, to grace Dholera to install the idols of God in the new temple in Dholera. Pleased at the prayer from his devotees, Lord Shriji Maharaj asked Brahmin priests to find out an auspicious time for the installation ceremony.

Lord Shriji Maharaj graced Dholera on the request from Punjaji and other devotees, and on the auspicious 13th day of the bright half of Vaishakha in V.S. 1882, Lord Shriji Maharaj installed with his blessed hands the idols of Lord Madan Mohan dev and His own form Harikrishna Maharaj at the Principal seat of the temple and invoked Gods amidst Vedic hymns.

Besides the Gods in the inner temple and sanctum sanctorum, Lord Hanuman and Lord Ganapati grace Roop Chowki near the main stairway of the temple. On the west, near the steps, there are the idols of Lord Sheshashayi, Suryanarayan, Dharm-Bhakti and Lord Ghanshyam Maharaj. The idols of Shankar and Parvati are on the right hand side. The temple site itself is a prasadi place touched closely and constantly by the blissful touch of Lord Shriji Maharaj.

Shri Swaminarayan Mandir, Gadhada

This Mandir was built by Lord Swaminarayan himself.

About this Mandir

The land for constructing this majestic temple in Gadhada, was donated by the court of Dada Khachar in Gadhada. Darbar

Shri Dada Khachar and his family were firm devotees of Shriji Maharaj. The temple work was planned and executed directly under the consultation and guidance of Shri Hari. Lord Shriji Maharaj had graced the place constantly and shared in the manual service in the construction of the temple, by lifting stones and mortar. Thus every stone and each of the joints have the prized treasure of the blissful personal touch of Shriji Maharaj. This great shrine has two stories and three domes. It is adorned with fine and attractive carvings.

Lord Shriji Maharaj had installed the idols with his blessed hands in this temple on the 12th day of the bright half of Ashwin, Vikram Samvat 1885. Lord Gopinath and Harikrishna Maharaj in the middle, Lord Dharmdev Bhaktimata and Vasudevanarayan on the western side and Lord Revti Baldevji, Shri Krishna and Suryanarayan in the eastern temple.

Besides the idols installed by Shriji Maharaj himself, the temple has many graced memories of Lord Shriji Maharaj. On the path of the worship circuit of the inner temple, there is the idol of Lord Ghanshyam Maharaj facing northward. This prasadi temple has blessed prasadi items of Shriji Maharaj displayed in a museum at the temple.

On the southern side of the temple, there is a big margosa tree (neem tree) and the chamber of Lord Vasudevanarayan. Lord Shriji Maharaj gave several discourses at that place. The court of Dada Khachar has been preserved in its original form.

On the backside, there is the Akshar Oradi temple and Gangajalio well. The residency for the saints and the court of Jiva Khachar in the town are the places of grace. Lakshmi wadi is situated a little away from the town. There at Lakshmi wadi, a single dome temple has been constructed at the place of the funeral rituals of Shri Hari's earthen self. Slightly away, there is one canopy where Shri Hari used to sit and deliver the discourses, and just a little ahead, there is the room of Nishkulanand Muni, where he placed the palanquin prepared by him for Shri Hari's last journey. A neem tree faces this place, and on its western side, there is one more canopy where Shri Hari celebrated 'Sharadotsava.'

Lord Shri Hari and his saints used to take a bath in the river Ghelo. This graced river flows in the south side of the temple. There are prasadi river-beds-Narayan Dharo and Sahasra Dharo which Shri Hari visited frequently. There are small temples of Neelkanth Mahadev and Lord Hanuman on the bank of the river. Both these places are prasadi places of Shriji Maharaj. The main land of Gadhada is still blessed with the holy spirit of Shri Hari.

5

Hindu Temples in Jammu and Kashmir

Amarnath

Amarnath caves is one of the most famous of Hindu temples, dedicated to Lord Shiva, located in Jammu and Kashmir, Republic of India. The temple is reported to be around 5000 years old and is a popular pilgrimage destination for Hindus-about 400,000 people visit during the 45 day season around the festival of Shravani Mela in July-August, coinciding with the Hindu holy month of Shravan. Inside the Amarnath Cave lies the ice Shiva Linga (along with two other ice formations representing Ganesh and Parvati) a natural formation of an ice stalagmite in the form of lingam.

This lingam, of Shiva is said to grow and shrink with the phases of the moon, reaching it's height during the summer festival. According to Hindu mythology, this is the cave where Lord Shiva told about the secret of Life and eternity to His divine consort Parvati, and hence this shrine holds a very special value to the Hindus.

The cave is situated at an height of 3888 m about 141 km from the Kashmir's capital city of Srinagar. The area is under the control of the Indian Army due to terrorism threats and hence prior permission is needed from the government before making the pilgrimage. Devotees generally take the 45 km pilgrimage on foot from town of Pahalgam, about 96 km from Srinagar, and cover the journey in 4 to 5 days. There are two alternate routes to the temple, one the more traditional and the longer path from Srinagar and the other a shorter route from the town of Baltal. Some devotees, particularly the old, also use horseback riding to make the journey.

The Linga

The cylindrical ice formation resembling a Shiva-linga which waxes during May to August and gradually wanes thereafter is a stalagmite.

According to The Hindu (reported on July 2nd 2007), "The Shivlingam in the 200-cubic metre cave was around 12 feet high on June 9 (2007) but had gradually thawed due to warm weather." "The Shivlingam has melted owing to the rise in temperatures. It is a normal phenomenon; weather affects its shape and size," Shree Amarnathji Shrine Board (SASB) chief executive officer Arun Kumar said. The other ice 'lingams,' representing Parvati and Ganesh were, however, still intact, he said.

History

The temple is reported to be about 5000 years old and has been mentioned in ancient Hindu texts. The exact discovery of the cave is not clear, though it is commonly believed that a Gujjar (natives of Kashmir) shepherd found the cave and was given a bag by a saint in it. When he returned home he found them to be gold coins, and this got the entire village excited and believed that the cave is the home to the Lord. Another legend says that an Hindu rishi, Kashyap drained the lake of Kashmir and found the cave along with the lingam in it. This latter legend might be alluding to the geological transformation of this region, when the massive sea in this part was compressed by the Indian geological plate to form the Himalayas.

The Amarnath Yatra, according to Hindu beliefs, begins on Ashadha Poornima (Full Moon Day of Hindu Month 'Ashadha') and ends on Shravana Poornima (Full Moon Day of Hindu Month 'Shravana'). The two-month Yatra for the year 2007 began on July 1, 2007 amidst tight security and adverse weather conditions.

Hari Parbat

Hari Parbat is situated at the periphery of Srinagar city is an ancient and one of the holiest places of Kashmir. It is the abode of Mahashakti the Divine Mother Jagatamba Sharika Bhagwati, also known as Maha Tripursundhari or Rajrajeshwari (locally called as harie). The eighteen armed goddess Sharika is regarded as the Presiding Deity (Isht-Devi) of Srinagar city. The goddess Sharika is represented by a Sayambhu Shrichakra (Mahamaha Shrichakra), also called Mahashriyantra, which consists of circular mystic impressions and triangular patterns with a dot (bindhu) at the Centre.

History

The first fortifications on the site were constructed by the Mughal emperor Akbar in 1590. He built an outer wall for the fort, and planned a new capital called Nager Nagor to be built within the wall. That project was never completed. The present fort was built in 1808 under the reign of Shuja Shah Durrani.

Legendary Origin

According to legend, the Hari Parbat hill was once a huge lake inhabited by the demon Jalobhava. The inhabitants called on the goddess Parvati for help. She took the form of a bird and dropped a pebble on the demon's head, which grew larger and larger until it crushed the demon. Hari Parbat is revered as that pebble, and is said to have become the home for all the gods of the Hindu pantheon.

Another version of the myth says that two demons, Tsand and Mond, occupied the fair valley. Tsand hid in the water near the present location of Hari Parbat and Mond somewhere above the present Dal Gate, and both terrorized the people of the valley. The gods invoked Parvati who assumed the form of a Hor (myna) and flew to Sumer, picked up a pebble in her beak, and threw it on the demon Tsand to crush him. The pebble grew into a mountain. Parvati is worshipped as Sharika in Shri Tsakra (an emblem of cosmic energy pervading the universe) occupying the middle part of the western slope of the hill. The hill is also called Predemna Peet.

On the birthday of Sharika Bhagwati, the devotees make a sacrificial offering of `Taher-charvan' (Taher-rice boiled with turmeric powder and mixed with oil and salt; charvan-cooked liver of goat) to the supreme goddess. This day is celebrated as Har Navum.

Kalika Temple

Maha Kali Mandir is the most prominent temple in Reasi town situated in district Reasi of J&K state. It is located on a hilltop close to the Reasi Bus Stand in the heart of the main city. It is said that 300 years ago Kalika Mata came in the dream of Pandit Jagat Ram Sharma and indicated her presence in the form of a Pindi (stone) lying under ground on this hill. On excavation of the area the Pindi was found. Thereafter a small temple was constructed on the hill and Pandit Jagat Ram Sharma became the caretaker.

Over the years the temple has gained prominence due to a strong belief of the people in Kalika Mata. The local people have contributed to the development of this temple. The devotees visit the temple in large numbers during the days of Navratri.

Kheer Bhawani

The temple of Kheer Bhawani is situated at a distance of 14 miles east of Srinagar against the background of natural sight near the village of Tula Mula. This temple, is located in the middle of a spring, around which there is a vast area whose floor has been covered with smooth and beautiful stones. In it exist large and old chinar trees beneath which the pilgrims sit or sleep on mats of grass. The colour of the spring goes on changing. While most of the colours do not have any particular significance, the colour black is taken as an indication for inauspicious times for Kashmir. The second picture, which was taken at three different dates, clearly shows three different colours of the spring.

History: Maharagya was pleased with the devotion of Ravana and appeared before him and Ravana got an image of the goddess installed in Ceylone. But the goddess became displeased with the vicious and licentious life of Ravana and so didn't want to stay in Ceylone. Therefore, under the command of the goddess, Hanuman got the image from Ceylone and installed it at the holy spot of Tula Mulla.

The mention of Kheer Bhawani is found in Kalhana's Rajtarangini. Kalhana writes that the sacred spring of Tula Mula is situated in a marshy ground. The name of the spring is Mata Ragini Kund.

Maharagini is the form of Durga Bhagvati. The Brahmins of Kashmir worship this spring and pilgrims from every comer of the country visit to have the darshan of the place.

In Rajtarangini Tula Mula is considered very sacred and the Brahmins of Tula Mula were very great and powerful. The spring of Maharagya was very sacred. Thousands of years ago many floods occurred in Kashmir and the sacred spring of Tula Mula also was inundated under its sway and the holy place could nowhere be traced. All around was water. At last Kashmir's Yogi Krishna Pandit had a dream in which the goddess appeared to him and ordered that she would swim in the form of a snake at the proper place and that he should stick large poles and when the water subsided there the holy spot was discovered. This event happened during the Samvat 4041.

The mention of this temple is also found in Abu-i-Fazal's book Aini-Akbariin which is written that the area of Tula Mula extended over the area of hundred bighas of land, which got sunk in the summer season and formed into a marsh.

Swami Rama Tirtha and Swami Vivekananda also visited here to have the darshan of the place.

With the pouring of milk and throwing of sugar candy in the spring by the pilgrims, a thick and solid layer was formed at its bottom. When it was cleared, the ruins of an old temple and shrine slabs engraved with figures were discovered. Here many images were also found but nobody rebuilt the temple till the Samvat 1969 when Maharaja Pratap Singh who was the disciple and worshipped this goddess, got a marvellous temple of marble made in the midst of the spring which shines like a pearl in a shell.

Some people are of the opinion that there was a mulberry tree near holy spot of Kheer Bhawani which, in Kashmiri, is called Tul Mul.

But Tul Mul is also derived from the Sanskrit phrase-Tul Muli-that is of great value. This means that all other pilgrim centres are of lesser value than this one. It is said that after Ravana finished the worship of the goddess he offered the kheer (rice pudding) to the goddess which she accepted and since then it is called Kheer Bhawani.

Khrew

Khrew is a town and a notified area committee in Pulwama district in the Indian state of Jammu and Kashmir.

Raghunath Temple

Raghunath Temple, with seven shrines each with its own Sikhara, is one of the largest temple complex of north India, and is located in the Indian state of Jammu and Kashmir. The temple was built during the period 1835-1860 by Maharaja Gulab Singh and his son Maharaja Rambir Singh. The temple has many gods, but the presiding deity is Rama, an avatar of Vishnu.

While the Hindus were performing puja in the temple complex on 24th November 2002, fidayeen attack by terrorists took place, which resulted into at least 10 deaths, and injuries to several devotees.

Shankaracharya Temple

The Shankaracharya Temple, also known as the Jyesteshwara temple is located in Srinagar, India. It is dedicated to Lord Shiva. The temple is located on the summit of the Takt-e-suleiman hill overlooking Srinagar town.

The temple dates back to 200 B.C. although the present structure probably dates back to the 9th century C.E. The temple was supposedly visited by the Adishankaracharya and has ever since been associated with it.

Shankaragaurishvara Temple

The Shankaragaurishvara temple is dedicated to the Hindu God Shiva and located in Patan near Baramula, India. The temple was built by Shankaravarman of Kashmir's Utpala dynasty who ruled between 883-902 C.E. It is presently in a dilapidated condition and worship is no longer conducted. It is built in a style similar to the Shankaracharya temple.

Shivkhori

Shivkhori is a famous cave shrine of Hindus devoted to lord Shiva, situated in district Udhampur of Jammu and Kashmir state in India. In Udhampur district, there are many shrines such as Mata Vaishno Devi, Sudhmahadev, Pingla Mata, Mahamaya Chountra Mata, Merhada Mata, Baba Dhandar, Siad Baba. Shiv Khori is one of them located in village Ransoo of Pouni block in tehsil Reasi of the Udhampur district, which attracts lakhs of devotees in a year. Shiv Khori is situated in between the hillocks about 140 km north of Jammu, 120 km from Udhampur and 80 km from Katra.

Buses and light vehicles go up to Ransoo, the base camp of pilgrimage surrounded by lush green mountains. People have to traverse about 3 km track on foot which is recently being constructed by the Shiv Khori Shrine Board, Ransoo duly headed by the District Development Commissioner, Udhampur as chairman and Sub Divisional Magistrate, Reasi as Member Secretary.

Khori means cave (Guffa) and Shiv Khori thus denotes Shiva's cave. It is about 200 metres long, one metre wide and two to three metres high natural cave contains a self made lingam, which according to the people is unending. The first entrance of the cave is so much wide that 300 devotees can be accommodated at a time. It is double chamber being quite spacious to accommodate large number of people. The inner chamber of the cave is smaller.

The passage from outer to the inner chamber is low and small, at one spot it divides itself into two parts. One of these is believed to have led to Kashmir where Swami Amarnath cave is existing. It is now closed as some sadhus who dared to go ahead never returned. To reach the sanctum sanctorum, one has to stoop low, crawl or adjust his body sideward where a naturally created image of Lord Shiva, about 4 metres high, is visible. The cave abounds with a number of other natural objects having resemblance with Goddess Parvati, Ganesha and Nandigan. The cave roof is etched with snake formations, the water trickles through these on Shiva Lingam. Pigeons are also seen here like Swami Amar Nath cave which presents good omens for pilgrimages.

Legend

A number of legends have propounded about the discovery of this holy cave. One of the most important legends among them is that a demon named Bhasmasura after a long meditation of Lord Shiva obtained blessing to end the life of any one with that blessing.

After obtaining it, the said devil tried to end the Lord Shiva-On seeing the evil design of the demon, the Lord Shiva run to save himself from the power of the demon and entered in this cave which is presently known as Shiv Khori. After this, Lord Vishnu in the guise of Mohini came forward and asked the demon to dance with her according to her tune. As and when the demon started dancing as per the actions of Mohini, the said demon took his hand at his head and with his own power, he was himself destroyed. As per the legend 33 crores deities exist in this cave in shape of pindies and natural milky water is falling on them from the top of the cave.

As per the other legend regarding discovery of this cave is that the historic Shiv Khori cave is believed to be discovered by a Muslim shepherded. He was in fact in search of his missing goat and went by chance inside the cave to find the same.

However he was very much startled to see a number of saints inside the cave, who were impressed by Lord Shiva's divine power and he too started pooja there. Later on the shepherd disclosed this to a number of other people in spite of his promise made with the saints not to disclose about them or this cave. It is said that the shepherd after narrating it to other people handled. According to the legends it is believed that a number of famous saints have been closely associated with this cave, who had spent decades inside this cave for spiritual attainment and meditation.

Other Details

About 40 to 50 year ago, only a few people knew about the Shiv Khori shrine but it has gained much popularity during the last few decades. In earlier times the number of yatries was just in thousands but after the constitution of Shiv Khori Shrine Board during December 2003, the number of devotees has superseded previous records as the number of devotees in year 2005 crossed 3 lakhs (300 thousands). This year it is expected to cross 5 lakh tourists. 30 percent devotees reach the shrine from within the state and 70 percent from different states of the country like Punjab, Haryana, Delhi, UP., MP, Bihar, Gujrat and Rajasthan etc.

A 3-day Shiv Khori mela takes places annually on Maha Shivratri and thousands of pilgrims from different parts of the state and outside visit this cave shrine to seek blessings of Lord Shiva. Maha Shivratri festival is usually held in the month of February or during first week of March every year. Keeping in view the increasing rush of pilgrims to the holy cave shrine, the Shiv Khori Shrine Board has taken up a number of steps to develop this spot in a bid to provide more and more facilities to the devotees, like construction of Shrine Guest House at a cost of Rs.19 lakh at village Ransoo, the base camp of yatra, Reception Centre and Pony shed at an estimated cost of Rs.79.59 lakh, tile work of entire 3-km long track is nearing completion, plantation of ornamental and medicinal plants on track and development of parks etc.

Other arrangements like electrification of the cave with modern techniques, provision of oxygen and electric generators, exhaust fans, construction of shelter sheds for yatris with toilet facilities near the cave site, 15 shelter sheds enroute Ransoo to cave shrine, railing from the base camp to cave, additional facility of 15,000/Efnr King water reservoir, proper sanitation, provision of 25 KV capacity electric transformer, clock room, starting of permanent bus services from Katra, Udhampur and Jammu, Police post and Dispensary and a STD PCO are under active consideration of the Shiv Khori Shrine Development Board.

To meet the ever growing rush of devotees in having smooth darshans of the Lord Shiva, an exit tunnel has been constructed by the shri Shivkhori Shrine Board this year in February.

Vaishno Devi

Vaishno Devi Mandir is one of the holiest Hindu temples dedicated to Shakti, located in the hill of Vaishno Devi, Jammu and Kashmir, India. In Hinduism, Vaishno Devi, also known as Mata Rani and Vaishnavi, is a manifestation of the Mother Goddess.

The temple is near the town of Katra, in Udhampur district in the state of Jammu and Kashmir,. It is one of the most revered places of worship in Northern India. The shrine is at an altitude of 5200 feet and a distance of approximately 12 kilometres (7.45 miles) from Katra. Million of pilgrims visit the temple every year and is the second most visited religious shrine in India, after Tirupati Balaji Mandir. The Shri Mata Vaishno Devi Shrine Board maintains the shrine. A rail link from Udhampur to Katra is being built to facilitate pilgrimage.

Legend

According to Hindu epic, Ma Vaishno Devi took birth in the South of India in the home of Ratnakar Sagar, Her worldly parents had remained childless for a long time. Ratnakar had promised, the night before the birth of the Divine child, that he would not come in the way of whatever his child desired. Ma Vaishno Devi was called Trikuta as a child. Later She was called Vaishnavi because of Her taking birth from Lord Vishnu's lineage.

When Trikuta was 9 years old, She sought her father's permission for doing penance on the seashore. Trikuta prayed to Lord Vishnu in the form of Rama. During Shree Rama's search for Sita, He reached the seashore along with His army. His eyes fell on this Divine Girl in deep meditation. Trikuta told Shree Rama that She had accepted Him as Her husband. Shree Rama told Her that during this Incarnation He had vowed to be faithful to only Sita. However the Lord assured Her that in Kaliyuga He would manifest as Kalki and would marry Her.

In the meantime Shree Rama asked Trikuta to meditate in the cave found in the Trikuta Range of Manik Mountains, situated in Northern India. Ma decided to observe the 'Navratra' for the Victory of Shree Rama against Ravan. Hence one reads the Ramayana during the 9 days of Navratra, in remembrance of the above connection. Shree Rama promised that the whole world would sing Ma Vaishno Devi's praise. Trikuta was to become famous as Vaishno Devi and would become immortal forever.

With the passage of time many more stories about the Mother Goddess emerged. One such story is about Shree-Dhar.

Shree-Dhar was an ardent devotee of Ma Vaishno Devi. He resided in a village called Hansali, 2 Km away from the present Katra town. Once Ma appeared to him in the form of a young bewitching girl. The young girl asked the humble Pandit to hold a 'Bhandara'. (A feast to feed the mendicants and devotees) The Pandit set out to invite people from the village and nearby places. He also invited 'Bhairav Nath' a selfish demon. Bhairav Nath asked Shri-Dhar how he was planning to fulfil the requirements. He reminded him of the bad consequences in case of failure. As Panditji was lost in worry, the Divine girl appeared and told Him not to be despondent as everything had been arranged. She asked that over 360 devotees be seated in the small hut. True to Her word the Bhandara went smoothly with food and place to spare.

Bhairav Nath admitted that the girl had supernatural powers and decided to test Her further. He followed the Divine girl to Trikuta Hills. For 9 months Bhairav Nath was searching for the mystic girl in the mountains, whom he believed was an incarnation of the Mother Goddess. While running away from

Bhairav, Devi shot an arrow into the Earth from which water gushed out. The resultant river is known as Baanganga. It is believed that by taking a bath in Baanganga (Baan: Arrow), a believer of the Mother Goddess can wash away all his sins.

The banks of the river, known as Charan Paduka, are marked by Devi's foot imprints, which remains intact till date. Vaishno Devi then took shelter in a cave known as Garbh Joon near Adhkawari where she meditated for 9 months attaining spiritual wisdom and powers. Her meditation was cut short when Bhairav located her. Vaishno Devi was then compelled to take the form of Maha Kali when Bhairav tried to kill her. The manifestation of the Mother Goddess took place at the mouth of the Holy cave at Darbar. The Goddess then beheaded Bhairav with such sheer force, that his skull fell at a place known as Bhairav Ghati, 2.5 km from the Holy Cave.

In his dying moments, Bhairav pleaded for forgiveness. The Goddess knew that Bhairav's main intention in attacking her was to achieve salvation. She not only granted Bhairav liberation from the cycle of reincarnation, but also granted him a boon, whereby every devotee, in order to ensure completion of the pilgrimage, had to visit Bhairav Nath's temple near the Holy cave after the darshan of the goddess. Meanwhile Vaishno Devi assumed the shape of a rock with three pindis (heads) and immersed herself into meditation forever.

Meanwhile Pandit Shree-Dhar became impatient. He started to march towards Trikuta Mountain on the same path that he had witnessed in a dream. He ultimately reached the cave mouth. He made a daily routine of worshipping the 'Pindis' in several ways. His worship pleased the Goddess. She appeared in front of him and blessed him. Since that day, Shree-Dhar and his descendants have been worshipping the Goddess Mother Vaishno Devi.

6

Hindu Temples in Karnataka

Amriteshwara Temple

Hindu epics, Amriteshwara temple, Chikmagalur district. The temple is a fine example of Hoysala workmanship built with a wide open mandapa (hall). Surrounded by Palm and Coconut farms, the temple still has its original outer wall with interesting, equally spaced circular carvings.

The temple has one vimana (shrine), hence it is a ekakuta design and a closed mandapa (hall) connects the shrine to the large open mandapa. A mid sized Hoysala temple, it compares closely with the Viranarayana temple at Belavadi in mandapa structure and size. The open mandapa has 29 bays and the closed mantapa has 9 bays with a side porch that leads to another separate shrine on the south side.

The shrine is square in shape and still has the original superstructure (tower) richly adorned with sculptures of Kirthimukhas (demon faces), miniature towers etc. Below the superstructure, the usual panel of Hindu deities is not present. The base of the wall has five mouldings which is an older Hoysala style. The Sukanasi has the original Hoysala emblem of Sala fighting the tiger.

The speciality of the temple are the rows of shining lathe turned pillars that support the ceiling of the mantapa. The mantapa has many deeply domed inner ceiling structures adorned with floral designs. The outer parapet wall of the open mantapa has a total of 140 panels of sculptures depicting the Hindu epics. Unlike in many Hoysala temples where the panels are small and carvings miniature, these panels are large. The Ramayana is sculpted on the south side wall on 70 panels with the story proceeding anti clockwise which is unusual. On the north side wall, all depictions are clockwise, the normal Hoysala style. 25 panels depict the life of Lord Krishna and the remaining 45 panels depict the epic Mahabharata.

Ruvari Mallitamma, the famous Hoysala sculptor and architect started his career here working on the domed ceilings in the main mantapa. The large stone inscription near the porch is an excellent example of medieval Kannada poetry composed by the famous poet Janna.

Annapoorneshwari Temple

The Annapoorneshwari Temple is located at Horanadu 100 km from Chikmagalur in the thick forests and valleys of the Western Ghats of Karnataka. This ancient Hindu temple of Goddess Annapoorneshwari has been restored and renamed as the Adi-Shaktyatmaka Shree Annapoorneshwari. The single image is of the Goddess Annapoorneshwari standing on a peeta with Shanku, Chakra, Sri Chakra and Devi Gayathri in her four hands.

The name *Annapoorneshwari* means "Feeding one and all". All who visit this temple are provided with breakfast, lunch and dinner and place to sleep on the temple premises.

Badami Cave Temples

The Badami Cave Temples, an example of Indian rock-cut architecture, are at Badami, a town in the Bagalkot District in the north part of Karnataka, India. Badami, the capital of the Early Chalukyas, who ruled much of Karnataka in the 6th to 8th centuries, lies at the mouth of a ravine with rocky hills on either side and a town tank in which water from the ravine flows. The town is known for its ancient cave temples carved out of the sandstone hills above.

Temple Caves

The Badami Cave Temples are composed of four caves, all carved out of the soft Deccan sandstone on a hill cliff in the late 6th century. The four caves are simple in style. The entrance is a simple verandah with stone columns and brackets, a distinctive feature of these caves, leading to a columned mandapa and then to the small square shrine (sanctum sanctorum) cut deep into the cave. The temple caves represent different religious sects. Among them, two are dedicated to Lord Vishnu, one to Lord Shiva and the fourth is a Jain temple. The first three are devoted to the Vedic faith and the fourth cave is the only Jain temple at Badami.

The cave temples date back to 600 and 700 CE. Their architecture is a blend of North Indian Nagara Style and South Indian Dravidian style. As described above each cave has a sanctum sanctorum, a mandapa, a verandah and pillars. The cave temples also bear exquisite carvings, sculptures and beautiful murals.

Banashankari

Banashankari Badami is a temple dedicated to Goddess Banashankari also known as Shakambhari.

An important time to visit the temple is in the month of January during Pushya maasa, where a navrathri is held. This is also the time when the temple gets extremely crowded by people who worship Shakambhari as their household Deity. This is called Banashankari Jathre, which lasts for a month during January and February. In this event a chariot is pulled from the temple gate to another sculpture called padhkatte.

Situated close to Badami in a place called Cholachagudda or cholachagudd, in Bagalkot District of Karnataka. In front of the temple one finds a tank and ruins of the old temple.

All the priests in the temple are from Cholachagudd. During the Jathre event there will be nearly 30 touring cinema theatres and 10-15 drama companies. There is a belief that the pond infront of the temple will never dry and it has never dried in the history when all the neighbouring ponds had dried during a drought one more belief about this pond is that a new born baby will have a good luck in his future if he is taken in a boat made from banana stem across this pond.

Chamundeswari Temple

Chamundeswari Temple is located on the top of Chamundi Hills about 13 km from the palace city of Mysore in the state of Karnataka in India. The temple was named after Chamundeeswari or Durga, the fierce form of Shakti, a tutelary deity held in reverence for centuries by Mysore Maharajas.

Description

The original shrine is thought to have been built in the 12th century by Hoysala rulers while its tower was probably built by the Vijayanagar rulers of the 17th century. In 1659, a flight of one thousand steps was built leading up to the 3000 foot summit of the hill.

At the temple are several images of Nandi (the bull mount of Shiva). There is a huge granite Nandi on the 800th step on the hill in front of a small Shiva temple a short distance away. This Nandi is over 15 feet high, and 24 feet long and around its neck are exquisite bells.

The temple has a seven story tall 'gopuram' decorated with intricate carvings. The idol of the Chamunda Devi is said to be made of solid gold and the temple gates are made of silver.

Cheluvanarayana Swamy Temple

Cheluvanarayana Swamy Temple is located in Melkote in the Mandya District, Karnataka, India. The place is also known as Thirunarayanapura. It is built on rocky hills known as Yadavagiri or Yadugiri overlooking the Cauvery valley. It is about 30 miles from Mysore and 97 miles from Bangalore.

Temple Complex

Cheluva-Narayana Swamy Temple

The temple is a square building of large dimensions but very plain, dedicated to Lord Cheluva-Narayana Swamy or Tirunarayana. The utsavamurthi, which is a metallic image, representing the deity which is called Cheluvapille Raya or Cheluvanarayana Swamy whose original name appears to have been Ramapriya. According to a legend, this metallic image was lost and was recovered by Sri Ramanujacharya. The annual report of the Mysore Archeaelogical Department states on the strength of epigraphic evidence, that the presiding deity of this temple was already a well known object of worship before Sri Ramanujacharya worshipped at the shrine in December 1098 CE. and even before he came to the Mysore region and that very probably he used his influence to rebuild or renovate the temple. From the lithic records of the period, existence of Tamil influence and Vaishnava worship in the area are also evident.

The temple is richly endowed, having been under the special patronage of the Mysore Rajas, and has a most valuable collection of jewels. As early as 1614, the Mysore king Raja Wodeyar (who reigned 1578-1617) who first acquired Srirangapattna and adopted the Srivaishnava faith, handed over to the temple and the Brahmins at Melkote, the estate granted to him by Vijaynagar king Venkatapati Raya. On one of the pillars of navaranga of the Narayanaswami temple is a bas relief about one and a half feet high, of Raja Wodeyar, standing with folded hands, with the name inscribed on the base. He was said to be a great devotee of the presiding deity and a constant visitor to the temple. A gold crown set with precious jewels was presented by him to the temple.

This crown is known as the Raja-mudi after his name. A legend says that on the day of his death, he was observed entering the sanctum and was seen no more afterwards. From the inscriptions on some of the gold jewels and on gold and silver vessels in the temple it is learnt that they were presents from Krishnaraja Wodeyar III and his queens. Krishnaraja Wodeyar III also presented to the temple a crown set with precious jewels. It is known after him as Krishnaraja-mudi. Vairamudi or Vajramukuta, another crown of great value, seems to be older than Raja-mudi and Krishnaraja-mudi and it is not known as to who gave it to the temple.

All the three crowns are kept in the safe custody of the Government and brought to the temple on specific annual occasion for adoring the image of Cheluvanarayana Swamy. The vairamudi festival, which is the chief annual celebration is attended by more than 400,000 people.

Chennakesava Temple

The Chennakesava Temple originally called Vijayanarayana Temple was built on the banks of the Yagachi River in Belur, an early capital of the Hoysala Empire. Belur is 40 km from Hassan city and 220 km from Bangalore, in Hassan district of Karnataka state, India. Chennakesava means "handsome Kesava". Belur is well-known for its marvelous temples built during the rule of Hoysala dynasty. Belur along with near by Halebidu is also one of the most favored tourist destinations in Karnataka. Belur is an important Vaishnava pilgrim centre. Visitors are often humbled by the beauty of the sculptures that are present here which are popular with Hoysala architecture and craftsmanship.

History

The temple was commissioned by Hoysala king Vishnuvardhana in 1117 CE. Scholars hold their own opinions regarding the reasons for the construction of the temple. The popular belief is the military success of Vishnuvardhana was the reason. Some scholars opine that Vishnuvardhana commissioned the temple to surpass the Hoysala overlords, the Western Chalukyas who ruled from Basavakalyan, after his victories against the Chalukyas while another theory is he was celebrating his famous victory against the Cholas of Tamil country in the battle of Talakad after which the Hoysalas took control of Gangavadi (southern regions of Karnataka). Yet another explanation pertains to Vishnuvardhana's conversion from Jainism to Vaishnavism, considering this is predominantly a Vaishnava temple. The Hoysalas had many brilliant architects who developed a new architectural idiom. A total of 118 inscriptions have been recovered from the temple complex covering a period of 1117 to 18th century which give details of the artists employed, grants made to the temple and renovations.

Temple Complex

The main entrance to the complex is crowned by a Rayagopura built during the days of Vijayanagar empire. Within the temple complex, the Chennakesava temple is in the centre, facing east and flanked by Kappe Channigraya temple and a small Lakshmi temple on its right. On its left and to its back is an Andal temple. Of the two main Sthambha (pillar) that exist, the one facing the main temple was built in the Vijayanagar period and the one to the right was from the Hoysala time. While this is the first great Hoysala temple, the artistic idiom is still Western Chalukyan, hence the lack of over decoration unlike in other later Hoysala temples including the Hoysaleswara temple at Halebidu and the Keshava temple at Somanathapura.

During later years, the Hoysala art took an inclination towards craftsmanship, with a weakness for minutia. The temple has three entrances and the doorways have highly decorated sculptures of doorkeepers (dvarapalaka). While the Kappe Channigraya temple is smaller than the Chennakesava temple, it is architecturally equally significant but lacks any sculptural features. This became a dvikuta (two shrined) with the addition of a shrine to its original plan. The original shrine has a star shaped plan while the additional shrine is a simple square. The icon inside is also Kesava and was commissioned by Shantala Devi, queen of king Vishnuvardhana.

Temple Plan

The Chennakesava temple is built with Chloritic Schist (soapstone) and is essentially a simple Hoysala plan built with extraordinary detail. What differentiates this temple from other Hoysala temples of the same plan is the unusually large size of the basic parts of the temple. The temple is a ekakuta vimana design (single shrine) of 10.5 m by 10.5 m size. A large vestibule connects the shrine to the mandapa (hall) which is one of the main attractions of the temple.

The mandapa has 60 bays. The superstructure (tower) on top of the vimana has been lost over time. The temple is built on a jagati (platform). Hence there is one flight of steps leading to the jagati and another flight of steps to the mantapa. The jagati provides the devotee of an opportunity to do a pradakshina (circumambulation) around the temple before entering it. The jagati carefully follows the staggered square design of the mantapa and the star shape of the shrine. The mantapa was originally an open one. A visitor would be able to see the ornate pillars of the open mantapa from the platform.

The mantapa is perhaps the most magnificent one in all of medieval India. The open mantapa was converted into a closed one after about 50 years during the Hoysala rule. This was done by erecting walls with pierced window screens. The window screens are on top of 2 m high walls. There are 28 such windows, with star shaped piercing and bands of foliage, figures and mythological subjects. On one such screen, king Vishnuvardhana and his queen Shanatala Devi are depicted. An icon depicts the king in a standing posture.

Shrine

The vimana (shrine) is at the back of the mantapa. Each side of the vimana measures 10.5 m and has five vertical sections: a large double storeyed niche in the centre and two heavy pillar like sections on both sides of that niche. The two pillar like sections adjoining the niche are rotated about their vertical axis to produce a star shaped plan for the shrine. The pillar like section and the niche bear many ornate sculptures, belonging to an early style.

There are some 60 large sculptures and are of deities from both Vaishnava and Shaiva faiths. From the shape of the vimana it has been inferred that the tower above would have been of the Bhumija style and not the regular star shaped tower that follows the shape of the vimana. The Bhumija towers are present on the miniature shrines at the entrance of the hall and are actually a type of nagara design (being curvilinear in shape).

This shape of tower is quite uncommon in pure dravidian design. The shrine has a life size (about 6 feet) image of Kesava (a form of Vishnu) with four hands, each hand holding an attribute namely, the discus (chakra), mace (gadha), lotus-flower (padma) and conch (Shanka) in clockwise direction. The entrance to the shrine is flanked by life size sculptures of door guardians (dvarapalaka).

Pillars and Sculptures

The pillars inside the hall are a major attraction and the most popular is the Narasimha pillar which at one time is said to have been a revolving one (on its ball bearings). There is a rich diversity about their style. While all the 48 pillars and the many ceilings are well decorated, nothing surpasses the finish of the four central pillars and the central ceiling.

These pillars may have been hand churned while the others were lathe turned. All four pillars bear madanikas (celestial nymphs) and there are 42 of them, 4 inside the hall and the rest outside between the eaves on the outer walls of the hall. They are also called madanakai, salabanjika or shilabalika and epitomise the ideal female form.

They are depicted as dancers, musicians, drummers etc. and are rarely erotic in nature. Some madanika popular with tourists are the Darpana Sundari (beauty with mirror), "The lady with the parrot", "The huntress" and Bhasma mohini. Other interesting sculptures inside the mantapa are Sthamba buttalika (pillar images) which are more in the Chola idiom indicating that the Hoysalas may have employed Chola craftsman along with locals. These images have less decor than regular Hoysala sculptures. The mohini pillar is an example.

At the base of the outer walls are friezes of charging elephants (650 of them) which symbolise stability and strength, above them are lions which symbolise courage and further up are horses which symbolise speed. There are panels with floral designs signifying beauty. Above these are panels depicting Ramayana and Mahabharata. This is called horizontal treatment with friezes. Hoysala artistry preferred to be discreet about eroticism, mingling miniature erotic sculptures in not very conspicuous places like recesses and niches. Sculptures depict daily life in a broad sense.

The doorways to the mantapa have on both sides the sculpture of Sala slaying a Tiger. These are unusually large images. While Sala is popularly known to be the founder of the empire, there is no support for this myth from scholars. Normally this image is placed on the sukanasi (nose of the main tower formed by a lower tower on top of the vestibule) next to the main tower. The story is that Sala killed the Tiger that was ready to pounce on the meditating muni (saint) who sought Sala's help in killing the Tiger. Some historians speculate that the legend may have gained importance after the victory of Vishnuvardhana over the Cholas at Talakad, the tiger being the royal emblem of the Cholas.

Other important sculptures are the Narasimha image in the south western corner, Shiva-Gajasura (Shiva slaying demon in form of elephant) on the western side, the winged Garuda, consort of Lord Vishnu standing facing the temple, dancing Kali, a seated Ganesha, a pair consisting of a boy with an umbrella and a king (Vamana avatar or incarnation of Vishnu), Ravana shaking Mount Kailash, Durga slaying demon Mahishasura, standing Brahma, Varaha (avatar of Vishnu), Shiva dancing on demon (Andhakasura), Bhairava (avatar of Shiva) and Surya. The sculptural style of the wall images shows close similarity to wall images in contemporary temples in northern Karnataka and adjacent Maharashtra and hence a Western Chalukya idiom.

Chennakesava Temple at Somanathapura

The Chennakesava Temple located at Somanathapura is one of the finest examples of Hoysala architecture. This temple was built by Soma, a *Dandanayaka* (commander) in 1268 CE under Hoysala king Narasimha III, when the Hoysala Empire was the major power in South India.

Chitrapur Math

Chitrapur Maṭh is the central Math (community temple) for the Chitrapur Saraswat Brahmin sect. This Math is located in Shirali in North Kanara area of Karnataka and has been there since 1757. The other Maths of this community are located in Gokarn, Karla, Mangalore and Mallapur. All the Maths have the insignia of the saffron flag as shown above.

The chief deity worshipped in this Math is Shri Bhavanishankar (shown in the picture above) who is a form of Lord Shiva. The other 6-7 sanctorums of the temple are reserved for the Samadhis of the previous GuruSwami's of the community. Daily Puja is carried out at the shrine of Lord Bhavanishankar as well as the other Swamis.

H.H. Sadyojat Shankarashram Swamiji is currently the Head of the Math having ascended the Peetha in February 1997. Shree Sadyojat Swamiji is from the Mount Abu monastery and is not from the lineage of gurus which began in 1708.

Devarayana Durga

Devarayana Durga is a fortified hill, about nine miles east of Tumkur town, in Tumkur District in the state of Karnataka, India.

It consists of three elevations and seven gates leading to the top. On the lowest elevation situated is the Lakshmi-Narasimha Swamy Temple. Near by is a spring know as Ane-done. On the slope of the hill is a pond said to be the source of stream Mangali. Higher up is another small spring named Jaya-tirtha representing the source of another stream Jaya. Both the streams unite at Irukasandra at the foot of the hill and form the Jayamangali. Thc hills are also the source of the river Shimsha.

On the middle elevation are the Government Travellers Bungalow and few other places of rest. There are also two other springs known as Ramatirtha and Dhanustirtha. There is a large cave nearby with figures of Rama, Sita and Lakshmana.

History

The place was originally known as Anebiddasari, then as Jadakana Durga after a chief named Jadaka and finally as Devarayana Durga after its capture by Maisuru king Chikka Devaraja Wodeyar.

Tradition relates that a robber chief named Andhaka or Lingaka had his stronghold here, and he was subdued by sumati, a prince, whose father, Hemachandra, was the king of Karnata and ruled from Yadupattana. On accomplishing the enterprise on which he had set forth, Sumathi is said to have established the city of Bhumandana near the present Nelamangala and taken up residence there for the protection of that part of his fathers kingdom.

Under the Hoysalas, there seems to have been, on the hill, a town called Anebiddasari or the precipice where the elephant fell. A rogue elephant, which the sthala purana describes as a Gandharva suddenly appeared before the town to the great consternation of the people and after doing considerable mischief, tried to walk up the steep rock on the west, when it slipped, fell back and was killed. The hill is accordingly called as Karigiri in the Puranas.

Under the Vijayanagara Kings, the use of the same name continued, and a large tank, named Bukkasamudra, was formed after throwing an embankment across the gorge from which the river Jayamangali has its source. Remains of the embankment and of the adjacent town can still be traced.

Dharmasthala

Dharmasthala is perhaps the most highly revered and best known temple town in Karnataka. Located amidst the picturesque Western Ghats on the banks of the Nethravathi River, it is about 100 km from Udupi and about 70km from Mangalore.

This holy place is the home of the Sri Manjunatheshwara Temple, where devotees of all castes and creeds visit. The temple is devoted to Shiva and houses a lingam of gold. The temple is unusual in that it is run by a Jain administration and poojas are conducted by Madhva priests. Everyone enjoys the generous hospitality without any distinction of caste, creed or class whatsoever. On an average the flow of pilgrims is about 10,000 people a day. A mechanised and clean kitchen provides free food for all pilgrims. There are guest houses with modern amenities.The temple is unique example of unity in diversity.

Dodda Ganeshana Gudi

The Hindu temple is situated inside the boundaries of a park called 'Bugle Rock'. The bull referred to is a sacred Hindu demi-god, known as Nandi; Nandi is a close devotee and attendant of Shiva. Dodda Basavana Gudi is said to be the biggest temple to Nandi in the world. The stone cult image of Nandi is continually covered with new layers of butter, *benne* in the local language of Kannada. There is also a cult image of the elephant-headed Hindu deity Ganesha close by.

Every year on the last Monday and Tuesday of the hindu month of Karthika Maasa a Groundnut fair is held in the temple premisis and groundnut is offered to the deity. This fair is known as 'Kadalekaayi Parishe' in local tongue. Groundnut sellers and devotees throng the place during 'Kadalekaayi Parishe'.

Basavana Gudi is a regular place of visit for tourists and is covered by most of the tour operators including the Karnataka State Tourism Development Corporation.

Doddagaddavalli

Doddagaddavalli is a village in Hassan District in the South India state of Karnataka, India. It is located near the city of Hassan and lies on the route to Belur at a distance of 16 km from Hassan. Its main attraction is the Lakshmidevi temple built by the Hoysalas in the year 1114 CE during the rule of king Vishnuvardhana. The temple is situated amidst pristine coconut plantations and has a lake at its rear which adds to the scenic beauty.

Gavi Gangadhareshwara Temple

Gavi Gangadhareshwara Temple, an example of Indian rock-cut architecture, is located in Bangalore in the state of Karnataka in India.

Godachi Veerbhadhreshwar Temple

Godachi;-[Ramdurg tq ; 14 km form Ramdurg] a celebrated pilgrim centre with temples like Veerabhadra, Kalamma and Maruti. The Veerabhadra Temple in Vijayanagar style has a garbhagriha with chalukyan doorway and a spacious mukhamantapa. The Veerabhadra image is recent. Marriages are held in the temple in good number. People from places like Pune, Bangalore, Bombay, Bidar, Kalburgi, Kolhapur and other cities visit this place daily, and especially on Amavasya or Poornima days. The Temple has choultries all around. The annual Jatra is held n honour of Veerabhadra in the month of December when more than 30,000 people assemble. The placename appears to have originated from the plant kodachi [godachi, Zizypus xylopyrus, willd]. The copper plates of Chalukya Kirti-Varman were found here. According to a legend, Shivasharanas on way to Ulvi fought a battle here. The former Jahgirdar of torgal is the trustee of the Veerabhadra temple.

Gokarna

Gokarna or Gokarn is a village in the Uttara Kannada district of the Karnataka state, India. It is a Hindu pilgrimage centre as well as a tourist destination in India. Gokarna is a beach town with tourists enjoying the sun, the surf and the sea gulls.

Etymology

Gokarna means Cows' Ear. It is believed that Lord Shiva emerged from the ear of a cow (Prithvi, the Mother Earth) here. It is also located at the ear-shaped confluence of two rivers Gangavali and Aghanashini.

Legends

Legends in the Sahyadri Khand of the Puranas indicate that the State of Kerala was reclaimed from the sea by the Warrior-Sage Parashuram who came from the North (of the Vindhya ranges) after his wanderings in which he killed the kshatriyas 21 times and threw his axe, the weapon by which he annihilated the kshatriyas, in the sea to prevent the erosion of the land stretching from Gokarna to the Southernmost tip of India.

Gokarna is also mentioned in the Shrimad Bhagawat Purana as being the home of the two brothers Gokarna and Dhundhakari and the Bhagawat also gives details of the difference in their temperament and nature and their exploits.

Ravana, a demonic king from Lanka, did penance for the grace of Lord Shiva at Mount Kailash. Lord Shiva agrees to give Atmalingam with condition that the atmalingam should be physically carried and not placed anywhere on the ground, and it establishes wherever it is placed on earth.

On his way, Ravana stops for bath and gives the atmalingam to Lord Ganesha dressed like a Vatu (brahmin boy), who promptly puts it down. Ravan tries to extricate it resulting in throwing the coverings of the Linga to Dhareshwar, Gunavanteshwar, Murudeshwar and Shejjeshwar temples. Refer full story in article on Murudeshwar

History

The earliest history of the city is not known. It was a centre for India's traditional and ancient Ganja Culture. A sect of brahmins called Gaud Saraswat Brahmins fled from the Gomantak to escape forcible conversions by the Portuguese and British and settled in and around Gokarna in 15th century. It was part of Sodhe and Vijayanagar kingdoms.

Later when Konkan region including Goa was occupied by Portuguese, it became part of their rule. Few temples were destroyed by the Portuguese in 1714 and then rebuilt later in the 18th century and also under the supervision of Guru H.H. Shrimat Anandashram Swamiji in 1928.

Gokarnanatheshwara Temple

Kudroli Sri Gokarnanatha Kshetra was started by his holiness Narayana Guru in Kudroli near Mangalore in karnataka State of India.

Halebidu

Halebidu is located in Hassan District, Karnataka, India. Halebidu was the regal capital of the Hoysala Empire in the 12th century. It is home to one of the best examples of Hoysala architecture in the ornate Hoysaleswara and Kedareswara temples.

Hampi

Hampi is a village in northern Karnataka, on the banks of the Tungabhadra River in India. Hampi is located within the ruins of Vijayanagara, the former capital of the Vijayanagara empire. Possibly predating the city of Vijayanagara, this village continues to be an important religious centre, housing the Virupaksha Temple. The village of Hampi contains several other monuments belonging to the old city. It extends into some of the old ceremonial streets of Vijayanagara. As the village is at the original centre of Vijayanagara, it is sometimes confused with this ruined city. Hampi is also called "The City of Ruins". The Vijayanagara ruins are listed as the *Group of Monuments at Hampi* as a UNESCO World Heritage Site.

The name "Hampi" is an anglicized version of the Kannada *Hampe* (derived from *Pampa*, the ancient name for the Tungabhadra river). Over the years, it has also been referred to as Vijayanagara and Virupakshapura (from *Virupaksha*, the patron deity of the Vijayanagara rulers).

History

Hampi is identified with the mythological Kishkindha, the Vanara (monkey) kingdom which finds mention in the Ramayana. The first historical settlements in Hampi date back to 1 CE.

Hampi formed one of the cores of the capital of the Vijayanagara empire from 1336 to 1565. It was destroyed by Moslem emperors. Hampi was chosen because of its strategic location, bounded by the torrential Tungabhadra river on one side and surrounded by defensible hills on the other three sides.

The site is of great importance in terms of architecture and Historical significance.The demography is abundant with large stones which have been utilized to make larger than life statues of god. One can see a structure of hisoric importance every quater of a mile.

Sadly the city is in ruins as it was not able to defend itself against Islamic aggeressions who treat Idol worship as blasphemy, 'all' the idols have been destroyed or damaged, the successive governments have not been able to keep the place free from treasure seekers who claim further damage.

Recently the Archaeological Survey of India is conducting continious excavations in the area to discover more artifacts and temples.

Hoysaleswara Temple

Hoysaleswara temple is a temple dedicated to Lord Shiva. It was built in Halebidu by the Hoysala Empire in the 12th century during the reign of King Vishnuvardhana. The construction was completed in 1121 CE. During the early 14th century Halebidu was the sacked and looted by Muslim invaders from northern India and the temple fell into a state of ruin and neglect. The temple is located in the town of Halebidu. Previously known as Dorasamudra or Dwarasamudra, Halebidu is 16 km from Belur, 31 km from Hassan and 149 km from Mysore in the state of Karnataka, India.

Idagunji

Idagunji is a famous place of Hindu worship in Uttara Kannada district and Honnavar taluk. The Lord Ganesha temple is the main attraction, receiving more than 1 million devotees per year. Idugunji is close to Manki Mavinakatte and about 14 km from Honavar, 28 Km from Navilgona.

Ikkeri

Ikkeri is situated in Shimoga district of Karnataka state at about 3 km to the south of Sagar. The word *Ikkeri* in Kannada means "Two Streets". This place was the capital of Keladi Nayakas for some years. The walls of the city were of great extent, forming three concentric enclosures. In the citadel was a palace built with mud and timber, adorned with carvings. Today what remains is the temple of *Aghoreshvara* (one of the several names of Lord Shiva), a large and well proportioned stone-building, constructed in a mixed style with a unique conception.

There are intricate carvings on the stone walls of the temple. There are carvings & sculptures such as Temple Relief (sculpture consisting of shapes carved on a surface so as to stand out from the surrounding background), Erotica, Fingurine, Old Kannada Manuscript, Sculpted Elephant etc.

Kadri Manjunath Temple

The Kadri Manjunatha Temple located in Mangalore in the state of Karnataka, India, dates back to approximately 1068 The square temple built with nine water tanks, nestles at the foot of the highest hill at Kadri in Mangalore.

Kalasa

Kalasa is a holy temple-town located in Chickmagalur district in Karnataka. Kalasa is home to the Kalaseshwara Temple dedicated to Lord Shiva. Kalasa lies 92 Kilometres South-west of Chickmagalur and is located on the banks of the Bhadra River.

Kalikamba Temple

Sri Kalikamba Vinayaka Temple is located in Lower Car Street about 3 kms from the City bus Stand in the city of Mangalore in India.

This temple is mainly revered by people of Vishwakarma Brahmin community (people involved in goldsmith, blacksmith, carpentry & architecture business).

This temple underwent major renovation recently. The Garbhagrihas of Lord Ganesh & Goddess Kalikamba were rebuilt with granite.

Kanakagiri

Kanakagiri is Historical place of India, situated in Karnataka State, 20 km North West to Gangavati town. The old name of this town was Suvarnagiri. It was the headquarters of the southern area of the Mauryan Empire. During the Vijayanagar period, this was the chief town of the Bedar Rajas. Kanakachalapati temple with its spacious halls and massive pillars is a fine specimen of the South Indian architecture of Vijayanagar times.

Karikanamma

Karikanamma is a Hindu temple in the Western Ghats in Karnataka, India, located near the town of Honavar. It is dedicated to the deity Kali.

Kateel

Kateel or Kateelu is a temple town in the Dakshina Kannada district in Karnataka, India, about 29 kilometres away from Mangalore. It is considered a holy city in Hinduism; the deity at the temple in Kateel is Durga Parameshwari.

The holy temple is situated on an islet in the middle of the sacred river Nandini amidst panoramic scenes and fascinating greenery. Thousands of devotees visit Kateel everyday to seek blessings from goddess Durga Parameshwari.

There is a story behind this spiritual place. A severe draught hit this place, it did not rain for years. Even Brahmins were forced to eat meat and the people were on the verge of giving up their principles.The great Sage Jabaali was disturbed by this situation. Through his 'Jnana Drishti', Jabaali realized the root cause of all this. He found that Arunasura the 'rakshasa' who escaped from death and fled when Goddess Durga killed Shambasura had increased his life span by following the teachings of his Guru. He had made the people stop all yagas and yajnas as a revenge against the 'devas', and this has resulted in drought and scarcity for years.

Jabaali wanted to put an end to human sufferings and decided to perform a yajna to please the devas. He requested Devendra to permit him to take Kamadhenu for the yajna. Devendra (Indra) asked Jabali to take Kamadhenu's daughter Nandini instead. Nandini refused to accompany Jabaali to the earth where evil was prominent. After a lot of arguments, Jabali, in his anger, cursed that she be born as a river on earth. Realising the mistake, Nandini prayed for mercy. Relenting, Jabali advised her to pray to Goddess Durga to redeem her from the curse, Nandini appealed to Goddess Durga who appeared to her and informed her that though Nandini would be born as a river in fulfilment of the curse she, Durga, would be born as Nandini's daughter at the centre of the river, and in the process, Nandini would attain purification. On Magha shudda Poornima, Nandini emerged as a river from Kanakagiri. Jabali performed his yajna. The devas were pleased and the earth was once again happy.

Elsewhere Arunasura acquired a boon from Brahma that he would not suffer death from any two legged or four legged being or from any weapon. Brahma also powered him with Gayatri Mantra. After acquiring these powers, Arunasura defeated the devas and conquered heaven. The Devas prayed Goddess Durga for help.

One day Goddess appeared in Arunasura's garden as a beautiful woman. Seeing the lady, Arunasura approached her. The beautiful lady reminded him that she had killed Shambasura and from whom Arunasura had escaped death. Arunasura got angry and tries to kill the woman with sword. The Goddess suddenly turned into a stone. Arunasura slashed the stone with the sword, then a vast swarm of bees emerged from the stone and stung him.

The bees (dhumbi) stung him repeatedly till his last breath. Devas led by Jabali performed abhisheka with tender coconut water and requested the Bramarambhika (Queen of the bees) to bless the world. Goddess Durga then appeared in her 'Soumya Roopa' in middle of the river, where present structure of the temple imparts its glory to the world. 'Kati' being the word which means 'centre' (midway between the 'Kanakagiri' the place where the river was born, and the end, Pravanje, where the river joins the sea) and 'lla' means area. Thus the place is called 'Kati + lla' Kateel.

The temple's trust also encourages several forms of arts. Notable among them is the Yakshagana dashavathara mela which was started as an offering to the goddess. During dussera, navaratri and other annual celebrations several sacred rituals like, Chandika havana, thula bhaara, veda parayana, hari kathas etc are performed.

Lakkundi

Lakkundi in Gadag District of Karnataka is a place of antiquarian interest with as many as 50 temples, 101 stepped wells (called Kalyani or Pushkarni) and 29 inscriptions, spread over the period of the later Chalukyas, Kalachuris, Seuna and the Hoysalas. A great centre of Kalyani Chalukyan art, there are several temples of note here.

Among them *Kasi Vishwanatha* is the most ornate and elaborately furnished. There is also a Jain Temple dedicated to Mahavira, the largest & oldest shrines at Lakkundi. Lakkundi is also noted for its step wells, artistically built with small canopied niches inside the walls of the wells enshrining lingas. There is sculpture gallery maintained by the *Archaeological Survey of India*. The architecture of the Chalukyas of Kalyana are said to be a link between those of the early Chalukyas of Badami and the Hoysalas who succeeded them.

Kateel Sri Durga Parameshwari Temple

Kateel Sri Durga Parameshwari Temple is a Hindu temple in Kateel in Dakshina Kannada. This temple is dedicated to Goddess Durga Parameshwari, also known as Bhramari. The temple is situated in the middle of the river Nandini. Kateel is 29 km from Mangalore city.

Keladi

Keladi is a temple town in Shimoga district of the state of Karnataka in India.

Keshava Temple

The Keshava temple in Somnathpur, near the city of Mysore in the Indian state of Karnataka, is the last major temple of the Hoysala dynasty. Somnathpur is around 38 kilometres from Mysore, Karnataka state.

The Keshava temple is the best-preserved most complete monument of Hoysala architecture. The temple is believed to have been built (around AD 1268) under Somnatha, a general in the army of Narasimha III.

Kotilingeshwara

Kotilingeshwara is the presiding deity of the temple of the same name in the village of Kammasandra in India. Kammasandra is a small village situated in Kolar district of Karnataka state. It is about five kilometres from Kolar Gold Fields. This place has the distinction of having the biggest Shivalinga in the world.

Kudalasangama

Kudala Sangama in India is an important centre of pilgrimage for people of the Lingayat faith. It is located about 15 kms from the Almatti dam site in Bagalkot district of Karnataka state. The Krishna and Ghataprabha rivers merge here and flow towards Srisaila (another pilgrim centre) of Andra Pradesh. The *Aikya Mantapa* or the holy *Samadhi* of Basavanna, the founder of the Lingayat faith along with Linga, which is believed to be self-born (*Swayambhu*), is situated here. The Kudala Sangama Development Board takes care of the maintanence and development of this place.

Kukke Subramanya Temple

Kukke Subramanya is a Hindu temple located in the small, rural village of Subramanya in the Western Ghats of Karnataka, India, about 105 km from Mangalore. This temple is one of the famous pilgrimage sites in India. Here the God Subrahmanya is worshipped for his divine power as a snake as the epics relate that the divine serpent Vasuki and other snakes found safety under God Subrahmanya.

Kurudumale

Kurudumale, a place in the Kolar district of Karnataka state, India, is famous for the Ganesha temple built by a Vijayanagara kings. This place was believed to be the place where Devas would descend from the heavens for recreation on earth. The ganesha temple is considered to be very powerful. Many people start new jobs or new work only after taking the blessing of Lord Ganesha.

There is another temple dedicated to Shiva called the Someshwara temple which is also situated in Kurudumale. The interesting thing about this temple is that it is built of a rock without any foundations. Another interesting thing is the artitectural style of the temple; this temple is considered to be older than the Ganesha temple and was built during the Cholas period. Half of the temple has different style of carving, believed to have been done by the legendary artist Jakanachari and the other half is believed to have been carved by his son Dankanachari. The part of the temple supposedly built by Dankana's has statues and carvings which are more intricate and sophisticated.

Lakshminarayana Temple, Hosaholalu

The Lakshminarayana Temple located in Hosaholalu, a small town in Mandya district of Karnataka, India was built by king Vira Someshwara of the Hoysala Empire in 1250 CE. The date of the temple has been ascertained by the style of the sculptures and architecture and compares closely with the contemporeneous Hoysala architecture at Javagalu, Nuggehalli, Somanathapura etc. The town of Hosaholalu is about 60 kilometres (37 mi) from Hassan and 45 kilometres (28 mi) from the heritage city Mysore, the cultural capital of Karnataka state.

Maha Ganapathi Mahammaya Temple

The Shirali Maha Ganapathi Mahammaya Temple is the Kuladevata Temple (family temple) to Bhats, Kamaths, Puraniks, Mallyas, Kudvas, Nayaks of the Gowda Saraswat community. The temple is located at Shirali in North Kanara (Uttar Kannada) district of Karnataka state. It is a five minute drive from Bhatkal.

These families are referred to as the Kulavis of the temple. The temple was established by devotees who migrated from Goa about 400-500 years ago. The presiding deities are Shri Mahaganapati (Vinayaka) and Shri Mahamaya (Shantadurga).

The deities were originally in Goa in the area called Golti and Naveli. On account of the hostile religious policies pursued by the Portuguese rulers around 1560 A.D., the devotees left Goa. Unable to take with them the idols, they invoked the 'saanidhya' or the presence of the deities in the silver trunk of Lord Ganesha and the mask of goddess Mahamaya.

When they reached Bhatkal they were unable to construct a temple immediately and kept these two symbols in a shop belonging to a devotee. Later on they constructed a temple in Shirali, a few miles north of Bhatkal, where it stands to this day. The deities are also called Pete Vinayaka and Shantadurga as they are located in a 'pete', which means a town in Kannada. The temple has a unique darshan seva called, "mali".

Today the temple conducts various pujas including Shasraganayaga, Rathotsav, Ganahoma and Sahasrachandikahavana.

The Rathotsav or the Car Festival is celebrated by the temple on Margashira Shudda Navami (in November or December.)

Its is estimated that currently the Shirali Maha Ganapathi and Mahammaya temple has 125 Kulavis, with a total of 600 persons. Most Kulavis visit the temple annually, and many Kulavis living abroad visit the temple every time they visit India.

Mangaladevi Temple

The Mangaladevi Temple (in full: Mahatobhara Shree MangalaDevi Temple) is a Hindu temple at Bolara in the city of Mangalore, India, situated about three km southwest of the city centre. This temple has influenced the name and importance of Mangalore. The name Mangalore is derived from Goddess Mangaladevi, the main deity of the temple.

Mariyamma Temple

This is a temple situated in Bolar, dedicated Goddess Mariyamma about 0.5 km from Mangaladevi Temple in Mangalore city. It is believed that Mariyamma & Mangaladevi were sisters.

Melukote

Melukote in Pandavapura taluk of Mandya District, Karnataka, is one of the sacred places in Karnataka. The place is also known as Thirunarayanapuram. It is built on rocky hills known as Yadavagiri or Yadugiri overlooking the Cauvery valley. It is about 30 miles from Mysore and 97 miles from Bangalore.

Mookambika

Mookambika Devi Temple of Kollur, dedicated to Mookambika Devi, is one of the most prominent shrines for people in the state of Karnataka and Kerala. Located at a distance of 147 km from Mangalore in the picturesque surroundings presented by the banks of the river Sauparnika and the lush green Kodachadri hill, the temple attracts millions of pilgrims every year.

The temple holds immense relevance for the devotees as it is associated with revered Hindu saint and Vedic scholar Adi Shankara. It is believed that Adi Shankara perceived the idea of having a Mookambika Devi temple at Kollur and himself installed the idol of deity in the temple some 1200 years ago. People have high faith in Mookambika Devi Temple as Goddess Mookambika is regarded as a manifestation of Shakti, Saraswathi and Mahalakshmi.

In fact Temple of Mookambika Devi is one of the 'Seven Muktistala' pilgrimage sites in Karnataka which are Kollur, Udupi, Subrahmanya, Kumbasi, Kodeshwara, Sankaranarayana and Gokarna.

The Mookambika Devi Temple stands on a spur of the Kodachadri peak. The deity is in the form of Jyotir-Linga incorporating both Shiva and Shakti. The Panchaloha image (five element mixed metal) of the Goddess on Shree Chakra is stated to have been consecrated by Adi Shankaracharya during his visit to this place. There is an exquisite sculpture of Panchamukha Ganesha here.

Kollur is regarded as one of the Seven Muktistala pilgrimage sites, of Parashurama Kshetra, in Karnataka which are (Kollur),

Udupi, Subrahmanya, Kumbasi, Kodeshwara, Sankaranarayana and Gokarna.

Legends

According to the legends, Kola Maharshi who was doing penance here, was disturbed by a demon who was also engaged in doing penance to please Lord Shiva, to get a boon from Him. To prevent the demon from fulfiling his evil desire, Adi Shakti made him dumb (mooka) and when the Lord appeared before him, he could not ask for anything. Thereupon he got enraged and soon began troubling Kola Maharshi who prayed to Adi Shakti for deliverance. Adi Shakti who vanquished demon Mookasura, was extolled by the gods as Mookambika. At Kola Maharshi's prayer, the Divine Mother accompanied by all the Gods; stayed there to be perpetually worshipped by the devotees.

Significance of Swayambhulinga

Swayambhulinga manifested itself when Parameshwara drew the Srichakra with his toe and Kola Maharshi performed a long lasting penance in its vicinity, as a result of which power of meditation spread far and wide on the earth. Udhbhava linga is the tangible form of Sri Chakra Bindu that is said to have the proximity of all gods.

It has a very high significance since Shri Mookambika Devi has merged with this Linga and fulfils the desires of devotees. A golden line has formed in the swayambhu Linga and it is wider on the left side as also taller. It is believed that Goddess Lakshmi, Parvathi and Saraswathi have all merged in the left side and the Lord Parameshwara, Lord Vishnu and Lord Brahma resides in the right side of the Linga. Besides the golden line, it is also said there is an image (carving) of Shiva injured by Arjuna's blow during the clash of Kiratharjuna, on the right side of the Linga. Towards the left, we may find the image (carving) of Gopada (foot of the Holy cow) at the Shakthi Peeta.

Adi Shankara (Vedic scholar and saint) has perceived and realized Goddess Mookambika as residing thus. Adi Shankaracharya appeared here leading Shri Saraswathi with a view to finding a place for enshrining her. He stopped at this temple, fixed Shrichakram and on it installed the idol of Mookambika which is the central idol behind the lingam. On the either side of this are idols of Kali or Parvathi and Saraswathi.

The place where sage stayed and did penance and the gate by which he left are at the back of the Mulasthana and to north respectively. Votaries to the temple are allowed the privilege of sitting at the place and passing under that gate for a fee. The temple has been patronized by ancient Hindu Kings and several parts in it are still believed to contain valuable treasure. This was the state temple for the Nagara or Bednore Rajas and many of the jewels now adorning the idol are said to have been presented by them and by their overlords of Vijayanagara.

Sanctum of Shri Mookambika

The installation of the idol at Mookambika temple has a history as ancient as about 1200 years. As suggested by Rani Chennammaji, the feudal lord by name Halugallu Veera Sangayya has covered the inside of the temple with stone. When we look at the temple structure, we find the sanctorum, then entrance hall and then the Lakshmi Mantapa. There are four pillars at Lakshmi Mantapa and on upper portion of each of these pillars, we find beautifully carved images of various gods. Prominently, they have sculpted the images of Ganesha, Subrahmanya, Naga, Mahishasura Mardini and the goddess in different postures as delineated in Devi Mahatma. Earlier, this made up the total temple structure and the outer prakara was not present. So Veera Sangayya also took up the prakara, as per the principles of temple architecture. We may also find beautiful images of Ganapathi atop the doors situated at the entrance to Garbhagriha, Lakshmi Mantapa and the Mukhya Dwara (main entrance). It is normal practice in any temple to depict the main deity over the entrance, and the fact that all three doors carry the carvings of Ganesha is considered to be of special significance.

There are many inscriptions at Kodachadri that relate the tale of time. The Prakaras, which underwent renovation from time to time, hold a mirror to the changing mores in architecture during bygone cultures. Specifically the Vaasthu of Garbhagriha structure is very ancient and extraordinary.

The Garbhagriha is single yoni flag size (Eka yoni pramana dwaja aya). Pre entrance has a three flag proportion and is about 3½ feet wide and 12 feet long. Lakshmi Mantapa measures 134'. 11". Then comes the prakara. Beyond that, is Navaranga Mantapa. Outside the temple is a large and beautiful Deepa Sthambha (a pillar to hold lamps). This has 21 concentric circles in which the lamps can be lighted, and when viewed from Kodachadri, one would feel as though we were looking at the Divine Makara Jyothi at Lord Manikanta's Shabarimale. This beautiful Deepa Sthambha rests on a Koorma Peeta (seat with tortoise head); on this tortoise is a huge elephant upon which Lord Ganapathi is astride, looking westward and facing Goddess Mookambika Devi.

During Navarathri, and during the Rathotsava on Phalghuni Masa Krishna Paksha Ashtami day (the day after Holi), the age-old practice of starting the pooja by praying to Lord Ganesha present on the pillar is kept up even today. In the inner corridor, just beyond the Garbhagriha, as we move around the shrine in a pradakshina, we will find totally four different idols of Ganapathi being worshipped, beginning with the Dashabhuja Ganapathi.

Of these, the Balamuri Ganapathi idol that is made of white marble is beautiful and high of significance. Then we have the image of serpent which has formed on the stone in the south-west corner. It is believed that, as we move in pradakshina, if we touch this serpent and offer our prayers, it results in several benefits, like warding of Sarpadosha, averting all doshas, and most importantly, acquiring good fortune.

Then we see the Shankara Peeta, where Adi Shankara Bhagavathpada meditated, and by virtue of his ascetic powers, visualized the form of Devi in all totality and realized the Devi herself. As we move in a pradakshina at the outer enclosure, we first find Subrahmanya swamy, then Saraswathi and then Pranalingeshwara, Partheshwara, the deity of Mukhya Prana (with a bell on the tail) installed by Vadiraja, Vishnu Brindavana, a beautiful idol of Gopalakrishna within the Brindaana (Considered as upa-pradhana Devatha), the platform for Tulasi and then the temple of Veerabhadraswamy who is the presiding deity. Entrance to this shrine being made of wood, we may see an excellent image, of Nrutya Ganapathi, right at the centre of the arch. It is said that the deity of Mukhya Prana has been situated right opposite the Veerabhadraswamy shrine with a view to balance its frightful appearance.

Pooja Practices

Here pooja practices are based on two disciplines-one as per vathula, which is one of the 28 vedas of Shaivagama, and which includes the rituals of Bali (sacrifice); secondly, as per Vijaya yagama Shastra. The five different poojas performed at the temple everyday are during Dantadavana (brushing the teeth), morning, afternoon, evening (pradhosha) and night. Pradosha Pooja is also called as "Salam Mangalarathi". It is said that Tippu Sultan, the ruler of Srirangapatna, once arrived here during pradosha pooja, witnessed the Mangalarathi, and became so impressed with the Devi, that he offered a Salaam in Muslim tradition to the Goddess, hence the name came into use. Complementary to this account is the practice observed every year, when the Muslim brethren visit the temple on a specific day for the darshana of the Goddess.

This special feature has been in vogue for many years now. Of the various festivals and other celebrations held at the temple, "Sharannavarathri" which is held usually during October, and "Brahma Rathotsava" held usually in the month of March are both very prominently observed. There are several instances of childless couples, the dumb, the blind and many such other people making a vow to the Goddess and realizing their desires.

Ornamental Jewels of Sri Devi Mookambika

There is vast collection of jewels at the temple received as gifts of acknowledgement from the community of devotees who have realized their dreams and desires with the blessings of the Goddess. Of the various jewels of the Devi, the one in emerald is very valuable. Emerald represents knowledge. This temple has two processional deities of gold. One is offered by Rani Chennamma as a substitute for the missing of original one. But subsequently the missing one found and thus there are two processional idols. Former Chief Minister of Tamil Nadu Sri. M.G.R. gifted a gold sword, which weighs one kg. And are 2½ feet long.

The former Chief Minister of Karnataka-Sri Gundu Rao, has gifted a similar type sword made of silver. The facial mask of Goddess Mookambika is completely of gold and gifted by Vijaya Nagara Empire. The gold face mask of Jyothirlinga gifted by Chennammaji of Keladi is another unique ornament.

Sowparnika River

The two rivers Agnithirtha & Sowparnika which flow in the sanctuary of mookambika descend from Kodachadri hills. The wee spring of cool water situated in between the temples of Kalabhairava and Umamaheshwara is the source of river Sowparnika. Legend says that Suparna (Garuda) did a penance on the banks of this river praying to the Goddess for the abatement of his mother Vinutha's sorrows.

When the Goddess appeared before him, he prayed that the river be henceforth known after him, Suparna, and therefore came to be called as Sowparnika. At the location where he is said to have sat in penance, there is a small cave even today which is known as "Garuda's Cave".

This holy river takes birth at the Kodachadri and flows up to the edge of Anthargami (now oluru) region where two more streams called Bhrungisha and Pippalada join it. Then it flows westward, surrounding Kollur in the name of "Sampara", and proceeds to join the sea near the temple of "Maharajaswamy" (Varahaswamy) at Maravanthe.

It is believed that river absorbs the elements of 64 different medicinal plants and roots as it flows, therefore it cures all the diseases of those who bathe in it. Hence a bath in this river assumes significance and is considered sacred.

Murudeshwara

Murudeshwara is a town in the Bhatkal Taluk of Uttara Kannada district in the state of Karnataka, India. Murudeshwara is another name of the Hindu god Shiva. Famous for the world's tallest Shiva statue, this beach town lies on the coast of the Arabian Sea and is also famous for the *Murudeshwara Temple*.

Etymology

The origin of the name Murudeshwara dates to the time of Ramayana. The Hindu gods attained immortality and invincibility by worshipping a divine lingam called the AtmaLinga. The Lanka king Ravana wanted to attain immortality by obtaining the AtmaLinga. Since the AtmaLinga belonged to Lord Shiva, Ravana worshipped Shiva with devotion. Pleased by his prayers, Lord Shiva appeared before him and granted him a boon. Ravana asked the AtmaLinga as the boon. Lord Shiva agreed to give him the boon with a condition that it should never be placed on the ground. If the AtmaLinga was ever placed on the ground, it will get stuck to that place. Having obtained his boon, Ravana started back on his journey to Lanka.

Sage Narada, who came to know of this incident, realised that with the AtmaLinga, Ravana may obtain immortality and create havoc on earth. He approached the Lord Vishnu and requested him to prevent the AtmaLinga from reaching Lanka. Lord Vishnu knew that Ravana was a very devoted person who used to peform prayer ritual in the evening every day without fail. He decided to make use of this fact and with the help of Lord Ganesh came up with a plan to confiscate the AtmaLinga from Ravana.

As Ravana was nearing Gokarna, Lord Vishnu blotted the sun to make it look like evening had appeared. Ravana now had to perform his evening rituals but was worried because with the AtmaLinga in his hands, he would not be able to do his rituals. At this time, Lord Ganesh in the disguise of a Brahmin boy came near him. Seeing him, Ravana requested him to hold the AtmaLinga until he performed his rituals, and asked him not to place it on the ground. Ganesh struck a deal with him saying that he will call Ravana thrice, and if Ravana does not return within that time, he would place the AtmaLinga on the ground.

As predicted, before Ravana could return after completing his rituals, Ganesh had already placed the AtmaLinga on the ground. Vishnu then removed his illusion and it was daylight again. Ravana, realising that he had been tricked, got really angry and tried to uproot and destroy it but could not.

Then he decided to destroy the covering of the AtmaLinga, and threw the case covering it to a place called Sajjeshwara, 23 miles away. Then he threw the lid of the case to a placed called Guneshwara, 27 miles away. Finally, he threw the cloth covering the AtmaLinga to a placed called Mrideshwara in Kanduka-Giri (Kanduka Hill). Mrideshwara has been rechristened to Murudeshwara.

Nanjangud

Nanjangud is a town in Mysore district in the Indian state of Karnataka. It is a temple town and is on the banks of the river Kapila (a.k.a Kabini). It is at a distance of 23 km from the city of Mysore. Nanjangud is also called as "Dakshina Kashi" (southern Kashi).

Origin of Name

The main temple at Nanjangud is dedicated to the Hindu god Shiva, whose another name is Nanjundeshwara. Nanjundeshwara means the God who drank poison. Hindu mythology quotes an interesting legend in which the Gods and demons churned the ocean in search of the nectar of immortality. During this churning, there were lots of artefacts that emanated out of the ocean, including poison.

To prevent the poison from spreading across the universe and destroying it, Shiva came to the rescue and drank the poison. His wife Parvati then held his throat tightly to prevent the poison from spreading to the rest of his body. Nanjanagud literally means the place where Nanjundeshwara resides.

History

Nanjangud has been a major Shaiva centre since times immemorial. The original Nanjundeshwara temple is said to be of Ganga period (325-1000 CE). This temple has then been renovated by the Hoysala kings. Both Hyder Ali and Tipu Sultan had close associations with this temple. Wodeyar kings have provided various grants to renovate the temple.

Nandi Temple

Nandi Temple (or Basavanagudi Nandi Temple) is located in Basavanagudi, a neighborhood of Bangalore, the capital of the state of Karnataka, India. The temple is exclusively for the worship of the sacred Hindu demi-god, the bull Nandi, Lord Shiva's vahana. The temple was built in 1537 by a local ruler under the Vijayanagara empire in the Vijayanagara architectural style. The ruler, a feudatory chief named Kempe Gowda, also founded the city of Bangalore. The temple is named after the large granite Nandi monolith placed on a plinth in the temple shrine (*garbhagriha*) which has become blackened from years of being rubbed with charcoal and oil. The temple is a small one, consisting only of the shrine fronted by a porch in the Vijayanagara style. The current tower (vimana) over the shrine was constructed in the early 20th century and is adorned with Shaiva figures and motifs.

It is said to house one of the largest Nandi idols in the world. The height of the idol is approximately 15 ft and it is approximately 20 feet long.

Nellitheertha Cave Temple

Nellitheertha Cave Temple in Nellitheertha, Karnataka, India is dedicated to the Indian deity Sri Somanatheshwara, or Shiva. The temple dates back to at least 1487.

The most interesting aspect of this temple is the natural cave situated to the right of the temple. The cave is about 200 metres long and one needs to crawl on ones knees to reach the inside of the cave. Inside, one can find a beautiful lake and a Shiva Lingam.

Nuggehalli

Nuggehalli also known as Nuggihalli is a town in Hassan district in Karnataka, India. It is located on the Tiptur-Channarayanapatna state highway. It is about 50 kms from Hassan city. It is connected by road with Bangalore, the state capital. Nuggehalli is home to two beautiful Hoysala temples, the Lakshminarasimha temple built in 1246 CE and the Sadashiva temple built in 1249 CE by Bommanna Dandanayaka, a commander in the Hoysala Empire during he rule of King Vira Someshwara. The town was called Vijaya Somanathapura in ancient times and was founded as an *agrahara* (place of learning) by Bommanna Dandanayaka. Prior to coming under the control of the Hoysalas, the area was ruled by the Chola dynasty who had built a Jayagondeshwara temple. The temple later was also patronised by King Vishnuvardhana in 1121 CE.

Pattadakal

Pattadakal is a town in the Indian state of Karnataka famous for its group of monuments that are the culmination of earliest experiments in vesara style of Hindu temple architecture. The temples were built in the 8th century CE. The uniqueness of this place derives from the presence of both the Dravidian or the Southern and the Nagara or the Northern (Indo-Aryan) styles of temple architecture.

Pattadakal is 22 kms from Badami, the capital of the Chalukya dynasty of Southern India, who built the temples in the seventh and eighth centuries. There are ten temples including a Jain sanctuary sourrounded by numerous small shrines and plinths. Four temples were built in Dravidian style, four in *nagara* style of Northern India and the Papanatha temple in mixed style. The group of mounuments in Pattadakal was designated a World Heritage Site in 1987.

Polali

Polali is a village in Bantwal taluk, in the Dakshina Kannada (South Canara) district of Karnataka state in India. Polali is famous for the Raja Rajeshwari Temple. Raja Rajeswari is an icon of Shakti.

Ranganathaswamy Temple, Bangalore

A temple dating back to the 16th century C.E dedicated to Lord Ranganathaswamy.The temple is built in the Vijayanagara style of architecture and has beautifully carved granite pillars. The temple is located on Ranganathaswamy Temple Street off Avenue Road, Bangalore, India

Shree Vishnumurthy Temple

Shree Vishnumurthy Temple is located in the town of Kulai(Suratkal) near Surathkal about 15 km north of Mangalore in the state of Karnataka, India. This is an ancient Vishnu shrine has a statue estimated to be about 600 years old. The temple's presiding deity is Shree Vishnumurthy who is another form of Lord Vishnu. Initially no temple complex was evident but Mr. Venkatramana Hebbar, a local archeologist and historian, found a small shrine in a state of ruin in the forest around 1911. The temple has been repeatedly renovated and is in use today with an active schedule of worship and festival celebrations.

Shri Vinayaka Shankaranarayana Durgamba Temple

Situated on the banks on Netravathi river the Shri Vinayaka Shankaranarayana Durgamba temple is fascinating not only for its artistic and scenic view but also for the spiritual energy it provides for the visitiors. It is the Sanctum-Sanctorum of thousands of devotees from all over the world.

Devotees whole-heartedly participate in the grand age-old JATHRA MAHOTSAVA and many other religious activities conducted at the Kshethra. In spite of this natural deterioration the Kshethra has maintained its OLD GLORY through its numerous religion and social activities. Under the able guideness of Shri A.C.Bhandary, the current Managing Trustee of the Temple, development works are going in a rapid phase.

The newly built all purpose "NANDA DEEPA" AUDITORIUM, the spacious new Bhojanashala, "The Community Tower", have all added new glory to the historically famous Kshethra. The Thirtha Mantap and Gharbhagudi of the Lord Vinayaka, Lord Shankara Narayana, Lord Shri Durgamba have been remodeled. New Main Entrance to the Temple and Swagatha Gopuram at the Entrance have been built. Also a new erection of a Brass Covered Holy Flag Pole is done. Much more development activities are planned at the Kshethra.

"AKHAYA, NEYHRAVATHI", which caters to the Mid-day meals programme and FREE MEDICAL CHECK-UP CAMP has also been set up at the Kshethra to serve the people of the region.

Shringeri

Sringeri, also written as Shringeri, is a taluk located in Chikmagalur district in the Indian state of Karnataka, is the site of the first maþha established by Adi Shankaracharya, Hindu theologian and exponent of the Advaita Vedanta philosophy, in the 8th century C.E. It is located on the banks of the river Tunga.

Shringeri Sharadamba Temple

Sri Sharadamba temple is a famous Hindu dedicated to goddess Saraswati located in the holy town of Shringeri in Karnataka, India

Shivasamudram

Shivasamudram (also called ShivanaSamudram or Bluff) is an island town dividing the Kaveri River into twin waterfalls, the Gaganachukki and the Barachukki, dropping 90 m. The town is located 27 km from Somanathapura and 80 km from Mysore in the Mysore district of the state of Karnataka, India.

Someshwara

Someshwara is the presiding deity in the temple of same name. The temple is situated in the heart of Kolar town. Lord Shiva is worshipped as someshwara. The temple was built by the chola kings who ruled the region in about 11th century.

The cholas were eventually driven out by the Kannada-speaking Chalukyas, but the temples which they buit still remain a testimony to the magnificent architecture of the Cholas. The someshawara temple is built in the typical Chola style of temple building with a huge gopuram at the entrance of the temple.

Sri Ranganathaswamy Temple (Shivanasamudra)

The Sri Ranganthaswamy temple in Shivanasamudra, in the Indian state of Karnataka, is a temple dedicated to the Hindu God Ranganatha, a manifestation of Vishnu. The temple is one of a set of three major temples that are built on three different islands on the Kaveri and are dedicated to lord Ranganatha, the others being those at Srirangapatna and Srirangam

Sri Ranganathaswamy Temple (Srirangapatna)

The Sri Ranganthaswamy temple in Srirangapatna, in the Indian state of Karnataka, is a temple dedicated to the Hindu God Ranganatha, a manifestation of Vishnu and is one of the Pancharanga Kshetrams. The town of Srirangapatna, which derives its name from the temple, is located on an island in the river Kaveri. The temple is one of a set of three major temples that are built on three different islands on the Kaveri and are dedicated to lord Ranganatha.

Sudi

Sudi is a panchayat town in the Gadag District of Karnataka, India. At one time it was a key town of the Kalyani Chalukyas during 1000 AD. It is famous for rare stone carved monuments like twin towered temple and large well built of stone and carvings, and few other structural temples. For long time these amazing structures were abandoned, but recently they caught the eye of the Indian Archeological Department.

Talakad

Talakad is a town on the left bank of the Kaveri river at a spot where the river makes a sharp bend. It is 45 kms from

Mysore and 185 kms from Bangalore in Karnataka, India. A historic site, Talakad once had over 30 temples that today are buried in sand. Now it is a scenic and spiritual pilgrimage centre. Here the eastward flowing Kaveri river changes course and seems magnificiently vast as here the sand on its banks spreads over a wide area.

Talapady

Talapady (Talapadi) is a village in Mangalore Taluk (Tehsil) of the Dakshina Kannada district of Karnataka state in India.

Talapady borders the state of Kerala. National Highway 17(NH-17), connecting Mangalore (Kudla or Mangaluru) to Kasaragod, passes through it. There is a checkpost here. A temple of Durga is at Devipura,Talapady. Goddess Durga parameshwari is the icon of Shakti. Goddess Durga parameshwari is the family deity (Kuladevata) of many people, especially Shivalli Madhva brahmins (Tulu brahmins). The temple is very old and considered to be very sacred.The temple practices some strict traditions like men can enter temple only,when they are bare chested.

Trikuteshwara

The beautifully-carved Trikuteshwara temple is located in the town of Gadag, 50 km south east of Hubli in Karnataka, India. The temple is dedicated to Shiva, and has three lingams mounted on the same stone. There is a shrine dedicated to Saraswathi in this temple and it has nicely carved columns. The temple dates back to the Kalyani Chalukyas who ruled this region from around 1050 to 1200 CE, during which time about 50 temples were built.

Udayagiri and Khandagiri Caves

Udayagiri and Khandagiri Caves are the caves of archaeological, historical and religious importance near Bhubaneswar in Orissa (India), situated on two hills Udayagiri and Khandagiri, mentioned as *Kumari Parvat* in Hathigumpha inscription, facing each other across the roads and have a number of finchy and ornately carved caves. It is believed that most of these caves were carved out huge residential blocks for the Jain monks, during the reign of King Kharavela. Udayagiri meaning Sunrise Hill, has 18 caves while Khandagiri has 15 caves. The caves of Udayagiri and Khandagiri, called lena or lena in the inscriptions, were dug out mostly during the reign of Kharavela for the above of Jaina ascetics. The most important of this group is Ranigumpha in Udayagiri which is a double storeyed monastery.

Udupi Krishna Temple

Udupi Krishna Temple is a famous Hindu temple dedicated to Lord Krishna located in the town of Udupi in Karnataka, India. The temple area resembles a living ashram, a holy place for daily devotion and living, founded by Madhvacharya founder of the Dvaita school of Vedanta. Legend has it that once Kanakadasa a worshipper who was not allowed into the temple was so piously dedicated, that one day the Krishna statue miraculously turned around to allow the disciple to gaze upon his heavenly form through a small window at the back of the mutt (matha). There are several temples here, the most ancient as basic wood and stone of 1,500 years origin.

Virupaksha Temple

Virupaksha Temple is located in Hampi 350 kms from Bangalore, in the state of Karnataka in southern India.

Hampi sits on the banks of the Tungabhadra River in the ruins of the ancient city of Vijayanagar, capital of the Vijayanagara empire. Virupaksha Temple is the main centre of pilgrimage at Hampi and has been considered the most sacred over the centuries. It is fully intact among the surrounding ruins and is still used in worship. The temple is dedicated to Shiva, known here as Virupaksha, as the consort of the local goddess Pampa who is associated by local mythology with the Tungabhadra River.

7

Hindu Temples in Kerala

Alathiyur Hanuman Temple

The Hanuman Temple is located at Alathiyur near Tirur in the Malappuram district of Kerala. According to legend, the Purumthrikkovil idol of Hanuman was consecrated by Sage Vasastha 3000 years ago in 1000 BC. Over the years the custodians of the temple were Alathiur Grama Namboodiri, Sri Vittath Raja, and the Zamorin Raja of Korikode.

Even though the main deity of the temple is Sri Rama this temple is famous and known as a Hanuman temple. Sage Vasatha installed the temple at the place where Sri Rama gives instructions to Sri Hanuman before his going to Lanka in search of Sita. The idol of Hanuman is adjacent to the main temple of Sree Rama. Sree Hanuman stands leaning forward as if to hear his master's words with a club in his hand. The temple of Sri Lakshmanan is situated a few metres outside the main temple.

It is believed Sri Lakshmanan was keeping away allowing Sri Rama and Hanuman to talk confidentialy. Here there is a platform commemorating Sri Hanuman's jump over to Lanka over the sea. In one end of the platform there is a Long Granite stone (Symbolizes the Sea) where devotees run on the platform and jump over the long Granite Stone. It is said that doing this jump in this temple brings great luck, health, long life, and wealth to all who perform this jump. Sri Hanuman of Alathiyur not only eliminates all mental agonies and fear of his devotees but fulfils all their desires.

Present State of the Temple

The Indian Government nationalized all Hindu temples. Years of neglect by the Indian government have resulted in extensive damage and presently the Temple needs to be renovated. The local population and the devotees have now embarked on a renovation programme under the guidance of the temple manager.

Ambalappuzha Sri Krishna Temple

Ambalappuzha Sri Krishna Temple, Malayalam is a Hindu temple in Ambalappuzha, Alapuzha district of Kerala, in south India.

The Temple

The Ambalappuzha Sri Krishna Temple is believed to have been built in the in the year AD 790 by the local ruler Chembakasserry Pooradam Thirunal-Devanarayanan Thampuran.

This temple is directly associated to the Guruvayoor Sri Krishna Temple. During the raids of Tipu Sultan in 1789, the idol of Sri Krishna from the Guruvayoor Temple was brought to the Ambalappuzha Temple for safe keeping.

The payasam served in the Ambalappuzha Temple is famous among Hindu devotees. This sweet pudding made of rice and milk has an interesting mythological legend behind it.

Ambalapuzha is a coastal town besides the NH 47 about 13 kms to the south of Allepey. The temple of Sree Krishna is located 1.5 kms east of the town junction. In the olden the headquarters of the Ambalapuzha rajahs were near the temple. There was a time when the Ambalapuzha territory had been under the rule of Chempakasseri rajahs. But when Marthanda Varma, the valorous ruler of Travancore conquered Chempakasseri territory in 925 M.E., there occurred a gradual declension of the royal family of Chempakasseri.Some people worship the presiding deity of the Ambalapuzha temple as 'Parathasarthy' while others as Gopalakrishna but both the names of course, are the two sides of the same coin.As it is said commonly, the legend about the origin and exaltation of the temple goes like this:

> *At one time in the history of Ambalapuzha, the place where the present temple is situated, was under water. While the rajah of Ambalapuzha dynasty and Vilwamangalam Swamiyar were going throught the waterways, it so happened that they could hear a luscious sound of flute coming from a nearby huge and luxuriant peepul tree. Swamiyar was so attracted by the music that the wanted the oarsman to row the boat to the shore. On landing they went in search of the origin of the melodious song.To his astonishment Swamiyar saw Sree Krishna sitting on a branch of the peepul tree playing his flute.*
>
> *At first he could not believe his eyes. He folded his hands and bowed his head, so did rajah. Both of them went round the tree singing praises of the Lord. The rajah thought that at last prosperity had come to his kingdom. He was so much pleased with the presence of the Almighty in his kingdom that he considered it as a blessing in disguise for the smooth functioning of his duties as well as the lofty administration of the territory.Vilwamangalam urged the king to build a suitable temple for the Lord where they had seen him. The place belonged to an Ezhava leader Ambanattu Panicker.*
>
> *The king bought the land, a major portion of which was submerged land, by giving him adequate compensation. The submerged land was filled up with soil and temple was built in a few months. It was decided to install the image made for the purpose in an astrologically suited time. But the high priest, after he examined the idol, expressed the view that the idol had certain inauspicious traits so that it was unsuitable for placement.*
>
> *The declaration of the priest fell upon the king like a thunder bolt. However, he wanted to get and idol placed at the stipulated time itself. He did not want to put off the function to a later period. It was a pity that the king*

could not make use of the original image meant for the purpose.Some people believe that the present idol was brought from Thiruvanvandoor, a village near Thiruvalla by bullying and coaxing a Brahmin priest. On the other hand some are of the opinion that it was brought from Koratti Thiruvampadi temple.

Anyhow, the king and his men were able to find an idol suitable to be fixed, and it was carried out on the day of 'Moolam' astericism in 'Midhunam (June/ July). Every year on the same day people in and around the place, forgetting themselves of their caste or creed, celebrate the eventful day by arranging colourful boat-race which is now known as the famous Champakulam boat-race.

Chempakasseri mana was the old royal palace on the southern part of the temple. Since ll the Chempakasseri kings were nampoothiries, the name of the 'mana' became the name of the kingdom. After having established the temple, Pooram Thirunal Maharajah handed over his kingdom into the divine hands of Lord Unnikrishna and left his kingdom to become one with the Brahma.

The sweet broth made of milk, sugar and rice, otherwise known as 'Ambalapuzha palpayasam' is well-known because of its speciality. No other sweet broth of any kind is as delicious and melodious as this payasam.

The folk-story behind the source of this broth, as handed down from generation to generation is as flows:

When there existed an acute financial difficulty at Chempakasseri kingdom, the king borrowed some money and paddy from a Patter and saved the country from a crisis. But the king was not able to repay the debt in time. So he became very sad. One day, when the king visited the temple as part of his daily routine, the Patter approached him and demanded the money and paddy. The king could not help avoiding the Patter and so he was completely at sea. At this time, as good luck would have it, Patter felt a sudden call of conscience and he told the king that he wouldn't have to repay the debt and in lieu of this he would make use of the money and paddy for a daily offering of palpayasam to Lord Krishna. The king heeded to this request and from the next day onwards he arranged for the preparation of the broth to be used for the noon offering to the deity. The ceremonial 10 day festival in 'Meenam' (March / April) is the most important festival at this temple. During this time there will be spectacular processions of deities on decorated elephants.

Besides, there will be a grand feast at the temple dining hall. It is believed that the Lord Unnikrishna will be present in disguise for the feast. So it is conducted with utmost care and sanctity. Once during festival Vilwamangalam Swamiyar had seen the Lord in the mess hall! 'Velakali' a kind of dance in imitation of battle, is an important ritualistic item which is being performed in front of the shrine. It reminds us of the old type of warfare using shield and sword which was once prevalent in the Chempakasseri kingdom.A 12-day 'Kalabham' festival (smearing of sandal paste) from the 1st of 'Makaram' (January / February) and 'Pallippana' which is held once in 12 years are special occasions of the temple.

The main gate of the temple is on the western side. The golden tope dome, a single-stone mandapam, the architectural stone images and the golden flag staff in front are a few signs of its eminence and splendour.The temple has neither a gate tower, nor shrines for gods outside the main sanctum sanctorum.The divine image is about 3 feet high.

Each day the holy face is adorned with gold when the rituals are being performed. In the right hand the divine holds a lash and in the left a conch which proclaims that the deity is none other than Parthasarathy himself. Link

An idol of Sri Krishna, The Lord Parthsarathy idol was installed in the temple.

The Aaraattu festival commences with the flag hoisting ceremony on the Atham star in Meenam (March-April). The important Aaraattu festival takes place on the Thiruvonam day of the same month.

In this temple 'Pallipana' is performed by 'Velans' (sorcerers) once in twelve years. Human sacrifice was conducted in ancient times. However, cocks have now replaced humans on the sacrificial altar.

Kalakkaththu Kunchan Nambiar(1705-1770) also spent his youth at Ambalappuzha.

Ammathiruvadi Temple

Ammathiruvadi Temple is located about 12 km away from Thrissur town in Kerala state, south India, in the village of Ûrakam. It is regarded as one of the great 108 Durga temples.

Ananthapura Lake Temple

Ananthapura Lake Temple is a Hindu temple located in the middle of a lake in the Kasargod District of Kerala, South India, 5 km from Kumbla. This is the only lake temple in Kerala and the original seat (*Moolasthana*) of *Ananthapadmanabha Swami (Padmanabhaswamy Temple) Thiruvananthapuram.*

Local legend has it that this is the original site where Ananthapadmanabha settled down. The temple's lake is also home to a venerable crocodile, which is supposed to be the guard of the temple. When one dies another mysteriously takes its place. Kumbla (or Kumbala) can easily be reached from Mangalore via a number of bus routes, as well as by train and taxi.

Ananthanatha Swami Temple

Ananthanatha Swami Temple (also known as the Puliyarmala Jain Temple) is a Jain temple located at Puliyarmala, 6 km from Kalpetta in the Wayanad district in the state of Kerala in India. It is dedicated to Ananthanatha Swami, one of the prominent saints of Jain faith.

Description

The outer entrance of the temple has a large pillar of carved granite in front of the main gate. The entrance doors contain intricately carved panels. Constructed in the traditional Dravidian style, the ornate carvings of the stupa are colorfully painted as they rise in a pyramid shape to the top where there is a carving of Mahavir. The small steps of the temple's main shrine are covered with many different Jain idols and symbols constructed of stone, brass and gold.

Aranmula Parthasarathy Temple

The Aranmula Parthasarathy Temple is a Hindu temple near Aranmula, a village in Kerala, South India.

The temple is on the left bank of the Pampa River. It is from here that the sacred jewels of Ayyappan are taken in procession to Sabarimalai each year. Aranmula is also known for the watersports involving a spectacular procession of snake boats. It is also linked with legends from the Mahabharata.

It is one of the most important Krishna temples in Kerala, the others being at Guruvayur, Trichambaram, Tiruvarppu and Ambalappuzha.

Also, it is one of the five ancient shrines in the Chengannur area of Kerala, connected with the Mahabharata. The Chengannur temple is related to Yuddhishtra; the Tiruppuliyur temple to Bheema; Aranmula to Arjuna; Tiruvamundur to Nakula and Tirukkadittaanam to Sahadeva). It has been glorified by the Tamil hymns of Nammalwar of the 1st millennium CE.

The temple has four towers over its entrances on its outer wall. The eastern tower is accessed through a flight of 18 steps. Descending 57 steps through the northern tower, one can reach the Pampa River.

Arattupuzha Temple

The Arattupuzha Temple is the famous Sree Sastha temple situated at Aarattupuzha, a beautiful village located 15 km away from Thrissur town in Kerala, India. The road that leads to this temple is 2 km to the east from *Tevar Road Bus stop* on the Thrissur-Kodungallur route.

Brahmeeswaran Temple, Palakkad

Brahmeeswaran Temple is a Hindu temple in the Palakkad district of Kerala state, south India. It is situated in Karimpuzha village, 25 km from Palakkad town.

The old temple was in an abandoned state for quite some time, till late 2001. A Nair family called "Chalapurathu" whose *tharavadu* (House) is situated in Karimpuzha came with an offering to Lord Shiva. The Chalapurathu family had renovated the temple, which took almost three years to complete. Businessman Mr B G Menon and famous Malayalam cine artist Mr Ravi Menon, who are members of Chalapurathu family took the lead role in getting the renovation completed.

Cherai Gowreeshwara Temple

Cherai Gowreeshwara Temple is one of the main Hindu temple in Kerala state, south India. This temple is in Cherai village in Ernakulam district of Kerala. Temple is mainatained by *Vinjhana Vardhini Sabha* (V. V Sabha). It also known as *Malyala palani*. The festival in the temple is biggest festival in Eranakulam district. The festival happens every year towards the last 2 weeks of January or first 2 weeks of February. The main attractions are Elephant march(around 20-30 elephants).

There is one more famous temple in Cherai, which is *Azheekkal Sree Varaha Temple* famous for its beautiful chariot.

Chottanikkara Temple

The Chottanikkara Temple is a famous temple of the Hindu mother goddess Bhagawati. The temple is located near Ernakulam in the southern Indian state of Kerala and is one of the most popular temple in the state, along with Sabarimala. Bhagawati is one of the most popular deities in the area, and she is worshipped at the temple, along with Lord Vishnu, in three different forms: as Saraswati in the morning, draped in white; as Bhadrakali at noon, draped in crimson; and as Durga in the evening, decked in blue.

People suffering from mental illnesses commonly visit the temple, as Bhagawati is thought to cure her devotees. One should not miss the 'Guruthi Pooja' in the 'Keezhkkaavu' temple at Chottanikkara. This is a ritual done at late evening to invoke the goddess.

'Chottanikara Magam' is the famous religious festival in the temple.

Ezhumanthuruthu Poonkavil Devi Temple

Poonkavil Sri.Balabhadra temple is one of the rarest temples of the deity Sri.Bala Bhadra. It is situated in a village called Ezhumanthuruthu in Kaduthuruthy Grama Panchayat, Kottayam District, Kerala State in India.

Guruvayur Temple

The Guruvayur Shri Krishna Temple is one of the most important and sacred pilgrim centres of Kerala. It is located in Guruvayur town of Thrissur district in Kerala,India and is easily accessible by road and rail. The presiding deity is MahaVishnu, in the standing posture with four hands which carry a Sankhu(conch), Sudarshana chakram (a serrated disk),lotus and mace. He is worshipped as Balakrishna, the full avatar (*Purnaavatara*) of Mahavishnu. The idol is made of a rare stone known as *Patala Anjana*.

Kallil Temple

Kallil Temple is 22 km away from Kalady, the birth place of Adi Sankaracharya. It is a 9th century Jain Temple in Kerala, South India. Kallil is malayalam for 'in stone'.

The temple, located in 28 acre (113,000 m^2) plot, is cut from a huge rock and a climb of 120 steps leads to the temple. To reach the temple one has to travel a distance of about 2 km from Odakkali, on the Aluva Munnar Road and 10 km from Perumbavoor.

The temple is under the administrative control of Chenkottukonam Sree Ramadasashramam. Earlier the temple was owned by the Kallil Pisharody family.

Durgadevi is the main deity of the temple. The idol of Brahma is seen carved at the top of the rock. *Brahma* is also worshipped along with Shiva and Vishnu. The temple closes after Poojas at noon every day and poojas are not being done at night. The annual festival of the temple is conducted eight days starting from the 'Karthika day' in *Vrischikam* (November-December). The procession is being conducted by carrying the idol of the deity on a female elephant.

The Jain deities of Parshvanath, Mahavira and Padmavati devi (worshipped as Bhagawathi by the local population) point to the Jain antecedents of the Kallil Pisharody.

Karppillikkavu Sree Mahadeva Temple

The Karppillikkavu Sree Mahadeva Temple is a Hindu temple to Shiva located in Manjapra, a village in the Ernakulam district of the Kerala region of India.

There is an important festival associated with the temple called Karpillikkavu Pooram. It lasts eight days during the month of Makara, a period corresponding to late January and early February. During this time, Shiva is believed to be in a pleasant mood and willing to grant all of the requests of his devotees.

Killikkurussimangalam

Killikkurussimangalam (also known as *Lakkidi*) is a small village around 8 km from nearby town Ottappalam in Palakkad district of Kerala, south India. The river Nila (Bharatapuzha) flows through the southern border of Lakkidi.

The village got its name from the famous Lord Shiva temple-Sri Killikkurussi Mahadeva Kshetram situated in the village. The temple is very old and legends say it has been founded by the sage *Sree Suka Brahma Hrishi*.

The village is the birth place of famous Malayalam satire poet and founder of the Ottamthullal art form, Kunchan Nambiar (Rama panivada). The house, where Kunchan Nambiar was born-Kalakkathu Bhavanam, is now a cultural central, under taken by Department of Culture of Kerala State

Government. There is also a library situated here in memory of Kunchan Nambiar called *Kunchan Smaraka Vayanasala*-Kunchan Memorial Library.

Kodikkunnu Bhagavathy Temple

The Kodikkunnu Bhagavathy Temple or Kodikkunnu Ambalam is a famous Hindu temple dedicated to Goddess Durga located in the village of Pallippuram, near Pattambi, in Palakkad district of Kerala, India. The goddess is commonly referred to as the Bhagavathy or Kodikkunnathamma.

The word "kunnu" means hill in Malayalam language. Literally, Kodikkunnu Temple would thus mean the temple situated on top of the hill called "Kodi". Kodikkunnu is near to Pallippuram railway station and can be accessed from Valanchery, Pattambi and Thrithala, by road. The main deity is *Amma* means Mother and there is Shiva also with almost same importance. To the left of Bhagavathy is the idol of Ganapathi. People come from distant places to worship the goddess. The temple has *nada* (holy entrance) from 3 directions, *viz.*, north, east and west. The door towards the south is permanently closed. Vehicles cannot reach the immediate temple premises as there is no road reaching the temple. From all three directions there are granite stone-paved steps to reach the temple.

Koodalmanikyam Temple

Koodalmanikyam Temple is the only Hindu temple in India where Bharata (Lord Sangameshwara), the brother of Sree Rama is worshipped. This beautiful ancient temple is situated in Irinjalakuda a small town in Trissur district of Kerala state, south India.

The speciality of this temple is that there is only one place of worship, even Ganapathy is not be found inside the temple. Usually all big temples in India will have more than one deity inside the temple, especially Sree Ganapathy.

Kshetram—The Hindu Temple of Kerala

Kerala is a land of temples. And Temples here, in a sense,

were the pivot of religious, social, economic and cultural life of the Malayalam people." (Sarkar 1978:1)

Apart from the economic aspects this statement of the archaeologist H Sarkar is still valid in present-day Kerala. In comparison to the mighty dravidian stone temples of the neighbouring state of Tamil Nadu, the view of the horizontal structured Kerala temple surprises with its modest proportions, the flat wooden and stone buildings, pillars, its enclosure by a low stone wall, the temple pond (kolam) attached to this small place of worship. Each part of the temple seems to be shaped according to the beautifully green surrounding, the coconut trees and paddy fields, serving the spiritual and social needs of the people living in villages nearby.

They call the temples kshetram, ambalam, or (in the north) tali. One could think of an ancient naturally grown socio-ecological concept. Sarkar (1978) shows how geographical factors ("high precipitation, the availability of laterite formation and dense jungles"), politics, culture and economy "influenced greatly the evolution of Kerala's temple-architecture". Sanskrit treatises, especially the Tantrasamuccya, codified the rules for temple architecture, thus the Kerala temple presents "a uniform level of achievement, and reflects more or less a common doctrinal approach and rituals".

The present-day kshetram were built from the ninth century onwards, amalgamating the dravidian goddess shrine (kavu) with aryan temple construction practices (Sarkar 1978:2-3). The centre of each temple is the srikovil, the tiny shrine where the main deity (murti) is seated. The sopana (steps) lead to the srikovil, which can be square, apsidal, rectangular, or circular. Nalambalam (the inner wall) surrounds the srikovil, the namaskara mandapan (pillared community space), various bali (minor gods symbolised by stone plinths) and the sapta madriga (the seven mother goddesses).

An outer wall (prakaram) encloses a courtyard where the dhvaja-stambha (the temple flagstaff), balipitha (the main bali plinth, also called velia balikal), the astha digbali (minor vedic gods positioned at the eight wind directions), and possibly other smaller shrines of major gods, are placed. The temple is posed in an east-west direction, the east nada (side) being the main entrance. Traditionally temple entry was strictly regulated for each community in Kerala.

Only members of the higher castes were allowed into the nalambalam, and the access to the temple precinct was completely denied to the lower castes. However, from 1936 onwards (the Travancore Temple Proclamation) the restrictions were lessened and finally abandoned. Then and now the entry to the srikovil and physical contact with the deity image is reserved to the Namputiri ritual experts, the pujari and tantri.

Kunnathoor Padi

Kunnathur Padi is the *Aaroodam* of Sree Muthappan. It is in the Kannur District of Kerala state, South India. It is 3,000 feet above sea level, atop Udumbamala of the Sahyadri mountains.

The famous Kunnathur Padi festival is conducted here, but there is no temple for Sree Muthappan. The festival is conducted in a natural setting, because Sree Muthappan frequently reminds that "fallen leaves, a spring, a large mountain, a round stone, forest and palm trees are enough, for me".

Lokanarkavu Temple

Lokanarkavu Temple is situated 5 km from Vatakara, a small town in Kerala state of south India. Lokanarkavu is a short form of *Lokamalayarkavu* which means *lokam* (world) made of *mala* (mountain), *aaru* (river) and *kavu* (grove).

In the vicinity of the temple, there are three rock cut caves. The candid murals and carvings here are of great fascination to the visitors. The main deity is Goddess Durga, with two adjacent shrines dedicated to the gods Vishnu and Shiva. The festival, locally called Pooram, is celebrated during March/April. It is believed that the temple is 1500 years old.

The week-long festival begins with Kodiyettam (flag hoisting) and concludes with Arattu. The temple dedicated to goddess Bhadrakaali has great historical importance as Thacholi

Othenan, the legendary martial hero of Kerala, used to worship here every day.

Lokanarkavu and Kalarippayattu

Forty-one day Mandala Utsavam is the annual festival at the Lokanarkavu Bhagavathy Temple. This is the only temple where a peculiar folk dance called Thacholikali is presented during festivals. The dance, performed during the festival resembles the martial art Kalarippayattu. Even today, all Kalaripayattu artists seek the blessings of the deity before their debut. This temple is associated with the heroes like Aromal Chekavar, Thacholi Othenan, Aringodar etc and heroins like Unniyarcha, Thumbolarcha of Vadakkan Pattukal.

History of Durga Temple

The Durga temple was built by Aryans Vaishya Brahmins who migrated to this place some 1500 years back. They were Brahmins who took up trade as their main occupation. The Aryan successors of these temple still are of prime importance in the temple. They gradually began to accept some of the traditions of local Nairs and made martial relationship with them. But on close examination their customs and beliefs are evidently different from local Nair community. It is believed that the goddess travelled with them to Lokanarkavu in the form of a lady who followed the five hundred Aryans.

The successors still see this goddess as their mother and not as goddess. Often the name of Thacholi Othenan is misquoted with the origin of temple. Othenan was a great devotee,but never had any holding rights or anything to do with the establishment of Durga temple. It is evident from the fact that the goddess is Durga at Lokanarkavu and not the Kali form. The heroes of Vadakkan Pattukal had their ancestral goddesses as Kali form and not Durga form.

The same applies to the local rulers who later claimed Lokanarkavu as their family goddess. All the rulers of Kerala had Goddesses with Thamasa pooja or shakteya pooja; ie poojas in which either man or animal was sacrificed. It was a more local tradition and most family temples of Kerala kings and locals had followed such tradition until it was modified. Later due to Aryanisation of temples, modifications were made by replacing human sacrifice with cutting plantain or performing poojas with tender coconut and cereals meant to replace liquor and meat. Unlike this local tradition Lokanarkavu durga temple do not have any such traditions and never had such practices as it was established by Aryans itself.

It is said that most other goddess temples in kerala are in Madhyama and rarely in Uthama state. But this temple is said to be in Athyuthama state. The Aryans though manifested as locals they strongly upheld their ethical roots through a complex of differences from rest of the people.

The race spirit was so high at older times that it is said that they refused to pay taxes to the local kings of Kkerala, as none of them was an Aryan. But at the same time or say at a later period they began to ignore the cast restrictions and even seemed to threaten the cast equations. But slowly they became adjusted and more reclusive and settles around the temple areas and withdrew from all other matters of Local people. Among the mandala vilakku festival, the successors of these Aryan Vaishya Brahmins migrants conduct the 16th vilakku, thats on 16th day and is of prime importance.

As we enter the temple we must pray to the stage kept in memory of these Aryan Brahmin Ancestors who built the temple. The stage is at right side to the main entrance and all devotees must seek their permission and pray to them to see the godess inside. This is to show that the Lokanarkavu Durga holds these people to the highest esteem and she had followed them wherever they went and their happiness is her prime importance. It is said that the prayers done without praying to these ancestors goes much unheard. In short it is a place of a never experienced tradition in Kerala.

Madai Vadukunda Shiva Temple

The Madai Vadukunda Shiva Temple is believed to have been constructed by "Kolathiri" Kings during medieval period on a plateau land generally known now as "Madai Para" in

Madai Village, Kannur Taluk and District of Kerala State. This is situating 22 km north of Kannur, the Head Quarter Town. The "Kolathiri" Kingdom is an inherent branch of erstwhile "Mooshaka" Dynasty, which ruled "Ezhimala" empire during 5th to 8th Century.

About 1200 years back a branch of their dynasty had migrated and settled down at Madai, which was then an important port and trading centre, 4 km south of Ezhimala. They constructed castles and temples and established their head quarters on "Madai Para", a significant plateau land lying at about 150 ft height from the sea level having sight to an extent of 20 km from all sides. Sree Vadukunda Shiva Temple was thus constructed on "Madai Para" in the southwest corner of it at a holy spot due to the presence of the divine power of "Swayambhoo" of lord Shiva.

Madhur Temple

History: Madhur temple was originally a Mahaligeshwara (Madanantheshwara-Shiva) temple and as the lore goes, an old lady named Madaru from so called backward caste was discovered an "Udbhava Murthy" (a statue that was not made by a human) of Shivalingam. The statue is made of alluvial soil. This statue was later installed in the temple and that's how then it was named as Madhur Madanantheshwara temple. Mahaganapathi devotion came later in the temple when this Elephant faced God appeared to some childrens as drawing art image in a South-side Wall of the temple. After ward the temple became as Madhur Mahaganapathi Temple. Local people used to call the God as 'Boddajja' also. Tipu Sultan is supposed to have visited the temple to drink water, during one of his fights in the area. A cut from his sword is still visible in the building that is built around the temple well. sadhandhan kanhangad, AYKumar Bela.

Makara Jyothi

Makara Jyothi is a beacon that appears at dusk on the day of Makara Sankaranthi (14 January) on the *Kantamala* hills facing (north-eastern side) the Sabarimala temple, a popular Hindu pilgrim centre in Kerala, India. It is widely believed by the devotees (especially those coming from outside the state of Kerala) that this *Jyothi* appears miraculously at Ponnambalamedu (believed to be the abode of Swami Ayyappan, the presiding deity of Sabarimala temple) and is the celestial manifestation of the god Ayyappan himself. Some others believe that the *Jyothi* is the Arati performed by the rishis and devas residing in the Kantamala hills. The *Makara Jyothi* marks the climax of the *Makaravilakku* season of Sabarimala pilgrimage lasting 41 days.

Mammiyoor Temple

Mammiyoor temple is a Shiva temple near Guruvayoor temple, Kerala, south India. Every devotee who goes to Guruvayoor is supposed to go to Mammiyoor also, as the ritual goes. Only Hindus are allowed inside the temple premises.

Legends

Bhagwan Vishnu himself worshipped idol at Guruvayoor made out of Pathala Anjanam. Vishnu gave the idol to Brahma. Prajapati Sutapa and his wife Prsni did penance to Brahma, and pleased with their devotion Brahma gave them this idol. Sutapa and his wife Prsni worshipped the idol with such devotion that Mahavishnu himself appeared before them for granting boon. In their over enthusiasm they asked thrice "We need a son equivalent to you". Mahavishnu told that them he himself will be born as their son in three different janmas (birth) and in all the three janmas you will get the vigraha given to you by Brahma.

In the first janma in Satya yuga, Mahavishnu was born as Prsnigarba, as son of Sutapa and Prsni. Psrigarba instructed the world the importance of Brahmacharya to the world.

In the second janma, Sutapa and his wife Prsni were born as Kashayap and Aditi and Mahavishnu was born as Vamana, their son in Treta yuga.

In Dwapara yuga, Lord Krishna' was born as son of Vasudeva and Devaki.

The idol was given to them by Daumya for worship. Sri Krishna established a big temple at Dwaraka and installed this idol. At the time of swargaarohana Lord Krishna instructed his devotee Udhava to install the idol at a sacred place with the help of Brihaspathi, the guru of the Devas and Vayu, the wind God. They (Guru and Vayu) took the idol and came down to a place down south and installed it.

This is why the place got its name Guruvayoor, where oor means place. It is also said that Lord Shiva and his Wife Parvathy were present at the auspicious moment and because there was a lack of space in the temple premises, Shiva moved a little further away, and gives his blessings from Mammiyoor Temple, which is a ten minute walk from the Guruvayoor Temple.

Mangottu Kavu Temple

Mangottu Kavu is a Hindu temple located in Athipotta, a small village in the Palakkad district of Kerala, India.

The presiding deity is Mangottu Bhagwathy. Every year the annual festival (*vela*) is conducted on the second Sunday after *Vishu* (in April), the starting of the Malayalam new year.

The *Mangottu Kavu* vela is preceded by a lot of festivities starting exactly a week before the actual festival. On the first Sunday after *vishu* the *Kodiyattum* (Flag raising) ceremony is performed. On Monday there is a *kari-kali* dance festival, wherein members of the *Nair* community visit all the Hindu homes in the locality and dance and sing the deities devotional songs. On Tuesday *chamanz-kali* follows. Here too members of the Nair community sing devotional songs visiting each Hindu home in the locality.

Wednesday there is *Kumati* festival. There are other cultural events like *chakiyaar kutt*, *pavva kutt* and so on during this festival period. A host of devotees arrive for the main *vela* festival.

Mannarasala Temple

Mannarasala Sree Nagaraja Temple is a very ancient and

internationally-known centre of pilgrimage for the devotees of serpent gods (Nagaraja).

Mezhuveli Temple

Mezhuveli Anandabhootheshawara Temple is situated at the heart of Mezhuveli. This temple was built by the villagers under the leadership of famous social reformer and poet Sri.Muloor S.Padmanabha Panicker. This century old temple was built on a place called 'Tholekavu' which was surrounded by a small hill called 'Meenchirakkal Hill' on the southern side, 'Ambottimodi' also called 'Kailasam' on the east, a beautiful stream flowing on the western side near "Pottanmala' and at the north side 'Padmanabhan Kunnu', a small hill. Tholekavu was a small forest, which is believed to be a part of the Pandalam Kingdom.

Muthappan Temple

Sree Muthappan is the most popular local god in the Kannur District of north Kerala state, south India.

Muthappan is also the theyyam performed in the famous Parassinikkadavu temple 16 km north of Kannur town.

Other theyyams are seasonal (the season lasting October to May), but Muthappan theyyam is performed year round.

This temple is in the banks of Valapattam river.

Oachira Temple

The Oachira Temple is an ancient temple in the Indian town of Karunagappally in Kollam district of Kerala State, in southern India. Every year the Oachira Vrishchikam festival is celebrated. *Oachirakkali* is a famous ritual performed during this festival and it involves mock-fighting in muddy water by traditional martial art experts.And also "Eruvathattam onam" is also celeberated.It is the festavle for catteles.In this festavel Asias tallest "EDUPPU KALA" is shown.It is from "Vayanakam kalakettu samathi".And also in this day 50s of others are shown.It is the famous festavel in "Onattu Kara".

The Oachira Temple is unique in the sense that it does not have a building or a Vigraha. People worship Lord Shiva at the base of a Banyan tree.

Padmanabhaswamy Temple

Padmanabhaswamy temple (aka Sri Padmanabhaswamy temple), is a famous Hindu temple of Lord Vishnu, located inside the Fort in city of Thiruvananthapuram, Kerala, India. The temple is one of the 108 divya desam, the holiest abodes of Lord Vishnu and the main deity, Padmanabhaswamy is a form of Vishnu in Ananthasayanam posture (in eternal sleep of *yognidra*). This is an ancient temple and the city of Thiruvananthapuram derives its name from the name of the presiding deity enshrined in the temple.

History

King Marthanda Varma, Maharaja of the erstwhile princely state of Travancore, did the last major renovation. He dedicated his kingdom to the deity, and pledged that he and his descendants would serve the kingdom as Padmanabha Dasa, meaning "servants of the Lord Padmanabha". With this, Sri Padmanabha became the nominal head of the state of Travancore, assuming the title Perumal, the Emperor.

The British Government saluted the Lord with 21-gun salute, a military tradition of colonial days, which was continued by the Indian Army until the abolition of the privy purses by Government of India with Indira Gandhi as the Prime Minister. The royal insignia of the Lord, The Valampiri Shankhu or sinistral conch-shell, served as the State emblem of Travancore and even continued so for some time after the re-organisation of the States. Sri Padmanabha is still regarded as regional deity of Travancore .

The two annual festivals of the Temple culminates with a grand procession, with the three deities (Sree Padmanabha, Narasimha Swamy and Krishna) carried on flower-decked and aesthetically decorated Garuda Vahanas to the Shankhu-mukhom beach, for 'aaraattu' (sacramental ablution). The 'aarattu' days are declared as local public holidays in Thiruvanathapuram.

The Temple

Gopuram: The temple has a seven-tier gopuram. The temple stands by the side of a tank, named Padma Theertham (meaning the lotus spring). The temple has a corridor with 365 and one-quarter sculptured granite-stone pillars with elaborate carvings. This corridor encompasses and leads one from the eastern side into the sanctum sanctorum. An eighty-foot flag-staff is erected in front of the main entry from the 'prakaram' (corridor). The ground floor under the gopuram (main entrance in the eastern side)is known as the 'Nataka Sala' where the famous temple art, Kathakali was staged in the night during the ten-day uthsavam (festival) conducted twice a year, during the Malayalam months of Meenam and Thulam.

The sanctum: In the sanctum sanctorum, Vishnu is in a reclining position over the Anantha or Adi Sesha, the serpent with his face pointed upwards, he is enjoying the smell emanating from the lotus held in his left hand, his right hand is hanging over Lord Shiva. Sridevi and Bhudevi, two consorts of Vishnu stand by his side and the Brahma is seen on a lotus, which emanates from the navel of Vishnu. The idol is made up of 10008 Saligram that compose the reclining lord. They are special because they are from Nepal, from the banks of river Gandaki and they were brought to the temple with all pomp and gaiety on elephant top. On top of them "katusarkara yogam", a special ayurvedic mix, was used to give a plaster.

In order to perform darshan and puja, one has to climb on a stone slab and different parts of the Vishnu's idol, namely, the face, the navel and the feet, are visible from three different door like openings. Only Travancore King should perform Namaskaram in the stone slap. It is made of single stone. Here, the King even the King is called "Padmanabha Dasa" who is a servant of Lord who actually rules the Travancore state.

There are other important shrines inside the temple for Lord Narasimha, Lord Krishna, Lord Ayyappa, Lord Ganesha and Lord Hanuman. Many other small shrines like Kshetrapalan(who guards the temple), Vishwaksena and Garuda.

Legend

Sage Divakara prayed to Lord Krishna for his darshan. Lord Krishna came in disguise as a small boy who was very mischievous. Once the small cute boy swallowed the Saligrama which was kept in Puja. The Sage got enraged and started chasing the boy and finally the boy hid himself behind the tree. Then, the tree broked down and became Lord Vishnu in Sayana Kolam (lying posture) around kilometres.

The Sage then prayed Lord Vishnu that he could not pray him fully as his form is so huge. Immediately, the Lord shrunk himself and told the sage that they would worship through three doors. First one where the Lord Vishnu offers worship to Lord Shiva, the second entrance is Lord Brahma praying Lord Vishnu from his lotus navel and third is Lord Vishnu holy feet which leads to salvation.

Mythology: Padmanabhaswamy Temple stands at a place considered as one of the seven Parasurama Kshetras; texts including the Puranas, particularly the Skanda Purana and Padma Purana, have references for this shrine. Tradition states that in this place, the Hindu deity Lord Vishnu gave darshan to Indian sages like Divakarmuni and Vilvamangalam Swami.

Another story tells of an ezhava couple seeing Vishnu in the form of a child. The child took morsels of rice from the hands of the couple. In memory of this legend, naivedyam or offering prepared from rice is offered to the deity here in a coconut shell. Link

Sri PadmanabhaSwamy Mahatyam

The idol is made up of 10008 salagramams that compose the reclining lord. They are special because they are from Nepal, from the banks of river Gandhaki and they were brought to the temple with all pomp and gaiety on elephant top. On top of them "katusarkara yogam",navaratnams, a special ayurvedic mix, was used to give a plaster. The Lord has personally come in disguise and had saved many times the Travancore Kingdom from the clutches of enemies. Here, we could see all the Trinity inside the sanctum.

Prasadam

Rice offered to the deity in coconut shell. Paal Payasam (Milk Kher) is very famous. During Tuesday, Panakam is offered to Lord Narasimha. Unni Appam, Aval with sugar is also offered to Lord.

Panachikkadu Temple

Panachikkadu Temple is a Hindu temple for the goddess Saraswathi, situated at Panachikkadu in Kerala, India. It is also known as the *Dakshina Mookambika* Temple as it is a Saraswathi temple located in the Southern region of the Indian peninsula. This temple is dedicated to Goddess Saraswathi, the Goddess for arts and learning. It is also one of the prominent Saraswathi Temples in Kerala.

The Panachikkadu Saraswathi temple has Vishnu as the main deity. Myths say that there once lived a poor but pious Brahmin who was a devotee of Kolur sri Mookambika devi and that he used to visit Kolloor temple every year. As the Brahmin grew old, his health worsened and on one of his trips to Kollur, he realized that he could no longer visit Mookambika again due to his poor health. As he returned to Panachikkadu, it is said that the Goddess Mookambika came mounted on his palm-leaf umbrella and settled at the present location at Panachikkadu Temple.

The major festival of this temple is the Saraswathi Pooja in the month of Thulam [A month in the Malayalam calendar known as Kollavarsham (Kolla era) which falls approximately in September-October]. During this festival, also known as Navaratri (Nine Nights), a large number of pilgrims congregate here to pay homage to the deity.

The ceremony of Vidyarambham (formal initiation into the letters of the alphabet) for the children is held on Vijayadashami (last day of Navaratri) day. On that day thousands of people arrive at this temple to initiate learning to their children.A major cultural festival of classical dance and music is held in the temple for the duration of the nine nights to coincide with the festival.

Panachikkadu can be reached from Chingavanam (4 km) by travelling through MC Road and from Eravinalloor (2.5 km).

Pundareekapuram Temple

Pundareekapuram is a small temple atop a little rise called Midayikunnam near Thalayolaparambu in Kottayam. Architecturally it is not very different from any typical village temple of Kerala. A tiled and saddle roofed square "cuttampalam"encloses a square sanctum sanctorum. Appended to the square enclosure is a small 'balikkalpura'. The idol worshipped here is the image of Vishnu sitting astride his celestial vehicle Garuda together with Bhoodevi. This is a rare icon.

There's a fine picture of Shiva and Parvathi sitting beneath the Kalpavriksha; a powerful picture of Durga vanquishing the buffalo-headed demon Mahisha, the pranks of Krishna the divine boy of Ambadi; a picture of a Yakshi the dangerous seductress of legends; Rama Pattabhishekham or the coronation of Sri Rama; Shiva Thandava and a picture of Sastha astride a horse to point out a few of the striking paintings at Pundareekapuram.

Since the temple is tucked away in off rarely trodden village road, these paintings have for long remained relatively obscure. But these murals, no doubt can hold their own against the better known wall-paintings of Padmanabhapuram and Mattancheri Palaces. In all probability these murals were painted during the later half of the 18 th century.

Another characteristic of the Pundareekapuram paintings and Kerala murals in general are the boldness and accuracy of the lines which give a unique force to the paintings.

Rajarajeshwara Temple

The Rajarajeswara temple is a beautiful Shiva temple (Rajarajeswara is one of the names of Shiva) and is located at Taliparamba in Kannur district of Kerala, south India.

The temple is regarded as one of the 108 ancient Shiva temples of Kerala. It has a prominent place amongst the numerous Shiva temples in south India. If any problem is encountered in temples of South India, the final solution is sought in this Temple through a *prasna*, a traditional method of astrological decision making. The *prasna* is conducted on a *peedha* (a raised platform) situated outside the temple.

The quadrangular sanctum has a two tiered pyramidal roof. In front of the sanctum is the *namaskara mandapam*. The temple has no *kodi maram* (flagstaff) as opposed to other temples in Kerala.

Sabarimala

Sabarimala is a pilgrim centre in Kerala in the Western Ghat mountain ranges of India. Lord Ayyappan's temple is situated here in the midst of 18 hills. The area is in the Sahya hilly regions of Kerala bordering Tamil Nadu. The temple is situated on a hilltop at an altitude of 1260 m/4135 ft. above mean sea level, and is surrounded by mountains and dense forests. Temples existed in each of the hills surrounding Sabarimala.

While functional and intact temples exist at many places in the surrounding areas like Nilackal, Kalaketi, and Karimala, remnants of old temples are visible in the remaining hills. Sabarimala is believed to be the place where Ayyappan meditated after killing the powerful demon, Mahishi.Sabarimala is one of the most visited piligrim centres in the world with crores of devotees coming every year. The world's second largest annual pilgrimage, after Haj in Mecca, is reported to be to Sabarimala.

The pilgrimage to Sabarimala is a singular example of one where pilgrims, without consideration of caste, creed, position or social status, go with one mind and one 'mantra' dreaming constantly of the darshan of the presiding deity at the Holy Sannidhanam. Vehicles can go up to Pampa. Thereafter, pilgrims have to follow a path approximately four kilometres up a steep hill. The path, now fully cemented, with shops and medical aid by the sides, used to be a mere trail through dense forest.

There is a place near the temple (east of Sannidhanam), dedicated to the Vavar, a Muslim who was the associate of

Ayyappan, called "Vavarunada". The temple is open for worship only during the days of *Mandalapooja* (November 15 to December 26), Makaravilakku (January 15) and Vishu (April 14), and the beginning of every month in the Malayalam calendar.

Shatrughna Temple

The Shatrughna Temple is situated at Payammal, which is 6 km from the Koodalmanikyam temple at Irinjalakuda in Thrissur District of Kerala in India. This is one of the few temples in India that is dedicated to Lord Shatrughna.

Sree Poornathrayesa Temple

Sree Poornathrayesa temple is situated in Tripunithura, Kerala, the capital of the former Indian state of Cochin. The temple has history of more than ten decades and was almost ruined to nothing in a major fire break out in the early 1900s. The current temple is a renovated one.

The temple is also famous for its yearly Utsavams or festivals. The main one being the Vrishchikoltsawam, which is conducted every year in the month of Vrishchikam (Nov-Dec).

The deity in this temple is Lord Vishnu who is in the form of Santhanagopala Murthy. It is well believed that childless couples will be blessed with children on praying Poornathrayesan.

Sree Ramaswami Temple

Sree Ramaswami or commonly known as Thiruvangad temple, dedicated to the Hindu god Sree Rama, is an important temple located in the east part of Thalassery. The temple is generally known as the Brass Pagoda from the copper sheeting of its roof. A part of the temple was damaged by Tipu Sultan's troops in the 18th century, but the temple itself is believed to have been saved from destruction. It was one of the outposts of the Thalassery fort in the eighteenth century. In its precincts were held many conferences between the officials of the East India Company and local leaders, at which political treaties and agreements were signed. The temple contains some interesting sculptures and lithic records. The annual festival of temple commences on Vishu day in Medam (April-May) and lasts for seven days.

Sree Venugopala

Sree Venugopla Krishna Swami Dewastan is a Hindu temple located in Chendamangalam, Kerala, India.

Sree Venugopala Krishna Swami Dewasthan was established in 1900 at Chennamangalam (earlier known as *Jayantha mangalam*), 42 km from Ernakulam, 22 km from Alwaye and 5 km from North Parur.

Its main deity is Venugopalakrishna Swamy, and its main idol is Shila Vigrah of Venugopalakrishna Swamy. It also contains an Utsav idol of the Lord and the idols of Garuda and Hanuman at his feet. The temple celebrates a six day-long annual festival in the month of Vaisakh.

Sri Devi Temple

Sri Bhagavathy Temple of Chettikulangara aka Sri Devi Temple is situated near Mavelikkara in Alappuzha district in the south Indian state of Kerala. According to the Travancore devaswam board it is next to Sabarimala in income generated.

Sri Nellikulangara Bhagavathi Temple

Sri Nellikulangara Bhagavathi temple is a beautiful temple in Nemmara village in Palakkad district of Kerala, a small state in south India. The deity of this temple is Sri Nellikulangara Bhagavathi.

This temple is famous for its festival conducted by the people of Nemmara and Vallangi villages on 20th Meenam (March-April) every year. This festival is called Nemmara Vallangi Vela.

Thirumanthamkunnu Temple

Thirumanthamkunnu Temple in Angadipuram is located about 1.5 km west of Perinthalmanna in the Malappuram district of Kerala state, south India. It was erected after the Angadipuram Temple. The temple courtyards are on a hill with a lovely view of the countryside spread out below.

The temple is an important pilgrim centre in Malappuram, especially for the annual 11 days Pooram festival celebrated in March and April. Mangalya pooja, Rigveda laksharchana, Chandattam and Kalampattu are important poojas here. The temple is dedicated to Goddess Durga. There are ceremonies and rituals specific to this temple that are not carried out at others.

A memorial for the martyrs of Mamankam is preserved near the Thirumandhamkunnu temple.

Thirunavaya Temple

Thirunavaya Temple is an ancient temple on the banks of the Bharathapuzha River dedicated to Lord Shiva with the other deities of Lord Ganapathy, and Goddess Lakshmi. It is located near the pilgrimage centre of Thirunavaya, a small village 8 km south of Tirur near Ponnani in the Malappuram district of Kerala, south India.

The temple was the traditional location for the ritual of the Mamankam festival, an enactment of traditional martial arts by suicide squades.

Thirunelli Temple

Thirunelli Temple (also *Tirunelli*) is an ancient temple dedicated to Lord Vishnu on the side of Brahmagiri hill in Kerala. Inscriptions in this temple date back to the period of Bhaskara Ravi Varma I (962–1019 CE). Thirunelli temple located in what is now the Wayanad district of Kerala, near the Papanasini River. The name *Thirunelli* derives from the *nelli*, the Malayalam word for Indian gooseberry of the Amla tree.

Thrikkakara Temple

Thrikkakara Temple (Thrikkakara Vamanamoorthy Temple) is one of the few temples in India dedicated to Lord

Vamana. It is situated in Thrikkakara, a village panchayat near Cochin in the state of Kerala, South India. The temple houses some lithic records of historic significance.

The most important event of the religious calendar here is Onam. The Onasadya or the Onam feast is held in a grand manner in the temple with a large number of people cutting across religious barriers participating in it.

Thrikkara Temple

Thrikkavu Sri Durga Bhagavathy Temple is an ancient Temple situated in Ponnani, Malapuram District, Kerala State, India. Goddess Durga is the main deity of this centuries old temple.

Even though authentic details are not available about the age of the temple, it is considered as one of the 108 Durga temples consecrated by Lord Parasurama in kerala. It is believed that the name Thrikkavu originated from "Thrikkani Kaadu".

Thrikodithanam Mahavishnu Temple

The Mahavishnu Kshetram (temple) at Thrikodithanam is one of the five Vishnu temples associated with the five Pandava brothers, the principal characters of the Mahabharata. It is believed that Sahadeva, one of the brothers, performed penance at this site. This temple is also counted among the *108 Temples & Celestial Abodes of Vishnu*, which make a Vaishnavite's pilgrimage itinerary, in India.

Earliest references to this temple appear in the poems and hymns composed by the greatest of Alvar saints-Nammalvar, in circa 800 AD. Stone inscriptions in the temple date it back to the Second Chera Empire (800-1102 AD).

Thrikodithanam Mahavishnu Kshetram is administered by the Travancore Devaswom Board (TDB), an autonomous body under Government of Kerala. TDB has classified this shrine among 224 "Major Temples" of Kerala.

Thrikodithanam is located is located 2.5 KM from Changanassery town, in Kottayam district, Kerala, India.

Trichambaram Temple

Trichambaram Temple is situated 20 km from Kannur district of Kerala state, south India. It is near Taliparamba town, famous for its spices trade. The temple is believed to have got the name from *Thiru Shambara* or the holy shambara in reverence to *Maharishi Shambara*.

The deity of the temple is Krishna. The sculptures on the walls of the sanctum sanctorum are a class by themselves. The temple also contains one of the most exquisite collection of mural paintings in south India. Trichambaram Temple has three ponds attached to it, with the temple for Durga being surrounded by water on all sides.

The annual temple festival (*Utsavam*) is a colourful event. The fortnight-long festival begins on *Kumbham* 22 of Malayalam calendar (which generally falls on March 6) every year with the *kodiyettam* (hoisting of a religious flag) and comes to an end on *Meenam* 6 (which generallay falls on March 20) with *Koodipiriyal* (Ending of this festival). In between these dates, for 11 days, *thitambu nriththam* (a sort of dance with the deities of Krishna and Balarama) is held at Pookoth Nada (1 km from Trichambaram temple).

Vadakkunnathan Temple

Vadakkkunnathan Temple is one of the largest Shiva temples in Kerala. Vadakkkunnathan temple is located in Thrissur in Kerala and is considered to be over a 1000 years old. This temple is a classic example of the Kerala style of architecture with beautiful murals of the seventeenth century delineating graphically the story of Mahabharata. The shrines and the Koothambalam display exquisite vignettes carved in wood. It is believed that this temple was built by Parasurama.

Legends say that Adi Sankaracharya was born, after his parents, who were childless for many years, prayed at the Vadakkumnathan (vRashAcala) temple.

The sprawling Thekkinkadu maidan, en circling the Vadakumnathan temple, is the main venue of the Thrissur Pooram.

Vailikulangara Bhabavathi Temple

Vailikulangara Bhagavathi Temple is a Bhadrakali temple in Thrissur district of Kerala, south India. It is near to Guruvayoor. The main festival of this temple is *Makara Chowa* (The first Tuesday (Chowa in Makara Masam in Malayalam Calendar). *Navaratri Sangeethothsavam* is another festival in this temple."Thazhthe Kaavu Vela" will be celibrated on next day of the Makrachovva. The Nadan Kalaroopam "Kaali Kali" will be conducted on that day.

Valliyoorkav

Valliyoorkav is a Hindu Temple in Wayanad district of Kerala state in south India. This Temple is only 3 km from Mananthavady town. Valliyoorkav Temple is dedicated to Mother Goddess and is worshipped in three principal forms of Vana Durga, Bhadrakali and Jala Durga. It is the most important place of worship for the tribal communities in Wayanad.

Valliyoorkkavu

Valliyoorkkavu is an ancient temple located high in the Hills at Valliyoorkkavu, 3 kilometres from Mananthavady town of Wayanad district in Kerala. The temple is dedicated to goddess Bhagavathy or Durga. The idol of the temple is believed to be self-manifested and the annual festival is held in March which lasts for 14 days. The festival is a major event and thousands of people from all over the places takes part in this biggest event in wayanad. The festival is very important to the tribal people in Wayanad. The traditional ritual of the Kalamezhuthu is performed during all nights of the festival. On the final day of the festival, the array of folk art forms are presented. The dances performed by the local tribals, using native percussion instruments, are a major attraction.Also the senic beauty of the place with hillocks and kabani river is worth a watch.

Velorvattom

Velorvattom is a place near Cherthala, Kerala State, India.

The place is famous for a temple "Velorvattom Maha deva temple", worshipping lord Shiva. The temple has two "nada" (entries) which is rare in Kerala. The temple is owned by "Aazvancherry thamprakkal" and now running by Kerala Urazma Devasam Board (KUDB). It is believed that the temple was created by Villimangalm swami, around 700 years ago.

Viswanatha Swamy Temple, Palakkad

Sri Visalakshi Sametha Sri Viswanathaswamy temple, popularly known as *Kasi Viswanathaswamy Temple* or locally as *kundukovil* is a famous Hindu temple located in the Kalpathy village of Palakkad in Kerala, India. It is the site of the annual Kalpathi Ratholsavam which is one of the most famous temple festivals of Kerala. This ancient temple nestles by the banks of the serene Kalpathy river (*Nila Nadhi*). Dedicated to Lord Shiva and his consort Visalakshi (another name for Parvati), it dates back to early fifteenth century. The similarity to the Varanasi Kashi Viswanatha temple on the banks of Ganges is responsible for the moniker *kasiyil pakuthi kalpathy* and the name *Dakshina Kashi* associated with this temple. The Temple is surrounded by the four Tamil Brahmin *agraharams* or traditional villages: New Kalpathy, Old Kalpathy, Chathapuram and Govindarajapuram.

Viwadrinatha Temple

Lord Vilwadrinatha Temple situated in Thiruvilwamala is one of the ancient temples in India. The temple attracts pilgrims from all over India, every year especially during the Ekadasi Festival around February. The temple is situated in a hill from which one can obtain a fantastic view of adjoining places. The heritage of this temple is very rich. Lord Vilwadrinatha is believed to maintain peace and calm in the region of Thiruvilwamala. This is evident given the fact that mixed proportions of people from different religions, castes etc. co-exist in harmony. Thiruvilwamala is closely located to Ottapalam (10 km distance). The place is also close to Trissur by 40 km and 35 km from Palghat.

8

Hindu Temples in Maharashtra

Alandi

Alandi is a city and a municipal council in Pune district in the state of Maharashtra, India.

Geography

Alandi (18°40'37.42?N, 73°53'47.76?E) is located on the banks of the Indrayani River, 25 km east of Pune, India. It has an average elevation of 577 metres (1893 feet).

Demographics

As of 2001 India census, Alandi had a population of 17,561. Males constitute 56% of the population and females 44%. Alandi has an average literacy rate of 73%, higher than the national average of 59.5%; with 62% of the males and 38% of females literate. 13% of the population is under 6 years of age.

Pilgrimage Centre

Saint Dnyaneshwar, after translating the Bhagavad Gita into Marathi attained Samadhi in a cave at Alandi. Alandi is thus a place of pilgrimage and is venerated by many Hindus. A temple complex has been built near the spot of Sant Dnyaneshwar's samadhi. It is visited by thousands of pilgrims, and in particular, those of the Varkari Sect. On every Kartika Ekadashi (eleventh day of the Hindu month of Kartik), a big festival is held at Alandi, when the Yatra (procession of pilgrims) reaches the town.

Among other important sites at Alandi are the Vitthala-Rakhumai temple, Siddhabet, Jalaram mandir (just like the one at Virpur Gujarat) and Dnyaneshwar's wall. The town of Dehu, where the samadhi of Sant Tukaram is located, lies not far from Alandi.

Alandi has also the distinction of having a prehistoric collection of Shivling. In one of the Saint Dnyaneshwar's verses he speaks of it being called "Sidheshwar". The name of the reigning deity of the place as also one of the names of Shiva. He states then that a collection of eighty-four Sidha]s meet or exist here.

Under a dense green and flower laden canopy emitting a heavenly fragrance and birds singing celestal tunes. This stanza is to be found in Saint Dnyaneshwar's book about the power of chanting Hari's name. The book is called Haripath. Even till this day Haripath is recited by countless rich and poor in Maharashtra. They experience its beauty and believe in its powers as also in the person who created them.

Alandi has become known as a place for mass-marriage ceremonies for impoverished eloped lovers and parents who would avoid expenses for a daughter's marriage. An "Alandi marriage" has therefore become a derogatory term in urban area around Pune.

Ashtavinayak

Ashtavinayak literally means “eight Ganeshas” in Sanskrit. Ganesha is the Hindu deity of prosperity and learning. The term also refers to a pilgrimage to the eight temples in Maharashtra state of India that house eight distinct idols of Ganesh, in a pre-ascertained sequence.

The Ashtavinayak tour covers the eight ancient holy temples of Lord Ganesha which are situated around Pune. Each of these temples has its own individual mythology and history, as distinct from each other as the idols in each temple.

The position of each idol, and its trunk are some of their differentiating aspects.

Babulnath

Babulnath is an ancient Shiva temple in Mumbai, India. Shiva in the form of the Lord of the Babul tree is the Main deity in this temple. The faithful climb up to the temple and obtain Darshan of the shivling and obtain blessings of the Lord. It is also possible to take an elevator up to the temple. The Bombay International School lies opposite the temple.

Ballaleshwar Pali

Ballaleshwar Pali temple is one of the eight temples of Lord Ganesha, Ashtavinayak. Among Astavinayakas, Pali's Ballaleshwar is the only vinayak who is famous by his devotee's name. It is located in village Pali which is at a distance of 30kms from Karjat in Sudhagad taluka of Raigad district. It is situated between fort Sarasgad and the river Amba.

Bhavani

Bhavani is a ferocious aspect of Hindu goddess Shakti or Devi. Bhavani means "giver of life", the power of nature or the source of creative energy. In addition to her ferocious aspect, she is also known as *Karunaswaroopini*, "filled with mercy".

Bhavani was the tutelary deity of the Maratha leader Shivaji. A temple to Bhavani, at Tuljapur in Maharashtra, dates back to the 12th century. The temple contains a meter-high granite image of the goddess, with eight arms holding weapons, and bearing the head of the demon Mahishasura, who she is said to have slain in Mysore.

Bhimashankar Temple

Bhimashankar is located in the village of Bhavagiri 50 km north west of Khed, near Pune. It is located 110 km away from Pune in the Ghat region of the Sahyadri hills. Bhimashankar is also the source of the Bhima river, which flows south east and merges with the Krishna river near Raichur. The other Jyotirlinga shrines in Maharashtra are Tryambakeshwar and Grishneshwar. Regular pilgrims near Mumbai visit Bhimashankar from Karjat via Khandas. The Bhimashankar

Wildlife Sanctuary located here is a popular weekend getaway from Mumbai and Pune.

Bhuleshwar Temple

Bhuleshwar is famous for the Hindu Temple of Lord Shiva, situated around 55 kilometres from Pune. The temple is situated on a hill and was built in the 13th century. There are beautiful carvings on the walls. Bhuleshwar has a mythological & historical significance. It is said that Devi Parvati danced for Lord Shiva and from here they went to Kailash and got married. This place is very crowded during Mahashivratri.

Chatursbringi Temple

The Chatursbringi Temple is a Hindu temple in Pune, in the Maharashtra state of India. The temple is located on the slope of a hill on Senapati Bapat Road. It is said to have been built during the reign of the marathi king Chhatrapati Shivaji Raje Bhosle.

The presiding deity of the temple is Goddess Chatursbringi. She is also considered as the presiding deity of the city of Pune. The temple is maintained by the Chatursbringi Devasthan Trust. Every year a fair is held at the foothill on the eve of navratri. Thousands of people gather pay respects and homage the Goddess Chatursbringi.

Dashabhuja Temple

The Dashabhuja Temple is a Hindu temple in Pune, in the Maharashtra state of India. The temple is located on Karve road, just below the Paud Phata flyover.

The presiding god of the temple is Lord Ganapati also known as Ganesh.

Elephanta Caves

The Elephanta Caves are the focal point of the Elephanta Island, located in the Mumbai harbour off the coast of Mumbai (Bombay), India. In 1987, the caves were designated a UNESCO World Heritage Site.

It is visited by many domestic and foreign tourists. In recent years, complaints have been made that visitors mistreat this important cultural and historic site. Most of the sculptures here were defaced by the Portuguese, who used the sculptures as target practice in the 17th century. The Portuguese also gave the island its modern name,*Elephanta* from *Gharapuri*.

The caves are thought to date back to the Silhara kings of the 9th through 13th centuries (810–1260). Some of the sculptures of this site are also attributed to the imperial Rashtrakutas of Manyakheta (in present day Karnataka), the *Trimurti* of Elephanta showing the three faces of Shiva almost akin to the Trinity of Brahma, Vishnu, and Mahesh. This was also the royal insignia of the Rashtrakutas. Other Rashtrakuta sculptures here are the reliefs of Nataraja and Sadashiva and the splendid sculptures of Ardhanarishvara.

The rock-cut temple complex cover an area of 60,000 sq ft consisting of a main chamber, 2 lateral ones, courtyards and subsidiary shrines. The site of these magnificent caves contained beautiful reliefs, sculptures, and a temple to the Hindu god Œiva. The caves are hewn from solid rock. The temple complex is said to be the abode of Shiva.

Ellora Caves

Ellora is an archeological site, 30 km (18.6 miles) from the city of Aurangabad in the Indian state of Maharashtra. Famous for its monumental caves, Ellora is a World Heritage Site.

Ellora represents the epitome of Indian rock-cut architecture.The 35 "caves" – actually structures excavated out of the vertical face of the Charanandri hills – comprised of Buddhist, Hindu and Jain cave temples and monasteries, were built between the 5th century and 10th century. The 12 Buddhist (caves 1-12), 17 Hindu (caves 13-29) and 5 Jain caves (caves 30-34), built in proximity, demonstrate the religious tolerance prevalent during this period of Indian history.

Grishneshwar

Grishneshwar, also known as Ghushmeshwar, is a famous

Hindu temple dedicated to Lord Shiva and is one of the twelve Jyotirlingas, the sacred abodes of Shiva. The temple is located eleven km from Daulatabad, near Aurangabad in Maharashtra India.

The Grishneswar temple was re-constructed by Maloji Raje Bhosale of Verul(Grand Father of Chhatrapati Shivaji Maharaj) in 16th century and later by Ahilyabai Holkar in 18th century, who also re-constructed the Kashi Vishwanath temple at Benares, and the Vishnu Paada temple at Gaya.

Kailash Temple

Kailash Temple, also Kailasanatha Temple is one of the 34 monasteries and temples, extending over more than 2 km, that were dug side by side in the wall of a high basalt cliff in the complex located at Ellora, Maharashtra, India, and represents the epitome of Indian rock-cut architecture. It is designed to recall Mount Kailash, the abode of Lord Shiva. While it exhibits typical Dravidian features, it was carved out of one single rock. It was built in the 8th century by the Rashtrakuta king Krishna I.

The Kailash Temple is notable for its *vertical* excavation—carvers started at the top of the original rock, and excavated downward, exhuming the temple out of the existing rock. The traditional methods were rigidly followed by the master architect which could not have been achieved by excavating from the front. The architects found to design this temple were from the southern Pallava kingdom.

It is estimated that about 400,000 tons of rocks was scooped out over hundreds of years to construct this monolithic structure. From the chisel marks on walls of this temple, archeologists could conclude that three types of chisels were used to carve this temple.

All the carvings are done in more than one level. A two-storeyed gateway opens to reveal a U-shaped courtyard. The courtyard is edged by a columned arcade three stories high. The arcades are punctuated by huge sculpted panels, and alcoves containing enormous sculptures of a variety of deities. Originally flying bridges of stone connected these galleries to central temple structures, but these have fallen.

Within the courtyard are two structures. As is traditional in Shiva temples, an image of the sacred bull Nandi fronts the central temple housing the lingam. In Cave 16, the Nandi Mandap and main Shiva temple are each about 7 meters high, and built on two stories. The lower stories of the Nandi Mandap are both solid structures, decorated with elaborate illustrative carvings. The base of the temple has been carved to suggest that elephants are holding the structure aloft.

A living rock bridge connects the Nandi Mandap to the porch of the temple. The temple itself is tall pyramidic structure reminiscent of a South Indian temple. The shrine – complete with pillars, windows, inner and outer rooms, gathering halls, and an enormous lingam at its heart – carved from stone, is carved with niches, plasters, windows as well as images of deities, *mithunas* (erotic male and female figures) and other figures. Most of the deities at the left of the entrance are Shaivaite (followers of Lord Shiva) while on the right hand side the deities are Vaishnavaites (followers of Lord Vishnu).

There are two Dhvajastambhas (pillars with the flagstaff) in the courtyard. The grand sculpture of Ravana attempting to lift Mount Kailasa, the abode of Lord Shiva, with his full might is a landmark in Indian art.

Kalaram Temple

The Kalaram temple is an old Hindu shrine dedicated to Rama in the Panchavati area of Nasik city in Maharashtra, India. It is probably the most important Hindu shrine in the city. The temple derives its name from the statue of Lord Rama that is black in colour.The literal translation of Kalaram means black Rama.

The sanctum sanctorum also houses the statues of goddess Sita and god Laxman. Thousands of devotees visit it every day. The temple formed a pivotal role in Dalit movement in India. The famous Dr. Ambedkar once held a protest outside the temple for allowance of Dalits into the temple.

Kaleshwar Temple, Nerur

The Kaleshwar Temple in Nerur, India is devoted to the God Shri Kaleshwar, an avatar of the God Shiva.

There is an ancient temple of Shri Kaleshwar in the Village Nerur, Dist. Sindhudurg, Maharashtra. Shri Kaleshwar is the Village Deity (Gramdevta) of all Nerurkars.

Kukdeshwar Temple

Kukdeshwar Temple is located in Pune District of Maharashtra, India. It is about 15 km west of Junnar and lies on the banks of Kukdi River. It is a Shiv temple noted for its beautiful sculptures and carvings. The roof of this temple is in a dilapidated state.

Lenyadri

Lenyadri is an Ashtavinayak temple located on the northwest bank of the River Kukadi in the state of Maharashtra in India. The temple is the only Ashtavinayak temple situated on a mountain, and the temple is also in the vicinity of Buddhist caves.

Mahalakshmi Temple

The Shri Mahalakshmi Temple of Kolhapur in Maharashtra, India, is one of the Shakti Peethas, listed in various puranas of Hinduism. According to these writings, a shakti peetha is a place associated with Shakti, the goddess of power. The Kolhapur peetha is of special religious significance, being one of the six places where it is believed one can either obtain salvation from desires or have them fulfiled. The temple takes its name from Mahalakshmi, the consort of Vishnu, and it is believed that the divine couple reside in the area.

The temple belongs, architecturally, to the Chalukya empire, and may have been first built circa 700 AD. Mounted on a stone platform, the image of the four armed and crowned goddess is made of gemstone and weighs about 40 kilograms. A stone lion, the vahana of the goddess, stands behind the statue. The crown contains an image of the Sheshnag — the serpent of Vishnu.

In Her four hands, the deity of Mahalakshmi holds objects of symbolic value. The lower right hand holds a mhalunga (a citrus fruit), in the upper right, a large mace (kaumodaki) with its head touching the ground, in the upper left a shield (khetaka), and in the lower left, a bowl (panpatra). Unlike most Hindu sacred images, which face north or east, the image of this deity looks west (Pashchim). There is a small open window on the western wall, through which the light of the setting sun falls on the face of the image for three days around the 21st of each March and September.

Mahalaxmi Temple

Mahalaxmi Temple is one of the most famous temples of Mumbai situated on Bhulabhai Desai Road. It is dedicated to Mahalaxmi, Lord Vishnu's consort. Built around 1785, the history of this temple is supposedly connected with the building of the Hornby Vellard (see History of Mumbai). Apparently after portions of the sea wall of the Vellard collapsed twice, the chief engineer, a Pathare prabhu, dreamt of a Lakshmi statue in the sea near Worli. A search recovered it, and he built a temple for it. After this, the work on the vellard could be completed without a hitch.

Mandher Devi Temple in Mandhradevi

Mandher Devi temple is the Kalubai temple in Mandhradevi near Wai (Satara District, Maharashtra, India). Located on a hill 4,650 feet above sea level, the temple, some 20 km from Satara, overlooks the picturesque Purandhar fort. Devotees attribute miraculous properties to a grove around the shrine. Local lore has it that the temple is more than 400 years old and was built during Shivaji's Maratha rule. However, no definite date on the temple's construction is available.

The title of the land is in the name of Lord Mandeshwar and Kaleshwari Devi. Most of the year there is little tourist traffic here. The nearest primary health centre is six kilometres away and a major hospital is at Satara town.

The temple is popular among lower caste Hindus who undertake the annual Kalubai Jatra pilgrimage over a ten day period every January. The main event is a 24-hour-long festival on the day of the full moon that includes animal sacrifices to the goddess. The religious event usually draws between 150,000 and 200,000 Hindu devotees. The annual fair is in honour of Kaleshwari Devi, fondly called Kalubai by the faithful.

The idol of Kalubai sports two silver masks and silk finery. The masks are carried in a procession by members of the Gurav family, seen as the hereditary custodians of the shrine. Members of this family take turns to conduct rituals.

Muktidham

Muktidham is a marble temple complex honouring various Hindu gods. It is a popular tourist attraction situated in the Nashik Road suburb of the city of Nashik in the western state of Maharashtra in India. It is privately operated through a trust and was built through a generous donation by the late Mr. J.D. Chauhan-Bytco, a local industrialist.

Mumba Devi Mandir

Mumba Devi Mandir, or Mumba Devi Temple, is an old Hindu temple in the city of Mumbai (formerly Bombay) dedicated to the goddess *Mumba*, the local incarnation of the Devi (Mother Goddess). Marathi *Mumba* derives from Sanskrit *Maha-Amba* "Great Mother", and *Mumbaî* combines the name with *aî*, the Marathi for "mother".

While Hindu sects devoted to the goddess Mumbadevi are attested to as far back as the 15th century, it is said that the temple was built in 1675 near the main landing site of the former Bori Bunder creek against the north wall of the English Fort Saint George by a Hindu woman also named Mumba. The creek and fort are now deteriorated to a point at which they are but derelict reminders of the city's past. The temple, on the other hand, is still active.

The goddess *Mumba* was patron of the *agri* (salt collectors) and *kolis* (fisherfolk), the original inhabitants of the seven islands of Bombay. She is depicted as a black stone sculpture in the temple. An etymology of Mumba that is popular is "Maha

Amba," or "Great Mother," one of the many of India's more well-known names for the Hindu Mother Goddess (Devi). Located in Bhuleshwar area in South Mumbai, the temple is in the heart of the steel and clothing markets. It is a sacred pilgrimage spot and place of worship for Hindus and is thus visited daily by hundreds of people. It is not uncommon for visitors of Mumbai to pay their respects at the temple and is one of the popular tourist destinations in the city.

Panchavati

Panchavati is a famous religious and pilgrimage place in India. The name is derived from the Sanskrit *pañca* five *vata* Banyan Tree. The area of five Banyan trees is situated on the banks of River Godavari in Nasik, Maharashtra, India.It has been proposed to identify it with the modern Nasik, because Lakshmana cut off Surpanakha's nose (nasika) at Panchavati.

In Panchavati today, there are five trees marked, one of which is an Ashoka tree, however. There is also a cave here where Sita, Ram and Lakshman prayed to Lord Shiva which is known as Sita Gumpha. The ancient Shivlinga still exists in the small place of worship in the cave and is visited by devotees.

According to Hindu legends and Ramayana Rama, along with his wife Sita and brother Laxman, stayed in Panchavati during their Vanwasa period. The famous Laxman Rekha is located in Panchavati about a kilometre away from Sita Gumpha. It was from this place that Ravana abducted goddess Sita. Today this area is a major pilgrimage and tourist attraction. Coordinates: 17°402 N, 75°202 E.

Sarasbaug Ganpati

The Sarasbaug temple houses the idol of Shree Siddhivinayak (God who makes wishes true). A sacred ground of faith for millions of devotees in Pune and around the world, on an average the Sarasbaug temple receives ten thousand visitors a day and this figure goes up to eighty thousand devotees per day on Ganesha Chaturthi and other special occasions.

Various dignitaries and luminaries throughout India have made it a point to visit this sacred temple to seek blessings of Shri Siddivinayak.

Siddhatek

Shree Siddhivinayak (Siddhatek) is one of the asthavinayak temples of lord Ganesh. Siddhatek, the town which houses this temple lies in Karjat,Ahmednagar taluka of Ahmednagar district. It is situated on the banks of river Bhima.

Shree Siddhivinayak's temple is on hill top facing north. Brass idols of Jay & Vijay are placed on both sides of Siddhivinayaka. In the Sanctum itself there is a Shivapanchayatan & goddess Shiva small temple. Hall of the temple was previously built by Baroda's landlord late Shri Mairal. It was broken in 1939 & was rebuilt by all Ganesh devotees in 1970. The idol is swayambhu, three feet tall, facing north with his trunk turned right. Idol is Gajmukh, however belly of the idol is not big. Riddhi & Siddhi are sitting on one lap of Vinayaka. Face is very calm & serene. The pradakshana (circumnavigation) of this God is said to be very fruitful. One has to travel 5 k.m. to comple one pradakshana as the idol is attached to the hill itself.

Siddhivinayak Temple

Shree Siddhivinayak Mandir seen in the evening from the corner of SK Bole and Kakasaheb Gadgil Marg.

The Shree Siddhivinayak Ganapati Mandir is a Hindu temple dedicated to Ganesha. It is located in Prabhadevi,Dadar, Mumbai, Maharashtra. It was originally built by Mr. Laxman Vithu and Mrs. Deubai Patil in November 19th, 1801.

The temple has a small mandapam (hall) with the shrine for Siddhi Vinayak ("Ganesha that grants your wish"). The wooden doors to the sanctum are carved with images of the Ashtavinayak (the eight manifestations of Ganesha in Maharashtra). The inner roof of the sanctum is plated with gold, and the central statute is of Ganesha. In the periphery of the temple, there is a Hanuman temple as well.

Shree Swaminarayan Temple Mumbai

This Temple (Mandir) is situated at Trijo Bhoiwado in Bhuleshwar area of Mumbai and is over a hundred years old. It was the first Shree Swaminarayan Mandir in Mumbai.

The present Mandir has a tri-spire structure and the Murti's installed are that of Shree Laxminarayan Dev, Shree Ghanshyam Maharaj, Shree Hari Krishna Maharaj, Shree Gaulokvihari and Shree Radhikaji. It is a Shikharband Mandir and comes under the Shree Laxminarayan Dev Gadi (Vadtal).

History of this Mandir

On Vaishakh Shukla Ekadashi, Vikram Samvat 1924, Param Pujya Param Bhakt, Shree Ranchhoddas Pranjeevandas built the first ever Shree Swaminarayan temple in Mumbai by breaking and rebuilding his own residence. The deities of Shree Hari Krishna Maharaj, Shree Gaulokvihari and Shree Radhikaji were instated by Acharya Maharajshri Bhagwatprasadji Maharaj. The Temple Trust instated by Shree Ranchhoddasji still contributes a monthly dakshina of Rs. 150/-to the Temple.

The present Tri spire temple structure was built and the deities of Shree Ghanshyam Maharaj and Shree Lakshminarayan Dev instated on Vaishakh Shukla Dwadashi, Vikram Samvat 1959 by Param Pujya Acharya Maharajshri Lakshmiprasadji Maharaj.

Shree Hari's absolute devotee, Rao Bahadur Sheth Curumsey Damjee contributed towards this temple's reinstatement with all material, physical and intellectual resources. His close associate and friend Shree Mathurdas Vaishnav too donated Rs. 25,000/-towards this sacred work.

Trimbakeshwar Shiva Temple

Triyambakeshwar or Triambkeshwar is an ancient Hindu temple in the town of Trimbak, in the Nashik District of Maharashtra, India, 28 km from the city of Nashik. It is dedicated to Lord Shiva and is one of the twelve Jyotirlingaas.

It is located at the source of the Godavari River, the longest river in peninsular India. The Godavari River, which is considered sacred within Hinduism, originates from Bramhagiri mountains and meets the sea near Rajahmudry. Kusavarta, a kund is considered the symbolic origin of the river Godavari, and revered by Hindus as a sacred bathing place.

In Mythology & Present

Triyambakeshwar or Triambhakeshwar is a religious centre having one of the twelve Jyotirlingas. The extraordinary feature of the Jyotirlinga located here is that it has three faces embodying Lord Brahma, Lord Vishnu and Lord Rudra (Shiva).

All other Jyotirlingas have Shiva as the main deity. The entire black stone temple is known for its appealing architecture and sculpture and is at the foothills of a mountain called Brahmagiri.

This place is famous for lots of religious rituals (vidhis). Narayan-Nagbali, Kalsarpa Shanti, Tripindi vidhi are done here. Narayan-Nagbalipuja is performed at Triyambakeshwar only. This puja is performed in three days. This puja is performed on special dates. Some days are not suitable to perform this puja. This puja is performed for many reasons like to cure an illness, going through bad times, killing a Cobra (Nag), childless couples, financial crisis or you want to perform some religious puja to have everything.

Triambakeshwar town has a large number of Brahmin households and is also a centre for Vedic Gurukuls (kind of boarding school). It also has Ashrams & Muths devoted to Ashtanga Yoga-the Hindu art of Living.

The place is known for its scenic beauty in rainy/ monsoon season and is surrounded by lush green hills untouched by pollution. Anjaneri mountain, the birth place of Lord Hanuman is 7 Km. from Triambakeshwar.

Shri Nilambika/Dattatreya Temple

This temple is on top of the Neel mountain. All goddesses ('Matamba','Renuka','Mananmba') came here to see 'Parashuram' when he was performing penance (tapas).After his penance he requested all goddesses to stay there and the temple was formed for these goddesses. There's a myth that God Dattatrya too was born here.

Vani (Nashik)

Vani is a small village located near Nashik in India. It is a holy place for the Hindu people. Devotees visit this place in large numbers every day. The image herewith is of the goddess who is worshipped in the holy temple. Since the temple is located on a mountain with 7 peaks, the goddess is known by name Saptashrungi Nivasini (one who lives on a mountain with 7 peaks).

Varadvinayak

Varadvinayak is one of the Asthavinayak temples of the Hindu deity Lord Ganesh. This is in Mahad village situated in Khalapur taluka near Karjat and Khopoli of Raigad District, Maharastra, India.

Legend has it that the childless great king, Bhima of Koudinyapur his wife meet Vishwamitra while they had come to forest for penance. Sage vishwamitra gave king, Ekashar Gajana Mantra (spell)to chant and thus prince Rukmaganda was born. Rukmaganda grew up into a beautiful young prince..

Rukmanganda during his hunting trip stopped at the hermitage of Rishi Vachaknavi. Mukunda, Rishi's wife fell in love prince's beauty and asked him to fulfil her desire. He flatly refused and left the ashram. Mukunda became very much lovesick. Knowing her plight, King Indra took the form of Rukmaganda and had pleasure with her. Mukunda became pregnant and gave birth to a son Gritsamada. Gritsamada curses his mother on knowing truth of his birth to become a throny plant bearing Bhor fruits.

Mukunda in turn cursed Gritsamada, that a cruel rakshas (demon) will born from him. Suddenly a heavenly voice said 'Gritsamada is Indra's son' leaving both of them shocked. Then Mukunda gets converted to Bhor plant and ashamed Gritsamada, leaves to Pushpak forest for penance. Lord Ganesh contented by Gritsamada's penance tells him that he will get a brave son who cannot be defeated by anybody other than Shankara. Gritsamada asks for the forest to become holy and so devotees get attainment of their aims here. He urged Ganapati to stay there permanently and asked for knowledge of Brahma. The forest is called Bhadraka today. Gritsamada built a temple there and the idol installed there is called Varadavinayaka.

It is said that if the coconut received as prasad during Maghi Chaturthi is consumed one will be blessed with a son. Hence there is heavy rush during Maghi Utsav.

Vithoba

Vithoba is a colloquial form of Vitthala, one of the manifestations of Vishnu (Krishna). Vithoba of Pandharpur is traditionally one of the most important deities in the Indian states of Maharashtra, Karnataka and Andhra Pradesh drawing millions of devotees across several cultures and languages of these states. Vithoba is a major focus of the Bhakti and Varkari movements in these states. A very substantial segment of spiritual literature in the Marathi and Kannada languages is dedicated to Vithoba.

9

Hindu Temples in Orissa

64 Joginis

64 Joginis Temple (Chausath Jogini Mandir) is situated in a hamlet called Hirapur, 20 Km outside Bhubaneswar (the capital of Orissa, a state in Eastern India).

The temple is supposed to be built by the Queen Hiradevi of Bramh dynesty during 9th century

It's built in a circular fashion, completely put together with blocks of sand stone. The inside of the circular wall has cavities, each housing the statue of a Goddess. There are almost 56 such idols, made of black granite, inscribed within the wall cavities, centring on the main idol which is the Goddess Kali, who stands on a human head representing the triumph of the heart over the mind. The temple houses a central altar (cuboid) which has the remaining 8 Goddess idols on all 4 sides.

64 Joginis Temple is a tantric temple, and is completely open on the top, as tantric prayer rituals involve worshipping the 'bhoomandal' (environment consisting all the 5 elements of nature-fire, water, earth, sky and ether).

The legend behind the temple according to local priests is of the Goddess Durga taking the form of 64 demi-goddesses in order to defeat a demon. After the fight the 64 goddesses (Joginis) asked Durga to commemorate them in the form of a temple structure.

The Jogini idols are generally representing a female figurine standing on an animal, a demon or a human head depicting the victory of Shakti (Feminine power). The Idols express everything from rage, sadness, pleasure, joy, desire and happiness.

Ananta Vasudeva Temple

Ananta Vasudeva Temple is situated at Bhubaneswar in Orissa state of India. The temple was constructed in the thirteenth century, and the images of Krishna, Balarama and Subhadra are worshipped there. Balarama stands under a seven hooded serpent, while Krishna holds a mace and a conch. Krisna being an avatara of Vishnu, this is basically a Vaishnavite temple, which dates back to the period of Chandrika, the daughter of Anangabhima III, during the reign of the king Bhanudeva.

Black Pagoda

The Black Pagoda is a temple of the Hindu god Surya, and is located in the village of Konark in the Indian state of Orissa. For its architecture and decoration, it is recognised as a major building of Orissa, a state that is famous in India for the beauty of its many temples. It is one of few notable temples of Surya, which are not numerous in India.

The temple is designed as the chariot of Surya.The first rays of sunlight fall on the main shrine.

Jagannath Temple (Koraput)

The Jagannath Temple in Koraput (also known as Sabara Srikhetra) was built in 1972.

Jagannath Temple (Puri)

The Jagannath Temple in Puri is a famous Hindu temple dedicated to Jagannath (Krishna) located in the coastal town of Puri in the state of Orissa, India. The name *Jagannath* (Lord of the Universe) is a combination of the Sanskrit words *Jagat* (Universe) and *Nath* (Lord of). The temple is an important pilgrimage destination for many Hindu traditions, particularly worshippers of Krishna and Vishnu. The temple is famous for its annual Rath Yatra, chariot festival where huge and elaborately decorated chariots are used for the procession of the three main temple deities.

The temple is famous for its annual Rath Yatra, or chariot festival, in which the three temple deities are hauled on huge and elaborately decorated chariots. Since medieval times, it is also associated with intense religious fervor.The temple is sacred to the Vaishnava traditions and saint Ramananda who was closely associated with the temple. It is also of particular significance to the followers of the Gaudiya Vaishnavism whose founder, Chaitanya Mahaprabhu, was attracted to the deity, Jagannath, and lived in Puri for many years.

Kedareswar Temple

Kanakeswar Temple, one of the eight Astasambhu Temples, is situated near the Ramachandi Temple, in Dhenkanal, Orissa. The presiding deity here is Lord Shiva, referred to locally by the name 'Kanakeswar'.

It stands in the yard of the Mukteswar Temple, with a striking 8 foott statute of Ram Bhakt Hanuman (the monkey God).

Konark Sun Temple

The 13th-century Sun Temple (also known as the Black Pagoda), built in Orissa red sandstone (Khandolite) and black granite by King Narasimhadeva I (AD 1236-1264) of the Ganga dynasty. The temple is one of the most well renowned temples in India and is a World Heritage Site.

Lingaraj Temple

Lingaraj Temple is a temple of the Hindu god Shiva and is one of the oldest temples of the Temple City Bhubaneswar, a revered pilgrimage centre and the capital of the state of Orissa.

Mausimaa Temple

Mausimaa Temple is an ancient shrine in Ganjam District

of Orissa. The temple can be approached by road from Bhubaneswar (140 km) and Chhatrapur (102 km). The nearest railway station is at Berhampur (88 km). It is about 8 km from Bhanja Nagar.

The presiding deity of the temple is Mother's Sister of Lord Jagannath).

The temple celebrates its festival during the Rath Yatra held in the Jagannath Temple (Puri). Upper Bagh Devi Temple and Ratneswar Mahadev temple are important shrines nearby.

This temple is located in Kullada, a village also famous for it's Bagdevi temple in Ganjam district.

Mukteswar Temple

Mukteswar Temple is in Bhubaneshwar in Orissa, not far from the Parsurameswar Temple.

This distinctive 10th century temple is one of the smallest and most compact, beautifully decorated with intricate carvings. There is a tank inside the compound that is still in use by devotees. Women toss coins into the tank, wishing to cure infertility. The local saint, Lakulisa is carved into the doorway.

The temple's red sanstone is covered with equisite carvings of lean Sadhus or holy men as well as voluptuous women encrusted with jewels.

The temples most striking feature is the arched gateway also called Torana dating back to about 900 A.D. and showing the influence of Buddhist architecture. The arched gateway has thick pillars that have strings of beads and other ornaments beautifully carved on statues of smiling women in languorous repose. In the yard stands the Kedareswar Temple with a striking 8 foot statue of Ram Bhakt Hanuman (the monkey God).

Mukteswara Temple

Mukteswara Temple is situated at Bhubaneswar in the Orissa state of India. It was constructed around the 10th century. Compared to the more well-known temples in Orissa, this is a small one with a height of only 35 feet. However, the sculptured gateway, diamond shaped latticed windows and decorated interiors and the large number of carvings have made it a unique monument. So much so that instead of its religious value, it is spoken of more due to to its architecture. Shiva is the presiding deity.

Parsurameswar Temple

Parsurameswar Temple is an Hindu temple dedicated to Lord Shiva located in Bhubaneshwar, Orissa, India. It is one of the oldest temples in Orissa. This 650 A.D. temple has all the main features of the pre-10th century Orissan style of architecture. Elements such as the pine spire that curves up to a point over the sanctum housing the presiding deity, and the pyramid-covered hall where people sit and pray.

The temple is ornamented with a bas-relief of prosessions of horses and elephant. Latticework covers the windows. In the temple courtyeard there are more exotic carvings of Ganesha, the elephant God and other deities.

On a corner of the temple compound is the exoticaly unique "Lingam of one thousand Lingas "shiva phallic symbol with 1,000 lingas engraved on it. Other interesting carvings are those of Shiva throwing down king "Ravana," who is trying to uproot Mount Kailasa, the resting place of Lord Shiva.

Ramachandi Temple

Ramachandi Temple, is on a beautiful spot on the banks of the Kusabhadra River where it flows into the Bay of Bengal. It is only 5 kms away from Konark in the Khordha District of Orissa.

Goddess Ramachandi, the deity of Konark is thought by some to be the presiding deity of this temple, while others thought it to be the temple of Mayadevi, wife of Surya (Sun god)

Now the temple has collapsed leaving remains of its broken walls and the empty throne. There is no historical evidence to conclude about its presiding deity.

Samaleswari Temple

Samaleswari Temple is a Hindu temple in Orissa, India dedicated to the goddess known as MAA, also known among the natives as *samalei maa*, meaning Mother Samaleswari.

MAA (mother) Samaleswari is the pristine goddess known in the Sambalpur region of India. Sambalpur is the headquarters of Sambalpur District, in the western portion of Orissa state.

She is worshipped with a great care and devotion by the natives in her temple, famously known as the samaleswari temple. Among the varieties of festivals observed before the goddess throughout the year three festivals are observed prominently. The first two are *navaratra puja* during the months of March and April and during the months of September and October. Among these two *navaratra pujas* (nine days continuous worship of the goddess) the second one is observed with a great splendour and devotion. The third festival which is said to be the chief festival of the whole western Orissa (sambalpur) region is *nuakhai*. In this festival the farmers offer the first produce from their lands to the goddess before using it for his personal use.

Upper Bagh Devi Temple

Upper Bagh Devi Temple is an ancient shrine at Kulada, Ganjam District in the state of Orissa in India. The temple is about 8 km from Bhanja Nagar, 102 km from Chhatrapur and 140 mk from Bhubaneswar. The nearest railway station is at Berhampur, 88 km away.

10

Hindu Temples in Rajasthan

Ambika Mata Temple

Ambika Mata Temple is a Durga temple in cleft of rock in the village of Jagat about 50 km southeast of Udaipur in the state of Rajasthan in India.

Temple

This is a little-known temple, dating back to 961 AD with images of Durga and many other female divinities. Ambika, a form of the Hindu mother goddess, is the principal image in the shrine and worshipped as Shakti, a primeval source of energy. She is associated with Durga through her lion mount and is connected to the Jains through a vision advising Vimala about building his Adinath temple at Mount Abu.

The many fine sculptures have been excellently preserved. Exquisite details appear high on the exterior walls of the temple, above larger sculptures of gods or goddesses, with musicians, dancers, and singers of the heavenly court, as well as countless beautiful women. The richess and arrrangement of the carving often has a curling vegetal motif.

The theme is of a mountain palace, a heavenly abode of the gods. The tower is covered with intricate motifs, including clouds, and is surrounded by small shikhara towers which echo the surrounding mountain peaks.

The architecture of the mountain palace, as the heavenly abode of the gods, echoes the temple which is their earthly residence.

Brahma Temple

Brahma temple is the temple situated at Pushkar in Rajasthan in India. The temple is dedicated to Lord Brahama and is said to be the only existing temple dedicated to Lord Brahama in India. This temple, built with marble, is decorated with silver coins, and there is a silver turtle on the floor of the temple. Legend also has it that the ancient lake Sarovar had appeared miraculously, when a lotus fell from the hands of Lord Brahma and dropped into the this valley. The image of Brahmaji in Pushkar is in a seated Palthi position.

Eklingji

Eklingji is a temple complex in Udaipur District of Rajasthan in western India. It is located 22 km north of Udaipur. Eklingji is believed to be the Ruling deity of Mewar Princely State and the Ruler *Maharana* rules as his *Dewan*.

Begun in 971, the temple complex was built by the Guhila (later called Sesodia) dynasty of Mewar, in honour of their presiding deity Eklingji, a form of Lord Shiva. The beautifully sculpted temple complex includes 108 temples within its high walls. The main temple dates to the 15th century, rebuilt from the ruins of an earlier destroyed temple. It is made of marble and granite, and has an enormous double-storied, elaborately-pillared hall or "mandap" under a vast pyramidal roof, with a four-faced image of Lord Shiva in black marble. Another temple in the complex is the Lakulish Temple, built in 971, it is the only temple of the Lakulish sect in the whole of India.

Galtaji

Galtaji is an ancient Hindu pilgrimage site situated 10 km from Jaipur in Indian state of Rajasthan on Jaipur-Agra highway near Sisodia Rani Ka Bagh.There are temples, pavilions, natural springs and holy 'kunds'.

It is believed that Saint Galav spent his life here and did meditation.

The main temple here is temple of Galtaji in pink stone and has a huge complex. The temple has a number of pavilions with rounded roofs, exquisitely carved pillars and painted walls. The temple is surrounded by natural springs and reservoirs that are considered holy.

There are seven tanks here and the Galta Kund is considered the holiest. A large number of people take a holy bath in these tanks especially on Makar Sankranti.

There is another temple in complex and that is temple of Balaji. Yet another notable temple at Galta is Surya Temple dedicated to the Sun God built in the 18th century.

Govind Dev Ji Temple

Govind Deo Ji temple is situated in the Jaipur in Rajasthan state of India.It is situated in City Palace complex. The temple is dedicated to Govind Deo Ji (Lord Krishna).The image of the deity was brought from Vrindavan here by Raja Sawai Jai Singh, the founder of Jaipur.

'Aartis' and 'Bhog' are offered to the deity seven times a day, when the idol is unveiled for 'Darshan'.Thousands of devotees visit the temple daily and even larger number visit during Janmashtami.

Jeenmata

Jeenmata is a village of religious importance in Sikar district of Rajasthan, India. It is located at a distance of 29 km from Sikar town in south. The population of town is 4359 out of which 1215 are SC and 113 ST people. There is an ancient Temple dedicated to Jeen Mata (Goddess of Power).

The sacred shrine of Jeenmata is believed to be a thousand years old. Millions of devotees assemble here for a colourful festival held twice in a year in the month of Chaitra and Ashvin during the Navratri. There are a number of dharamshalas to accommodate large number of visitors.

Jeenmata temple is situated near the hill 10 km from village Rewasa. It is surrounded by thick forest.Its full and real name was Jayantimala. The year of its construction is not known however the sabhamandapa and pillars are definitely very old.

The temple of Jeenmata was a place of pilgrimage from early times and was repaired and rebuilt several times. There is a popular belief which has come down to people through the centuries that in a village Ghoghu of Churu, King Ghangh loved and married an Apsara (nymph) on the condition that he would not visit her palace without prior information. King Ghangh got a son called Harsha and a daughter Jeen. Afterwards she again conceived but as chance would have it king Ghangh went to her palace without prior intimation and thus violated solemn vow he had made to the Apsara. Instantly she left the king and fled away with her son Harsha and daughter Jeen whom she abandoned at the place where presently the temple stands. The two children here practiced extreme asceticism. Later a Chauhan ruler built the temple at that place.

Kaila devi

Kaila devi temple is a temple situated 23 km from Karauli in Rajasthan state in India. The temple is located on the banks of the Kalisil river in the hills of Trikut, 2 km. to the north-west of Kaila village. The temple is dedicated to the tutelary deity, goddess Kaila, of the erstwhile princely rulers of the Karauli state. It is a marble structure with a large courtyard of a checkered floor. In one place are a number of red flags planted by devotees.

Kalika Mata Temple, Chittorgarh Fort

Kalika Mata Temple, Chittorgarh Fort is a very ancient temple that predates Maharana Pratap. It has thousands of visitors everyday. People come from far and near to visit this temple.

Karni Mata

Karni Mata temple is a 600 year old temple at Deshnoke, Rajasthan, India. Karni Mata is believed to be the incarnation of Hindu goddess Durga.The peculiarity of this temple is that thousands of rats are worshipped here. The temple in its present form was completed in the early 20th century in late Mughal style by Maharaja Ganga Singh.

This temple is dedicated to Karni Mata. There is a legend that she prophesied the victory of Rao Bika. The rats are seen as holy, owing to the belief that the souls of the followers of Karni Mata are in these rats and thus they must be looked after. The huge silver gates to the temple, and the marble carvings were a donation of Maharaja Ganga Singh. Throughout the year pilgrims from anywhere come to pay religious tribute to Karni Mata. Outside Rajasthan she is respected and loved in areas like Gujrat, Madhya Pradesh, Haryana. During Navratri thousands come to the temple on foot.

Nathdwara

Nathdwara is a town in Rajasthan state of western India. It is located on the Banas River in Rajsamand District, just north of Udaipur. This holy town is famous for its temple of Krishna which houses the Shrinathji, a 12th century idol (murti) of Krishna. The idol was moved in the 17th century from Govardhan hill, near Mathura, to protect it from the Mughal emperor Aurangzeb's campaign against Hindu worship in his empire. The Haveli of Shrinathji (as the temple is called), was once a royal palace of the Sesodia Rajput rulers of Mewar.

Salasar Balaji

Salasar Balaji is a religious place for the devotees of Lord Hanuman. It is situated in Churu district of Rajasthan. Salasar Dham attracts innumerable Indian worshippers throughout the year. On Chaitra Poornima and Ashvin Purnima large fairs take place in the area when more than 6 to 7 lacs of people assemble here to pay their homage to the deity. Hanuman Sewa Samiti looks after the management of the Temple and the fair. There are many Dharamshalas to stay and Indian restaurants to eat. Salasar Dham is situated in Salasar town.

Sanwaliaji Temple

The Sanwaliaji temple of the Dark Krishna is situated on the Chittorgarh-Udaipur Highway, at the town of Mandaphia, about 40 kilometres from Chittorgarh. This temple of Shri

Krishna is considered second only to the temple of the Lord Shrinathji at Nathdwara.

Shila Devi

Shila Devi is famous idol of Durga.Her temple is located in Amber fort.The idol was brought by Raja Man Singh I of Amber from Jessore, now in Bangladesh.On the sixth day of winter Navratris, special prayers are offered to this goddess.Lakhs of people from Jaipur and surrounding areas come here to pay offerings to Shila Devi.

Shrinathji

Shrinathji is a deity form of Krishna situated in the temple town of Nathdwara near Udaipur in Rajasthan. Shrinathji specifically refers to the story in the Bhagavata Purana wherein Krishna lifts Govardhan hill to protect the inhabitants of Vrindavan from a downpour of rain sent by Indra, king of the devas. Krishna in his form of Sri Nathji is also worshipped throughout India by followers of Bhakti Yoga and the Vaishnava traditions, especially within Gujarat. The town of Nathdwara itself is often referred to as 'Shrinathji', after the famous deity.

Sundha Mata Temple

Sundha Mata temple is about 900 years old temple of Mother goddess situated on a hill top called 'Sundha', located at Longitude 72°-22' E and Latitude 24°-50' N, in Jalore District of Rajasthan. It is 64 km from Mount Abu and 20 km from the town of Bhinmal. In the temple premises there are three historically significant inscriptions that lighten history of the region. First inscription is of year 1262 A.D, which describes victory of Chauhans and downfall of Parmaras. The second inscription is of 1326 A.D. and third one is 1727 A.D. There is a wildlife sanctuary nearby covering an area of 107 square kilometres. Ropeway (Udan Khatola) to the temple-first in Rajasthan is under construction.Ropeway (Udan Khatola) to the temple-first in Rajasthan is ready Rs 50 for both the ways.

11

Hindu Temples in Tamil Nadu

Adi Kumbeswarar Temple

Kumbeswarar Temple is a famous Hindu temple dedicated to Lord Shiva located at the centre of the Tamilnadu town Kumbakonam, India. The famous Hindu festival of Mahamaham is associated with this temple. The huge temple with built over an area of 30181 sq ft is reported to be more than 1300 years old.

Shri Adhi Kumbeswara is the presiding deity of Kumbakonam and Manthrapeeteswari Mangalambika is the lord's Consort. The temple complex is huge and has beautiful artwork. The Mahamaham festival takes place once every 12 years during the Tamil Month of Masi (February/March), when lakhs of pilgrims from various parts of India visit Kumbakonam to take a holy bath in the sacred Mahamaham tank which is located in the heart of the town.

Aeri Katha Ramar Temple

Aeri Katha Temple is a Hindu temple dedicated to Lord Vishnu located near the holy city of Chengalpattu, Tamilnadu, India. This is the stalam where Udayavar was named 'Ramanujar'. Ramanujar was instructed the Pancha Samskara Mantram. Mathuranthaka Chaturvedi Mangalam, Vaikunda Varthanam, Thirumathurai, Thirumanthira Tirupathi, Karunagara Vilagam are the other names of the stalam. Tirumisai Alwar got siddhi in this stalam.

Airavatesvara Temple

Airateswara Temple is a Hindu temple located in the town of Darasuram, near Kumbakonam in the South Indian state of Tamil Nadu. This temple, built by Rajaraja Chola II in the 12th century CE, along with the Brihadeeswara Temple at Thanjavur, the Gangaikondacholisvaram Temple at Gangaikonda Cholapuram are a UNESCO World Heritage Site referred to as the Great Living Chola Temples.

Legend

The Airateswara temple is dedicated to Lord Shiva. Shiva is here known as Airavateshwara, because he was worshipped at this temple by Airavata, the white elephant of the king of the gods, Indra.

It is said that the King of Death, Yama also worshipped Shiva here. Tradition has it Yama, who was suffering under a Rishi's curse from a burning sensation all over the body, was cured by the presiding deity Airavateswarar. Yama took bath in the sacred tank and got rid of the burning sensation. Since then the tank has been known as Yamateertham.

Aksheeswaraswamy Temple

Aksheeswaraswamy Temple is a Hindu temple dedicated to Lord Shiva located near the holy city of Chengalpattu, Tamilnadu, India. The temple is incarnated by the hymns of Tirugnana Sambandar.

History

The all powerful Asuras, Tarakan, Kamalatchan and Vithvan Mali built palaces in gold, silver and iron respectively and were troubling the Devas more frequently. The Devas along with Vishu and Brahma worshipped Lord Shiva. Lord Shiva personified sky as the roof, ground as base, Surya & Chandra as Wheels, Four Vedas as horses, Merumalai as the Bow, Vasuki as the string and Thirumal himself as the arrow. Brhma was steering the Chariot. Vinaya grew angry as he was not a part of the war and broke the caster bolt of the Chariot. Lord Shiva gave good deeds to Vinayagar and went ahead winning the Asuras at Thirvathikai. Since the Achu(Caster Bolt) was broken into pieces(Pakkam), this place is called Achirupakkam.

Alagar Koyil

Alagar Koyil (Alagar temple), also known as Azhagarkovil, is a temple dedicated to Lord Vishnu situated 21 km from the city of Madurai, which lies in the Tamil Nadu state of India.

Annamalaiyar Temple

Annamalaiyar(Arunachaleswara in Sanskrit) is a noted Hindu temple dedicated to Lord Shiva, located at the bottom of the Annamalai hill in Tamilnadu, India. It is the home of Annamalaiyar or Arunachaleswarar (Lord Shiva worshipped as a Shiva Lingam) and Unnamulaiyaal (Apitakuchambaal-Parvati), and is one of the largest temples in India.

It occupies a special place in the Saivite realm and is regarded as one of the Pancha Bhoota Stalams (one of the five grand temples associated with the five basic elements) – associated with the element Fire, the other four being Thiruvanaikaval Jambukeswara (water), Chidambaram Natarajar (sky),Kanchi Ekambareswara (earth) and Kalahasti Nathar (wind).

The earliest known record of the temple is in the works of the poet Nakkirar of the third Tamil Sangam period. This would date the temple's origins back at least 2000 years. At that time, the temple would have been a simple wooden structure. The present masonry structure and gopurams (temple towers) date back approximately 1200 years. This has been determined from an inscription in the structure that was made during the reign of Chola kings who ruled in the ninth century A.D.

Ashtabujakaram

The temple is called 'Ashtabujankaram' because the Lord Adhikesava Perumal has eight hands loaded with weapons. It is in Vishnu Kanchi.

Ashtalakshmi Kovil

The Ashtalakshmi Kovil lies on the shorelines near the Elliot's beach, in Chennai, India. It is a temple to the Goddess Lakshmi. Ashta means eight, and the eight forms of Lakshmi are worshipped in this temple. Lakshmi is the consort of Lord Vishnu.

Ayikudi Balasubramanya Swami Temple

The Ayikudi Balasubramanya Swami Temple is located in the village of Ayikudi, Thirunelveli district near Thenkasi.

Until 1947 this area was under the regime of Thiruvadhankur Kings. The temple is situated on the banks of Hanuman Nadhi. Sri Hanuman who was said to have stopped by and rested on the banks of this river on his way to Lanka, hence the river was named Hanuman nadhi. Obviously this is why Rama & Subramanya are popular names in this region.

Lord Karthikeya appears among five Vrikshas (trees) and the five Devatas in the form of a young Balasubramanya. The five Vrikshams are Arasu (Surya), Vembu neem (Ambhikai), Kariveppilai Curry leaves tree (Mahesha), Madhalai (Ganesha) & Mavilangu (Vishnu).

A devotee named Mallan at Nanjaipara, found the main deity Idol of the temple in the Mallam River. Once there lived a Brahmin Mugura Bhakthar sanyasi who obtained samadhi in that area. His samadhi was built on the shores of Hanuman Nadhi. An Arasa Tree was planted at that place & his community was conducting pujas & ceremonies there. The idol of Balasubramanya Idol that was found at Mallapuram was installed on the samadhi of that Sanyasi and the pujas were continued.

Until 1931 the top of the temple was only made by coconut & palm leaves. About 150 years back the Thiruvadhankur Royal family took up the temple management. Then the temple was renovated and festivals were organized. The Utsava Murthi was known as Muthukumara swami. The Balasubramanya Mulavar Pujas were conducted in the traditional way by the

Brahmins and the Utsava pujas & processions were conducted by Shivacharyas.

The Idol: Both the Mulavar & the Utsavar are identical, The idol is a small Vigraham, with the young baby faced Muruga, with four hands Vajram, Shaktivaram & Abhayam with a Peacock on the left and the lord sits on a lotus Padmapeetam.

Special ways of Prayer: The Arasa leaf Vibhuthi Prasadham (Holy Ash) available in this temple is very powerful. Padi Payasam, Kavadi, Pallkudam are some of the important ways in which the devotees show their love to the Lord. According to legend, on the steps leading to the Hanuman nadhi Sri Balamuruga takes payasam along with other children.

Special Days: During Aipasi month Nov 15-Dec 15, During Skandha shasti Soorasamharam festivities are popular for 7 days in this temple. Each day of the Utsavam the Lord is decorated differently and there is a Huge crowed of devotees attending the festivities. Special pujas are conducted in the temple during Chithirai Vishu, Vaigasi Vishakam & Masi Makam. The lord is taken on the Peacock on the streets as a procession around the temple.

Devotees believe that those who get the dharshan and pray to this Balasubramanya will attain all the prosperity.

Bakthavatsala Perumal Temple

Bhakthavatsala Sri Bakthavatsala Perumal temple is a Hindu temple, located at Thiruninravur near Chennai, India. It is one of the 108 Srivaishnavite divyadesams.

Brihadeeswarar Temple

The Brihadeeswarar temple (also spelled Brihadeshvara Temple or Birhadeeshwara temple),originally called as Peruvudaiyar Koil in Tamil, is an ancient Hindu temple located at Thanjavur in the state of Tamil Nadu, India. This 10th century CE temple, part of the UNESCO World Heritage Site "Great Living Chola Temples", is a prominent example of the Dravidian style of temple architecture. The central temple known as the *Periya Kovil* (Big Temple) stands within a fort, whose walls were later additions built during the 16th century. The name *periya kovil* came from its original name "periya aavudayar kovil" (*aavudayar* being a local name of Lord Shiva). The *vimana* (main tower) of the temple is approximately 65 m (215 ft) high and is the tallest in the world. It was so designed that the vimana never casts a shadow at noon during any period of the year.

Ekambareswarar Temple

Ekambareswarar Temple is one of the famous Hindu temples dedicated to Lord Shiva, located in Kanchipuram in the state of Tamilnadu, India. It is one of the five major Shiva temples (each representing a natural element), representing the element Earth. The other four temples in this category are Thiruvanaikaval Jambukeswara (water), Chidambaram Natarajar (sky), Thiruvannamalai Arunachaleswara (fire) and Kalahasti Nathar (wind).

Reaching a height of 57 meters, the temple's *gopuram* is one of the tallest in South India. One notable feature of the temple is the Aayiram Kaal Mandapam, or the "hallway with a thousand pillars". The temple's inner walls are decorated with an array of 1,008 Shiva lingams. The *sthala-virutcham* is a 3,500 year old mango tree whose branches are said to yield four different types of mangoes.

It is also one of the 108 Divya desam for Vaishnavaites. There is a small Sannidhi for Lord Vishnu named ThiruNilaaththingal Thundathan. Legend says that once Parvati was doing Tapas under the Mango Tree. In order to test her devotion Lord Shiva sent fire on her. Goddess Parvati prayed to her brother Lord Vishnu. In order to save her,he took the Moon from Lord Shiva's head and showed the rays which then cooled down the tree as well as Parvati. After that, Lord Shiva again sent River Ganga to disrupt the tapas. Parvati devi prayed to Ganga and convince her that both of them are sisters and should not harm her. Ganga did not disturb her penance after that. Then, Parvati made a Shiva Linga out of sand and got united with Lord Shiva. Here, Lord Vishnu is prayed as Vamana Murthy.

Chamundeswari Temple

Chamundeswari Temple is located on the top of Chamundi Hills about 13 km from the palace city of Mysore in the state of Karnataka in India. The temple was named after Chamundeeswari or Durga, the fierce form of Shakti, a tutelary deity held in reverence for centuries by Mysore Maharajas.

Description

The original shrine is thought to have been built in the 12th century by Hoysala rulers while its tower was probably built by the Vijayanagar rulers of the 17th century. In 1659, a flight of one thousand steps was built leading up to the 3000 foot summit of the hill.

At the temple are several images of Nandi (the bull mount of Shiva). There is a huge granite Nandi on the 800th step on the hill in front of a small Shiva temple a short distance away. This Nandi is over 15 feet high, and 24 feet long and around its neck are exquisite bells.

The temple has a seven story tall 'gopuram' decorated with intricate carvings. The idol of the Chamunda Devi is said to be made of solid gold and the temple gates are made of silver.

Gunaseelam Vishnu Temple

'Gunaseelam Vishnu Temple is a famous Vishnu temple near Trichy, in the state of Tamil Nadu India. An exceptional feature about this temple is that mentally challenged people are taken to the temple and kept in the temple premises for 48 days(*mandalam* in Tamil). At the end of the 48 days it is believed that their illness is cured by the grace of the Lord Prasanna Venkatachalapathi. The etymology of the name derives from "Gunam" (Cure) and "Seelam" (Place), meaning the place in which all illnesses are cured. This temple is around 20 miles from Trichy.

Getting Here Gunaseelam is connected by town buses originating from Trichy and the frequency is low. The buses to Gunaseelam start from Chatiram Bus Stand in Trichy. Private taxis are recommended due to convenience.

Kailasanathar Temple

The Kailasanath temple is located in the temple town of Kanchipuram in Tamil Nadu, India. It was built by the Pallavas in the early 8th century CE. It is famous for its splendid *vimana*. It also contains numerous panels showing lord Shiva as Nataraja in various postures.This temple was built by Pallava King Narasimhavarman II (Rajasimhan).

The Chola King Rajaraja Chola I visited this temple and named this temple as kachipettu periya thirukatrali(Stone Tenple of Kachipettu(ancient name of kanchipuram).It is believed by many archeologists that this kailasanathar temple must be the inspiration for Rajaraja Chola I to built the Tanjore Rajarajeeswaram temple.

Kalikambal Temple

The Kalikambal Temple is a Hindu temple dedicated to Kalikambal (Kamakshi) and Kamateswarar. The temple is located in Thambu Chetty Street, George Town a prominent financial centre of Chennai, India.

History

The temple was originally located closer to the sea shore, and was relocated to the current site at 1640 AD. The great Maratha ruler Shivaji had worshipped in this temple during October, 1667. It is believed that a fierce form of Goddess was held in worship earlier and that this form was replaced with the shanta swaroopa form of Kamakshi.

Kalyana Varadharaja Perumal Temple

Kalyana Varadharaja Perumal Templ at 31 Paruthiyur Sengalipuram, Thiruvarur District 612 604 was an ancient temple that exists in Paruthiyur. The main Idol Adhi Varadarajar is gracing with 'Prayoga-Chakra". This chakra was sent to protect Ambarisha, a Vishnu devotee, from the curse of Duruvasa, the famous saint. Panchaloka idols of this temple are very ancient and more than 1000 years old. Kalyana Varadarajar another Vishnu is also gracing the devotees from the same Shrine.

Paruthiyur Kodanda Rama Shrine is at this temple. When you visit this temple, if one feels that the main deities are so beautiful, they only have to wait to see the Utsava Murthis whose beauty is par-excellence. Shri Kodhanda Ramar, Janaki, Lakshmana and Anjaneya are the Utsava Murthis. The shilpa of Shri Rama is as per the vivid description given by Shri Anjaneya Swami in the Sundra kandam of Valmiki Ramayanam. This temple was the life and soul of a Mahaan Paruthiyur Krishna Sastri The idols in the temple belonged to the 10th century early Chola period.

Kamakshi Amman Temple

Kamakshi Amman Temple is a famous Hindu temple dedicated to Goddess Kamakshi a divine form of Parvati. It is located in the historic city Kanchipuram, near Chennai, India and is popularly associated with Adi Sankaracharya, one of the greatest Hindu saints. Along with Madurai Meenakshi, Thiruvanaikaval Akilandeswari, Vishalakshi Varanasi, Kamakshi is an important part of worship of Parvati.

The main deity is seated in a majestic Padmasana posture, an yogic posture signifying peace and prosperity, instead of the traditional standing pose in most other temples of Parvati. The goddess holds a sugarcane bow and lotus and parrot in the lower two of her arms (Many of the Hindu god forms generally have four arms) and has the two divine instruments *Pasa* and *Angusa* in her upper two arms. There are no traditional Parvati or Shakthi shrines in the city of Kanchipuram, apart from this temple, which is unusual in a traditional city that has hundreds of traditional temples.

There are various legends attributed to it. One of them according to *Kamkshivilasa* is that the Goddess had to absorb all the other shakthi forms to give boon to Manmatha (the Hindu god of fertility and love). Another legend attributes it to the Raja Rajeswari pose of the deity that signifies an absolute control over the land under its control, leaving no other forms of Shakthi. Legend has it that Kamakshi offered worship to a Shivalingam made out of sand, under a mango tree and gained Shiva's hand in marriage.

Kamakshi and Adi Sankaracharya

Adi Sankaracharya is significantly associated in the rich history of the temple. Like many other ancient goddesses, the form of Kamakshi was less benign than the current form. There used to be various forms of animal and human sacrifices in ancient Shakthi temples and it is believed that Adi Sankaracharya led to the more peaceful representation of the goddess by placing a divine Chakra before it.. And the goddess agreed to show her benign side in the temple, while the forms of Shakthi outside Kanchipuram still had more angrier forms of Shakthi.

There is no verifiable historical proof for this, though it is a part of the local folklore. Symbolic of this, during the festivals when the processional deity is taken for a procession around the temple streets, it takes leave from Sankaracharya, at his shrine in the inner corridor. It is also believed that Sankaracharya defeated Buddhist and other philosophers in this place, sparking a revival for Hinduism.

Kapaleeshwarar Temple

The Kapaleeshwarar temple is a Hindu temple located in Mylapore, Chennai, India. The original 8th century Shiva temple was built by the Pallavas and located on the shore but it was destroyed by the Portuguese and was re-built 300 years later.

The presiding deity of this temple is a form of Shiva called *Kapaleeshwarar*. The form of Shiva's wife Parvati at this temple is called *Karpagambal* (from the Tamil for "goddess of the wish-yielding tree"). Legend has it that Lord Shiva was once telling Lord Brahma, the Hindu god of creation, about the creation of the three lokas but Lord Brahma did not agree with what Shiva said. Shiva got angry and plucked out one of Brahma's four heads. Brahma begged for forgiveness and was asked to perform penance at Mayilai (Mylapore) and then he asked Lord Shiva to take the name of Kapaleeswarar.

History

It is believed and proven by the name of the area "Mylapore" where the temple is situated, and "architecture", "statues" inside the temple that it is indeed based on the story of shiva(kapaleeshwarar) turning parvati(karpagambal)into peahen. One day as lord Shiva was telling something important to his wife Parvathi,she was admiring a peacock dancing beautifully besides them.

Knowing that she was not listening to him, shiva got angry and turned her into a peahen and sent her to earth. After realising her mistake, parvathi as a peahen started doing pooja to shiva and prayed to take her back as his wife. Impressed with her sincere prayer and devotion, he changed her back and accepted her as his wife. Statues and arts depicting this story can be seen throughout the temple including Temple Tower(Gopuram).

The age of the temple is the source of much debate.

The commonly held view is that the temple was built in the 7th century CE by the ruling Pallavas, based on references to the temple in the hymns of the Nayanmars (which however place it at the shore). Further, the architecture of the temple appears to be 300-400 years old. The scholarly view that accounts for the discrepancies is that the original temple was built on the shore at the location of the current Santhome Church but was destroyed by the Portuguese, and the current temple (which is 1-1.5 km from the shore) was built more recently. A small minority of people believe that the original temple was indeed on the beach, but that the sea has receded over centuries.

Mythology

A legend associated with this temple is that Shiva's wife Parvati was distracted by a peacock and did not hear him call out to her. Annoyed, Shiva turned her into a peahen and sent her to earth. The peahen arrived at this temple and performed tapas (penance), and was eventually accepted again by Shiva. A temple was then built around the location of the peahen's tapas, and the place was named "Mayilapur" (Tamil: mayil: peacock, peahen; pur: generic place ending, like "-ville"), which was later anglicized to Mylapore.

The famous Saiva saint and poet Sambanthar (Thirugyanasambandar) turned the local

The Temple

Architecture: Architecturally, the temple is of typical Dravidian style with the gopuram overpowering the street on which the temple sits. There are two entrances to the temple marked by the gopuram on either side. The east gopuram is about 40m high, while the smaller western gopuram faces the sacred tank.

Shrines: The temple has other shrines dedicated to Ganesha (a dancing form called Nardana Vinayakar), Muruga (called Singara Velar), with his two consorts Valli and Deivayani. Smaller shrines are dedicated to other forms of Shiva (Annamalaiar, Sundareswarar and Jagatheswarar), Muruga (Palani Andavar) and others. In particular, there is a shrine with an image of a peahen, which is where Mylapore derives its name from. Navagraha shrine is also present. There is a separate shrine for Sani Bhagavan and special puja's will be done on saturday.

Sambanthar (Thirugyanasambandar), is said to have brought back to life the maiden Poompavai, daughter of Shivanesa Chettiar (a Shiva devotee) who was desirous of marrying him, at Mylapore. The saint poet Tiruvalluvar lived here. The bronze idols of the 63 Nayanmars, the saints who were devotees of Lord Shiva are placed in the Kapaleeswarar Sannadhi. Every year the Arupathumoovar festival is conducted & the 63 nayanmars (Nayanmar) are taken in procession.

Vahanas: The vahanas at the temple include the bull, elephant, bandicoot, peacock, goat and parrot among others, while a golden chariot is a recent addition. The God and the Goddess is seated on the vahana and brought around the temple with the temple band playing music throughout this occasion. Devotees gather around the vahanas and consider it a privilege to lift the God and the Goddess on the vahana.

Karpaka Vinayakar Temple

Karpaka Vinayakar Temple is an ancient rock-cut cave shrine dedicated to Lord Ganesh, located at Pillayarpatti 15 km west of Karaikkudi in the state of Tamil Nadu in India.

In the cave temple are rock cut images of Shiva and other gods as well as several shrines. The Agama texts found on stones in the temple help date the temple to the period between 1091 AD and 1238 AD. The presiding deity is Karpaka Vinayakar or Desi Vinayaka Pillaiyar. It is 6 feet high and 5 feet wide.

A unique Tamil image of Ganesha is found in the temple help verify the temples's date.

Today the Pillayarpatti Nagarathar worshippers are involved in maintaning and conducting daily worship services in the temple. People from all over the state come here everyday and great numbers of pilgrims gather here for the Ganesh Chaturthi festival held every year during Augues and September.

Kattalai Amman Temple

Kattalai Amman Temple is a Hindu Temple situated in Kanyakumari District at the southern part of Tamilnadu, India. The temple is located in the picturesque village, surrounded by mountains and canals. The temple was known originally as "Kandan Sasthankoil".

The current temple complex was built in 1981 and the first Amman Kudai Vizha (annual celebration of the Devi) was conducted on 9th November 1981 (24th Aippasi 1157 of Tamil Calendar). The star (Nakshatra) on this auspicious day was Revatî. There after every year annual celebration is conducted on Aippasi month on the day of Revatî nakshatra. Currently there are three main building for the temple. The renovated Nagaramman temple, the 1981 built Amman Temple and the later build "Shiva Maadan" temple which also houses the deity "Boothathan".

The Temple complex consists of the main campus which houses the main deities and the area surrounded. The surrounding areas also has bases for some deities and also the sacred temple spring water (ootrukuzhi) where year round fresh water flows, the temple pond and rocks and trees. The pond is also known as irumbittan kulam. Legend is that iron was melted and poured into this pond.

The temple is currently maintained by the Elur Chetty community.

Kunrakudy

It is a famous murugan temple, atop a small hill near Madurai, India.

Marudamalai

Marudamalai is one of the most popular abodes of Lord Muruga and in importance it is next only to the Arupadaiveedu ("The six Fort-Houses of Muruga"), for Muruga devotees. Some people consider Marudhamalai to be the unofficial seventh Padaiveedu of Muruga, along with a few other contenders for the spot, including Kunrakudy, Sikkal and Vayalur.

Like most Murugan temples, Maruthamalai Murugan temple is situated upon a scenic hill that is a part of the beautiful lush green Western Ghats and is about 15 km from the vibrant city of Coimbatore, Tamil Nadu, India.

This is an ancient temple. References to this temple are found in inscriptions in the Thirumuruganpoondi temple. ThirumuruganPoondi temple is a "Tevarapaadalpetrastalam" and is at least 1200 years old. So we can surmise that the Marudhamalai temple is older than 1200 years.

There is a shrine called the "Paambaatti Shithar Kugai" (Paambaatti Shithar cave) that is in proximity to the Murugan temple. Legend has it that a Sitthar referred to as the Paambaatti Sitthar lived here in Marudhamalai. Paambaatti Sitthar is one of the most notable 18 Sitthars. Pambaatti Sitthar as his name indicates that he was associated with snake charming. As is the custom of the Sitthars of Tamil Nadu, he too, in the interest of mankind, has written extensively on the medicinal values and applications of plants.

Near the foothills, there is a temple for Lord Pillayaar who is known as the "Thaanthondri Vinaayakar" (which means that the Pillayar idol appeared on its own without human intervention).

This temple is under the control of Religious endowments department of Government of Tamil Nadu.

This temple is located on a hilltop called *Marutha Maillai* (roughly translating to "hill of vegetation"), true to its name, the legend has it that this hill has many herbs of medicinal value. The hill is also home to a particular sect of tribal tamil people. The temple in recent years has been renovated and the local business community is supporting this activity. The temple also plans to have a rope car operate from the foothills. In recent years number of Nature cure clinics have come up nearby this hillside.

Meenakshi Amman Temple

The Meenakshi Sundareswarar Temple or Meenakshi Amman Temple is a historic Hindu temple located in the holy city of Madurai, Tamil Nadu, India. It is dedicated to Lord Shiva (in the form of *Sundareswarar* or *Beautiful Lord*) and his consort, Goddess Parvati (in the form of *Meenakshi* or *Fish-eyed Goddess*). The temple forms the heart and lifeline of the 2500 year old city of Madurai, home of the Tamil language.

According to Hindu legends, Lord Shiva, in the form of Sundareswarar, with his divine group of followers, appeared here in Madurai, to marry Pandya King Malayadwaja Pandya's daughter, Meenakshi, believed to be an incarnation of Hindu Goddess Parvati.

This temple is one of the most sacred abodes of Parvati, others being Kamakshi of Kanchipuram, Akilandeswari of Thiruvanaikaval and Vishalakshi of Varanasi.

The temple has a stunning architecture and it was a frontrunner in the election for the modern seven wonders of the world for its architectural importance. The complex houses 12 magnificent gopurams or towers that are elaborately sculptured and painted.

The temple is a significant symbol for the Tamil people, and has been mentioned since antiquity in Tamil literature, though the present structure is believed to have been built only recently in the early 17th century.

Navagraha Temples

Navagraha temples are temples devoted to the nine (nava) major celestial bodies (Grahas) of Hindu astronomy. These celestial bodies are named Surya (Sun), Chandra (Moon), Chevaai/Mangal(Mars), Budhan (Mercury), Guru/Brihaspati (Jupiter), Shukra (Venus), Shani (Saturn), Rahu (Head of Demon Snake) and Ketu (Tail of Demon Snake). Many temples in South India contain a shrine dedicated to the Navagrahas. However, the term Navagraha temples refers to a cluster of nine separate temples, each an abode of one of the Navagrahams.

Nellaiappar Temple

Nellaiappar Temple (also spelled Nellaiyappar) is located in the heart of the town of Tirunelveli in the state of Tamil Nadu, India. It is one of the famous Tamil Nadu temples, deep in tradition and history and also known for its musical pillars and brilliant sculptural splendours.

Palani Murugan Temple

'Palani Murugan Temple' is one of the most famous Murugan temples in India. It is located in the township of Palani, 100 km east of Madurai, and near the famous hill station, Kodaikanal. It is one of the major Arupadaiveedu of Lord Muruga. The other Arupadiveedus are Thiruchendur (100 km south-west of Madurai), Swamimalai (150 km east of Madurai), Thiruthani (50 km from Chennai), Pazhamudircholai (10 km north of Madurai) and Thiruparamkunram (10 km south of Madurai).

Pancha Rathas

Pancha Rathas an example of monolith Indian rock-cut architecture dating from the late 7th century located at Mamallapuram, a tiny village south of Madras in the state of Tamil Nadu, India. The village was a busy port during the 7th and 8th century reign of the Pallava dynasty. The site is famous for the rock-cut caves and the sculptured rock that line a granite hill, including one depicting Arjuna's Penance. It has been classified as a UNESCO World Heritage Site.

The Pancha Rathas shrines were carved during the reign of King Mahendravarman I and his son Narasimhavarman I. Each temple is a monolith, carved whole from a rock outcropping of pink granite. The five monolithic pyramidal structured shrines are named after the Pandavas (Arjuna, Bhima, Yudhishtra, Nakula and Sahadeva) and Draupadi. As noted, each shrine is not assembled from cut rock but carved from one single large piece of stone. It is likely their original design traces back to wood constructions.

Parthasarathy Temple

The Parthasarathy Temple is an 8th century Hindu Vaishnavite temple dedicated to Lord Krishna, located at Triplicane, Chennai, India. It is considered one of the 108 divyadesams or holy abodes of Lord Vishnu. The name 'Parthasarathy', in Sanskrit, means the 'charioteer of Arjuna', and Lord Krishna is worshipped in that role in this temple.

Pazhamudircholai

Pazhamudircholai is a Hindu temple located 10 miles north of Madurai, India atop a hill covered with dense forests. One of Arupadaiveedu of Muruga, is very close to the Vishnu temple of Azhagar Kovil.

Punnainallur Mariamman

The Punnai Nallur Mariamman temple is an Hindu temple located at Thanjavur in the state of Tamil Nadu, India. The temple of goddess Mariamman is one of the famous temples around Thanjavur District.

Ramanathaswamy Temple, Rameswaram

Ramanathaswamy Temple is a famous Hindu temple dedicated to Lord Shiva located in the island of Rameswaram in the state of Tamilnadu, India. According to Shaiva mythology, Lord Rama is believed to have prayed Lord Shiva here to absolve any sins that he might have committed during his war against the demon king Ravana. The temple along with Viswanathaswamy temple, Varanasi is one of the holiest Hindu shrines that has to be visited in one's lifetime and is one of the twelve Jyotirlingas the holy abodes of Shiva.

Rockfort Ucchi Pillayar Temple

Rockfort or Ucchi Pillayar koil, is a combination of two famous 7th century Hindu temples, one dedicated to Lord Ganesh and the other dedicated to Lord Shiva, located atop a small rock in Trichi, India. Geologically the 83m high rock is said to be one of the oldest in the world, dating over 3 billion years ago, and mythologically this rock is the place where Lord Ganesh ran from King Vibishana, after establishing the Ranganathaswamy deity in Srirangam. The name rockfort comes from the fact that the place was used for military fortification first by the Vijayanagar emperors and later by the British during the Carnatic wars.

The temple complex is composed of two parts-A shiva temple (Thayumanaswamy) carved in the middle of the rock and a Pillayar (Ganesh)temple at the top portion of the rock. The Shiva temple is the bigger one, housing a massive stone statue of Shiva in the form of Linga along with a separate sanctum for goddess Parvati. The temple is mystic in its nature with an awe-inspiring rock architecture. The Ganesh temple is much smaller with an access through steep steps carved on the rock and provides a stunning view of Trichi, Srirangam and the rivers Kaveri and Kollidam. Due to its ancient and impressive architecture created by the Pallavas, the temple is maintained by the Archaeological department of India.

Sangameswarar Temple

Sangameswarar Temple is a temple dedicated to Lord Shiva in Bhavani, Tamil Nadu.

Sangamam in Tamil means 'join'. As the Kaveri River and Bhavani River join in Bhavani, the deity here is named as Sangameswarar.

In the temple, near the Ambal Sannithi, two statues are seen, on which when water is poured, the statue's face may appear to either laughing or crying. When the kings ruled the place even some mines are been carved, from this place to Chdambaram.

Sarangapani Temple

Sarangapani Temple is a place of worship, dedicated to Vishnu as the Supreme God of the Vaishnava traditions of Hinduism.

It lies in the Tanjore district of Tamil Nadu. It's about 1½ miles away from Kumbakonam railway station. Which is on the Chennai-Tanjore main line. Bus facility and staying facilities are ample. It is one of the 108 Divya Desams.. This temple is along Kaveri and is one of the Pancharanga Kshetrams.

Sikkal Singaravelan Temple

Sikkal Singara Velan Temple is one of the most popular Hindu temples dedicated to Lord Muruga and a contender for a the unofficial seventh Padaiveedu of Muruga, along with the popular Arupadaiveedu (six bodes of Lord Muruga). It is located in the village of Sikkal, near Nagapattinam in Tamilnadu. It is believed in Hindu mythology that this place was once a jasmine forest and due to it pleasant smell, the semi-human goddess in Hindu mythology, Kamadenu lives here. It is one of the rare traditional Hindu temples that has both Shiva (Navaneeteswarar) and Vishnu (Venaipperuman) deities in the same complex.

The most important festival is associated with Lord Muruga getting the weapon Vel from his divine mother, Parvathi to destroy the demon king, Suran. During this time, it is believed by the devotees that the idol sweats and a major event is conducted. After receiving the weapon and the blessings from his divine mother, he proceeds to kill the demon in Sri Lanka, while setting up the base camp in Thiruchendur.

Sri Adikesavaperumal Temple

The Sri Adikesavaperumal Temple is a Hindu temple located in Thiruvattar, India an is one of the 108 Divya desam (holy shrines) of Vishnu. The temple is a picturesque setting surrounded on three sides by rivers (River Kothai, River Pahrali and River Thamirabarani).

The Temple

The temple architecture is Kerala Architecture with wooden pillars, doors and roofs. The lord is lying on his snake couch and has to be viewed through three doors. We could see Lord Shiva near the Lord Adikesava Perumal inside the sannidhi.Deepalakshmis are many but none resembles the other. The Otraikkal Mandapam (single stone hall) made of single stone 3 feet thick is a marvel. Oorthuva Thandavam, Venugopala, Rathi, Manmatha, Lakshmana and Indrajit are excellently carved. The temple is also renowned for its murals. This Temple is older than PadmanabhaSwamy Temple at Thiruvananthapuram. The style and the architechture of this temple is taken as the sample to construct the PadmanabhaSwamy Temple at Thiruvananthapuram. There is also a Small Shrine for Lord Lakshmi Narasimhaswamy near the River and opposite to the AdiKesavaPerumal Temple.

Legend

Legend says that Lord AdiKesavaSwamy defeated the demon kesi. The demon's wife prayed to River Ganga and to River Thamirabarani and create a destruction. But it was in vain and she surrendered to Lord. Thus, the formation of the rivers made in circle named to be known as Thiruvattaru.

Sri Appakkudathaan Perumal Temple (Thirupper Nagar)

This temple is situated in Tamil Nadu, three miles away from Tiru Anbil-Kollidam and along the south shore of Kollidam. This sthalam is on the way to Kumbakonam-Tiruvaiyaaru-Tirukkaattup palli and Kallanai. This is one of the 108 Divya Desams.

Sri Azhagiya Manavala Perumal Temple

Situated in Urayoor, Trichy district in Tamil Nadu. Urayoor is also known as Thirukkozhi,nikaLaapuri, uRanthai. It is also near to Naachiyar koil. A valiant rooster, believed to have warded off an elephant with its beak, here at Uraiyur; the name Thirukkozhi (Mookkeeswaram) possibly stems from this legend. The temple is in between Trichy-Main guard Gate. This temple is in walking distance from Srirangam across the Kaveri river. This is one of the 108 Divya Desams.

Sri Chandramouleeswarar Temple

Sri Chandramouleeswarar Temple is situated atop Hariharan Kundram, near Arungundram village.

Sri Devaadi Raja Perumal Temple

This Hindu temple is situated in Thiruvazhunthoor, a village in Tanjore district of Tamil Nadu.

It lies in between Mayavaram junctiont and Kuttalam station on the main railway line between Chennai (Madras) to Tajore.

This temple can also be reached by travelling around 7 Kms from Kuttalam and about 8 Kms from Mayavaram.

This Divyadesam is also called with other names such as Azhundoor, Azhundhai, Therazhunthur.

Sri Hara Saabha Vimocchana Perumal Temple

This temple is situated in Tanjoor, Tamil Nadu (6 miles away from Tanjoor, 2 miles from Tiruvayyaaru)

It is one of the 108 Divya Desams.

Sri Pundarikashan Perumal Temple

Thiruvellarai is situated in Tamil Nadu near Trichy. It is located at a distance of 27 km from Trichy, enroute to Turaiyur. This place has Sri Pundarikasha Perumal Temple, one of the 108 Divya desams.

Sri Purushothaman Perumal Temple

Sri Purushothaman Perumal Temple is a Hindu temple which has the shrines of Brahma, Vishnu and Shiva in the same complex, making this a unique temple with shrines for all three gods and their consorts in the same place. There are very few temples where Brahma, the first of the trinity, is worshipped in statue form, which makes this temple an important place of worship. The Purushothaman is sung by Thirumangai Alvar and hence this is one of the 108 Divya Desams.

Sri Ranganathaswamy Temple (Srirangam)

The Sri Ranganathaswamy Temple in Srirangam, Tamil Nadu India is a Hindu temple dedicated to Lord Ranganatha, a reclining form of Lord Vishnu. It is the first and foremost among the 108 Divya Desams, the holy abodes of Lord Vishnu.

The Temple

The temple occupies an area of 156 acres (6,31,000 m²) with a perimeter of 1,116m (10,710 feet) making it the largest temple in India and one of the largest religious complexes in the world. In fact, Srirangam temple can be easily termed as the largest functioning Hindu temple in the world (Angkor Wat being the largest non-functioning temple). The temple is enclosed by 7 concentric walls with a total length of 32,592 feet or over six miles. These walls are enclosed by 21 Gopurams (Towers). Among the marvels of the temple is a "hall of 1000 pillars" (actually 953).

Though the term Kovil is generically used in Tamil to signify any temple, for many Vaishnavas the term Kovil exclusively refers to this temple, indicating its extreme importance for them. The presiding deity Lord Ranganathar is praised in many names by His devotees, including "Nam-Perumal" (our Lord in Tamil), "Azhagiya Manavalan" (The beautiful groom in Tamil), while His divine wife Ranganayaki is affectionately called "Thayar" (Holy Mother). Apart from the main shrine of Ranganathar, the complex also houses shrines of dozens of forms of Lord Vishnu including Sudarshana Chakra, Narasimha, Rama, separate shrines for Ranganayaki and dozens of other shrines for the major saints in the Vaishnava tradition, including Ramanuja. The temple follows the traditional

Thenkalai sect of Iyengars, who are mainly identified by a "Y" shaped mark in the forehead.

Legend

Sriranga Mahathmiyam is the compilation of the mythological and religious account of the temple, detailing the origins of its greatness. According to it, Lord Brahma, the Lord of Creation in Hindu Mythology was once in a state of deep meditation and in His supreme trance received the gift of the Lord Vishnu's idol, "Ranga Vimana". He was told by the Supreme Lord that there would seven other appearances of such idols on earth-Srirangam, Srimushnam, Venkatadri(Tirumala), Saligram(Muktinath), Naimisaranya, Totadri, Pushkara and Badrinath.

The idol was then passed on by Brahma to Viraja, Vaiswatha, Manu, Ishwaku and finally to Rama. Lord Rama, himself an avatar of Vishnu, worshipped the idol for a long time, and when he returned victoriously from Sri Lanka after destroying Ravana, he gave it to King Vibhishana as a token of appreciation for the latter's support for Rama against his own brother, Ravana. When Vibhishana was going via Trichy en route to Sri Lanka, the Lord wanted to stay in Srirangam. Vibhishana, while on the way back to his Kingdom, passed through Trichy, and wanted to take a bath in the river Kaveri.

In order to do this without placing the idol on the ground, Vibishana found Lord Vinayaka, disguised as a cowherd boy. As per the plan, when Vibhishana was fully into water, Vinayaka kept the idol firmly on the sand in the banks of the Kaveri. On seeing this, the angry Vibhishana chased the boy to punish him, but the boy kept running and climbed over the rock near the Kaveri bank. Vibhishana finally caught the boy and hit him on the fore-head, upon which the boy revealed himself to be Lord Vinayaka. Vibhishana immediately apologized and the Lord gave him his blessings after which Vibhishana continued on his way to Lanka.

The place on which the Ranganathan idol was kept was later covered in deep forests, due to disuse and after a very long time, it is discovered when a Chola king chasing a parrot found the idol accidentally. He then established the Ranganathaswamy temple as one of the largest temple complexes in the world.

According to History, most dynasties that ruled the South-Cholas, Pandiyas, Hoysalas, Nayakkas-assisted renovation and assisted in the observance of the traditional customs. Even during the periods of internal conflicts amongst these dynasties, utter importance was thrown on the safety and maintenance of these temples.

The temple is mentioned in Tamil works of literature of the Sangam Era, including Silapadikaram. However, archaeological inscriptions are available only from the 10th century AD..

Invasion of Srirangam Temple: During the period of invasion by Malik Kafur and his forces in 1310-1311, Namperumal was stolen and taken to Delhi. In a daring exploit, devotees of Srirangam ventured to Delhi and enthralled the king with their histrionics. Moved by their talent, the King was pleased to gift them the presiding deity of Srirangam, which was requested by the performers.

Things took a drastic turn immediately. Surathani, his daughter fell in love with the deity and followed him to Srirangam. She prostrated to the God in front of the Sanctum Sanctorum and is believed to have attained the Heavenly Abode immediately. Even today, a painting of "Surathani" (known as "Thulukha Nachiyar" in Tamil) can be seen in the Arjuna Mandap adjacent to the Sanctum Sanctorum for whom, "chappathis" are made daily. This greatly explains the Secular nature of the temple and also its all inclusive nature.

Having assumed that the magical power of the deity had killed his daughter, there was a second invasion to Srirangam in 1323 A.D. This time it was more severe that the presiding deity, was taken away, before the Islamic invaders reached Srirangam, by the group led by the Vaishnavite Acharaya, Pillai Lokacharyar, who died en-route to Thirunelveli in Tamil Nadu. The Goddess "Renganayaki" was taken in another separate procession. Swami Vedanta Desika, instrumental in planning the operations during the siege of the temple, closed the Sanctum Sanctorum of the temple with bricks, after the processions of the presiding deities had left-thereby protected the temple for generations to come.

13000 Sri Vaishnavas-people of Srirangam-laid down their lives in the fierce battle ensuring that the instution was protected. In the end, "Devadasis", the danseuse of Srirangam, seduced the Army Chief, to save the temple.

Almost after six decades, the presiding deity returned to Srirangam and the same Swami Vedanta Desika, who built a brick wall in front of the sanctum sanctorum broke it open. We learn that the deity of Srirangam lived in the hills of Tirumala Tirupati for quite a long period of time.

It is not surprising therefore, to note that, the temple and the life of the people even today are intertwined. The Lord is their Ruler and also their Child. It is believed that Sriman Narayana presently lives in Srirangam and not in His abode, Vaikuntham.

Significance of the Temple: Religious documentation informs that this temple is the only one of its kind for Lord Vishnu that was sung in praise by all the Alwars (Divine saints of Tamil Bhakthi movement), having a total of 247 "pasurams" (hymns) in its name. Acharyas of all schools of thought-Advaita, Vishistadvaita and Dvaita, recognize the immense significance this temple, regardless of their affiliation.

The temple amazes us with its astounding architecture and sculptural beauty. The "hall of 1000 pillars" (actually 953) is a fine example of planned theatre-like structure and opposite to it, "Sesha Mandap" with its intricacy in sculpture is a delight. The Rajagopuram (the main gopuram that is one of the tallest religious structures in the world) did not reach its current height of 73 m. until 1987, when the 44th Jeer of Ahobila Mutt initiated the process with the help of philanthropists and others.

Sri Vadivazhagiya Nambi Perumal Temple (Thiru Anbil)

This is a Hindu temple located at a distance of about 8km from Lalgudi near Trichy; on the banks of the river Kollidam.

It is one of the Pancharanga Kshetrams along the course of the Kaveri are Srirangapatnam (Karnataka), Srirangam, Koyiladi (Anbil) and Kumbhakonam and Indalur (Mayiladuturai). Anbil is also known by the names Tirumaalayanturai, Mandookapuri, Bhrahmapuri.

This temple is referred to by a paasuram of Tirumazhisai Alwar where he addresses seven shrines featuring Vishnu in a reclining position-Tirukkudandai, Tiruvegkaa, Tiruvallur, Tiruvarangam, Tiruppernagar, Anbil and Tirupparkadal and hence is a Divya Desam.

Srivilliputhur Andal Koil

Srivilliputtur Divya Desam is a popular Hindu temple and one of the 108 Divya Desams, the most important abodes of Lord Vishnu and is the birthplace of two of the most important Alvars (saints) in the Vaishnavite tradition, Periyazhvar and Andal. The temple is located in the town of Srivilliputtur, about 74 km from Madurai, India. It is significant that the temple tower is used in the Tamilnadu government's official seal.

Swamimalai Murugan Temple

Swamimalai Murugan Temple is a Hindu temple located in the township of Swamimalai, 250 km from Chennai and is very close to Thanjavur and Kumbakonam in India.

It is one of the *Arupadaiveedu*, believed to be the six main abodes of Muruga. According to Hindu belief, Swamimalai is where Muruga preached to his own father, Shiva, at a tender age.

Thiruchendur Murugan Temple

Thiruchendur Murugan temple is a Hindu temple dedicated to Lord Muruga and one of the *Arupadaiveedu* (six major abodes) of Lord Muruga. It is located in the small town of Thiruchendur in the district of Tuticorin, Tamil Nadu, India and is 55 km south-east of Tirunelveli,40 km from Tuticorin and 75 km north-east of Kanyakumari. It is easily accessible either by bus or car.

Each Arupadaiveedu has an event mentioned in the 'puranas'. Thiruchendur is said to be second in importance among his six abodes. This place is also referred to by other names in religious poems and literature as Thirucheeralaivai, Thiruchenthil, Thiruchenthiyoor, etc. The deity is worshipped by various names such as Senthilandavan, Senthilkumaran and so on. The Arupadiveedus are Palani (120 km west of Madurai), Swamimalai (150 km east of Madurai), Thiruthani (50 km from Chennai), Pazhamudircholai (10 km north of Madurai) and Thiruparamkunram (10 km south of Madurai).

The temple is situated so close to the sea that waves from the Gulf of Mannar lap at the eastern perimeter wall of the temple.

Thirukadalmallai

The Sthalasayana Perumal Temple is at Mahabalipuram. The Temple resides as the first and foremost of Mahabalipuram sculputres. It is one of the 108 Divya desam.

Thirukkadaiyur

Thirukkadaiyur is a temple town on the east coast of Tamil Nadu, about 300 kilometres south of Chennai. The original temple, *Thirukkadaiyur Mayanam* now called *Thirumeignanam* built in circa 11th century A.D. was ravaged by sea and is in ruins now. Another temple on identical plan was built later and is now thronged by people who pray for long life.

This is one of the holy places of Saivism today. Legend has that *Mrikandu*, a sage and devotee of Lord Shiva, prayed to God to bless him with a son. God appeared and gave him a choice to select the type of child he wanted-A honest responsible and virtuous son who will live only for 16 years or a son who would live for 100 years but whose behaviour is bad. *Mrikandu* chose the former.

The boy, named *Markandeya* also grew up to be an ardent devotee of Shiva. The destined time came. When *Yama* tried to snatch the life of the boy, *Markandeya* went to the temple and clutched at the Shiva Lingam in a bid to escape death.

Pleased by the boy's belief, Shiva rescued him from death. It is possible that this legend was created as there was a conflict between the worship of *Yama* and the newly emerging brahminised form of the Lord and the latter sect won. Interestingly, the temple has an appellation as *Mayanam* which in Tamil means crematorium.

Thirukkadigai

There are three separate shrines dedicated to Lord Narsimha on top of the hill, Lord Bhaktavatsala Perumal on the base of the hill and Lord Anjaneya on a separate hill. It is one of the Divya desam.

Thirupparamkunram Murugan Temple

One of the *Aru Padaiveedu*, the six main abodes of Lord Muruga, Tiruparankunram offers a mystic beauty. It is carved in rock and is monstrous in size for such an architecture. It is where the lord marries Deivanai, the divine daughter of the king of heaven, Indra.

The temple is located 5 miles from Madurai in India. In the main shrine, apart from Muruga, deities of Lord Shiva, Lord Vishnu, Lord Vinayaka and Goddess Durga are housed. The other 'Arupadaiveedu's dedicated for Lord Muruga are Palani (120 km west of Madurai), Swamimalai (150 km east of Madurai), Thiruthani (50 km from Chennai), Pazhamudircholai (10 km north of Madurai) and Thiruchendur (100 km south of Madurai).

One of the curious thing about this temple is that, the Gods Shiva and Vishnu face each other in the main shrine, and this is a rare thing in ancient Hindu temples. This is because Hinduism always held two distinct worshipping groups- Shaivites (worshippers of Lord Shiva) and Vaishnavites (worshippers of Lord Vishnu).

Outside the temple there is a beautiful pond where, according to Temple tradition, the fishes are served with salt and rice flakes by the devotees. There is also a Vedic school adjacent to the banks of the temple pond.

Thiruppathisaram

Thiruppathisaram also known as Thiruvanparisaram is to the north-east of Nagercoil. The place derives its name from a 5000 years old temple dedicated to Thiruvazhimarban Lord Vishnu.

Thiruthani Murugan Temple

Tiruthani Murugan temple is one of the famous Hindu temples dedicated to Lord Muruga. It is one of the Arupadaiveedu, the six holy abodes of Lord Muruga, the others being Palani (100 km west of Madurai), Swamimalai (150 km east of Madurai), Tirupparangunram (5 km from Madurai), Pazhamudircholai (10 km north of Madurai) and Thiruchendur (100 km south of Madurai). It is located in the township of Tiruttani 50 km north of Chennai enroute to Thirupathi. According to Hindu mythology, Lord Murugan married Valli, the daughter of a hunter, here.

Thiruvanaikaval

Thiruvanaikal is a famous Shiva temple near Tiruchirapalli, India and adjacent to the Ranganathaswamy temple at Srirangam. It was built by Kocengannan, also called Kochenga Chola, who was one of the Early_Cholas, around 1800 years ago. It is one of the five major Shiva temples (Panchabhoota Sthalams), representing five major elements-Fire, Earth, Water, Sky and Wind. The main deity, Jambukeswara representing the element Water, sits under a Jambu tree over a small stream that engulfs the deity during the rainy season. The other Panchabhoota Sthalams are located at Chidambaram (space), Kalahasti (wind), Tiruvannamalai (fire) and Kanchipuram (earth).

The goddess Akilandeswari is one of the most famed forms of Parvati along with Meenakshi and Kamakshi. The massive outer wall-Vibudi Prakara, stretching over a mile, is said to have been built by Lord Shiva Himself, working with the laborers, in Tamil mythology. The temple is known as one of the hosts for the annual Natyanjali festival of the classical Indian dance.

Thiruvidandai

"Thiruvidandai" is one of 108 Divya desam. It is near Chennai around 40 kms. It is Varaha Kshetram. It is famous for marriages.

Tiruththanka

The Temple which is also called Tooppul in Kanchipuram. The Lord here is called 'Deepaprakasar' or 'Vilakoli Perumal' (One who had given light). Thayaar is worshipped as Maragathavalli Thayaar.

Tiruvekkaa

The temple is near Varadharaja Perumal Temple in Vishnu Kanchi. It is one of the 108 Divya desam. The Lord here is called 'Yathothkari' or 'Sonna Vannnam Seidha Perumal' (the Lord who had acted on what he had said).

Tiruvelukkai

The Tiruvelukkai Divya Desam is one among the 108 Divya desam which is located in the temple town of Kanchipuram. It is said to be the lord favourite place.

Uppiliappan Temple

The Uppiliappan Temple which is also called ThiruVinnagar is near Thirunaageshwaram, Kumbakonam, Tamil Nadu. The deity here is Lord Uppiliappan Perumal with his consort Bhumi Devi and her father Sage Markandeya.

Uttamar Kovil

Uttamar Kovil (also known as Thirukkarambanoor) is a temple town near Tiruchirapalli in Tamil Nadu, India. It is known for the Sri Purushothaman Perumal Temple or otherwise known as Uttamar Kovil (Uttamar means The good one and Kovil means Temple). It has the shrines of Brahma, Vishnu and Shiva in the same complex, making this a unique temple with shrines for all three gods and their consorts in the same place. There are very few temples where Brahma, the first of the trinity, is worshipped in statue form, which makes this temple an important place of worship.

Vaitheeswaran Temple

Vaitheeswaran Koil is 24 km (15 miles) from Chidambaram, Tamil Nadu, India. The place is famous for the Shiva temple dedicated to Lord Vaidyanatheeswarar, the healer of all diseases and his consort Thaiyalnayaki. It is believed that a bath in the holy waters of the Siddhamirtham tank within the temple complex will cure all diseases.

Varadharaja Perumal Temple

Varadharaja Perumal Temple or Hastagiri or Attiyuran is a famous Hindu temple dedicated to Lord Vishnu located in the holy city of Kanchipuram, Tamilnadu, India.

The Temple

It is an ancient temple built by the Cholas in 1053 and one of the 108 divyadesams the holy abodes of Vishnu. It is located in part of Kanchipuram called the Vishnu Kanchi that is a home for a lot of famous Vishnu temples, including this temple and one of the greatest Hindu scholars, Ramnujacharya is believed to have resided in this temple .

The temple is a huge one on a 23 acre complex and is famous for its holiness and ancient history. Another significant thing about the temple are beautiful carved lizards and platted with gold, over the sanctum. The temple is originally built in 1053 and it was expanded during the reings of the great Chola kings Kulottunga Chola I and Vikrama Chola. In 14th century another wall and a gopura was built by the later Chola kings. It has got a huge Prakaram.

The tower is also huge and beautifully carved. It is one of the 108 Divya desam. Lord Varadharaja Swamy resides in the upper prakaram. Beneath the sannidhi there is a shrine for Lord Narasimha. There is a separate Shrine for Perundevi Thayaar. Sudarshana, Azhwar's Shrine is near the temple tank and it is in the outer prakaram. The architecture was from

Chola and Vijayanagar kingdom. The stone chains in hundred pillared mandapam depicts the complicated architecture.

Legend

The Legend is that Lord Brahma worshipped Lord Varadharaja Swamy in Krita Yuga, Gajendra in Treta Yuga, Brihaspati in Dvapara Yuga and Ananta Shesha in Kali Yuga. It is believed that Airavata, the elephant of Indra in the form of a hill bears the image of Lord Varadharaja Swamy.

The wonders and the greatness of this temple and the Lord Sri Varadaraja, who is also in other forms in the nearby temples in the Kanchipuram and the holy water are very much elaborated in the sacred text called "Sri Hastigiri Mahatmayam".

Varaha Cave Temple

Varaha Cave Temple, an example of Indian rock-cut architecture dating from the late 7th century, is a rock-cut cave temple located at Mamallapuram, a tiny village south of Chennai in the state of Tamil Nadu, India.

The village was a busy port during the 7th and 8th century reign of the Pallava dynasty. The site is famous for the rock-cut caves and the sculptured rock that line a granite hill, including one depicting Arjuna's Penance. It has been classified as a UNESCO World Heritage Site.

Varasiddhi Vinayaka Temple

The Varasiddhi Vinayakar Temple in Besant Nagar, Chennai, India is a famous Hindu temple, located near the beach in Besant Nagar. It is dedicated to the Hindu elephant god Vinayaka or Ganesha. The temple participates in activities such as feeding the poor and holds poojas frequently.

Vayalur Murugan Temple

The Vayalur Murugan Temple is a Hindu temple dedicated to Lord Muruga, located near the city of Tiruchirapalli (Trichy) in Tamil Nadu, India.

Vedapureeswarar Temple

Vedapureeswarar temple is a sacred place on the northern banks of the Cheyyar River in the Tiruvannamalai District near Kanchipuram in the state of Tamil Nadu in South India. The temple is devoted to Lord Vedapuresswarar who came here and imparted his spiritual knowledge regarding the Vedas. This sacred place is now known as Cheyyar but was previously called Thiruvathipuram. It is a temple which has a few unique distinctions.The Nandi, which usually faces the Shiva lingam, is facing the opposite direction.Also,one can worship all the Pancha Bootha (lingams) in this temple.

It is in this sacred place that Saint Thirugnanasambanthar used his holy miraculous powers and transformed a male palm tree into a female palm tree, according to legend. Arunagirinathar, a devotee of Lord Muruga worshipped the God in this temple.

Yoga Narasimha Temple

Its original name was Gadikachalam or Chozhasimhapuram.

Image:Sholingaur.jpg It is believed that Moksha is certain for those who stays for just 1 kadigai (24 minutes) at this place. Saptarishis desirous of having darshan of Nrisimha performed Tapas here and were rewarded within one kadigai. Hence this Kshetra is called Kadikachalam and Tirukadigai. Vishwamitra obtained the title of Brahmarishi when he worshipped Lord Nrisimha here for a kadigai. On the hillock nearby is the Sannidhi of Karudaruda Varadaraja. This is an important prathana sthala. People come here for warding off evil spirits.

The Moolavar on top of the hill (500 ft) is Yoga Narasimhar (Akkaarakani) seen in seated posture facing east.

Thaayaar-Amruthavalli.

Theertham-Amrutha Theertham, Thakkan Kulam.

It is also believed that Vishwamitra maharishi worshipped the Lord here for 1 kadigai & attained the Brahmarishi status. There is a sannadhi for Varadaraja Perumal with Garudan on the banks of the tank on the way to the top. There is a popular belief that worhsip at this sthalam will rid devotees of diseases and mental disroders.

The utsavar at the foot of the hill is Bakthavatsala Perumal (Thakkan). There is a sannadhi for Adikesava Perumal behind the utsavar. There are also sanndahis for Andal, Erumbiyappa, Thottachariyar.

The Anjaneyar on the smaller hill is Yoga Anjaneyar with Changu & Chakram (four arms).

12

Hindu Temples in Uttar Pradesh

Belon Temple

Belon Temple is situated in Belon village near the town of Narora in Bulandshehar, Uttar Pradesh, India and around 60 kilometres from the industrial city of Aligarh. The temple of Belon, relatively small for the kind of fame it has in northern India, is devoted to Sarva Mangala Devi, the goddess of all wellbeing. A visit to the temple is believed to bring happiness in all aspects of one's life. Pilgrims come from many parts of Uttar Pradesh, the heart of northern India, to catch a glimpse of mother goddess, to recite prayers and to leave offerings.

Narora, a fairly small town, has gained recognition because of a nuclear power plant nearby. The District of Bulandshahr is located in the Meerut region of Utter Pradesh, between the Ganga and Yamuna rivers. This lies between 28.4 south and 28.0 north latitude and between 77.0 and 78.0 longitude.

Next to Belon village lies Rajghat, which translates to "Royal bank". Rajghat is situated on the bank of Ganga, and the area includes several temples, most notably one devoted to Lord Hanuman which has a 40-foot statue of a monkey god. Rajghat is another sacred place for followers of the Hindu religion because of its historic significance in occupying the banks of the holy Ganges.

Gorakhnath Math

The Gorakhnath Math (Gorakhnath Mutt) is a Hindu monastic group in the Nath tradition founded by

Matsyendranath. The name Gorakhnath derives from the medieval saint, Gorakshanath (ca. 11th c.), a famous yogi who travelled widely across India and authored a number of texts that form part of the canon of the Nath sampradaya (community).

Junglee Nath

Jangli Nath is a Hindu temple situated in a village named Aswa Mohmadpur of *Matera Town* situated in Nanpara Tehsil. According to local legend, Shiva Linga is made of wood and it is believed that it came out itself from the ground.

There is a festival on each Monday of the Shrwan month of the Hindu calendar, attended by thousands of devotees.

Kashi Vishwanath Temple

Kashi Vishwanath temple is one of the most famous Hindu temples dedicated to Lord Shiva and is in the holy city of Varanasi, India. The temple stands on the western bank of Hinduism's holiest river Ganges, and the deity is one of the twelve Jyotirlingas the holiest of Shiva deities. The main deity is known by the name *Vishwanatha* or *Vishweshwara* meaning the *Ruler of the world*. The temple town that claims to be the oldest living city in the world, with 3500 years of documented history is also called Kashi and hence the temple is popularly called as Kashi Vishwanath Temple. Due to this 15.5m high golden spire, the temple is sometimes called as the Golden Temple, similar to the Sikh Gurudwara at Amritsar.

The temple has been in Hindu mythology for a very long time and a central part of worship in the Shaiva philosophy. The original temple has not yet been found and due to invasions, the temple has been destroyed and rebuit a number of times. The current structure is believed to have been built by Maharani Ahilya Bai Holkar of Indore in 1780. Since 1983, the temple is being managed by Govt. of Uttar Pradesh.

History

The Shiva temple is believed to have been there in the site for thousands of years, as mentioned in old scriptures. The

Mughal emperor Akbar allowed the temple to be constructed but his grandson, the Islamic ruler Aurangzeb ordered its demolition in 1669 and constructed Gaynvapi Mosque, which still exists alongside the temple . This mosque has minarets towering 71 metres above the Ganges River and the traces of the old temple can be seen behind the mosque. The temple spire and the dome are plated with 1000 kg of gold donated by Maharaja Ranjit Singh of Punjab, in 1835.

The Temple Structure

The well in the templeThe temple complex consists of a series of smaller shrines, located in a small lane called the Vishwanatha Galli, near the river. The linga the main deity at the shrine is 60 cm tall and 90 cm in circumference housed in a silver altar . There are small temples for Mahakala, Dhandapani, Avimukteshwara, Vishnu, Vinayaka, Sanishwara, Virupaksha and Virupaksh Gauri in the complex. There is a small well in the temple called the Jnana Vapi (the wisdom well) and it is believed that the Jytorlinga was hidden in the well to protect it at the time of invasion.

Importance of the Temple

The temple is widely recognized as one of the most important places of worship in Hindu religion and most of the leading Hindu saints, including Adi Sankaracharya, Ramakrishna Paramhansa, Swami Vivekananda, Goswami Tulsidas, Swami Dayananda Saraswati, Gurunanak have vitied this site . According to Hindu mythology, a visit to the temple and a bath in the river Ganga is believed to lead one on a path to Moksha (liberation). Thus, people from all over the nation, try to visit the place at least once in their lifetime.

There is also a tradition that one should give up at least one desire after a pilgrimage the temple, and the pilgrimage would also include a visit to the temple at Rameswaram in South India, where people take the water samples of Ganga to perform prayer at the temple and bring back the sand from near that temple. Due to the immense popularity and holiness of this temple, hundreds of temples across the nation have been built with the same style and architecture.

Kesava Deo Temple

Kesava Deo Temple is among the most sacred of Hindu sites. It was built in Mathura over the prison which was believed to be the birth place of Lord Krishna. Mughal empreror Aurangzeb ordered the demolition of the temple and constructed Katra Masjid in 1661. Traces of the ancient Hindu temple can be seen from the back, where the modern temple Shri Krishnajanmabhoomi complex stands.

The name Kesava Deo Temple has been taken up by many other temples in and around Mathura. There is one temple just besides the main Krishna Janma Bhoomi complex which is gaining popularity among local people ever since the heavy security cover took over the main Krishna Janma Bhoomi complex.

Around the main Krishnajanmabhoomi complex there is another temple having same Hindi name as the Kesava Deo Temple. A separate page has been started for that temple at Keshav_Dev_Temple.

This temple has gained popularity after the Krishna Janma Bhoomi complex has been put under great security cover after incidents in Ayodhya 1990 and 1992.

Krishnajanmabhoomi

Krishnajanmabhoomi, which means 'the birth-place of Krishna', is a temple built on the birthplace of Krishna (an avatar of God in his original form in Mathura, India. It is believed that Lord Krishna was born here in a cell of a prison, which once stood there. Krishna was son of Vasudeva and Devaki. Devaki was cousin(sister) of the local King Kansa. Kansa was told that the eighth son of Vasudeva and Devaki will kill him. Fearing this he imprisoned his sister and brother-in-law and eventually killed first seven children of the couple.

Krishna was the eighth child of the couple, and he was transported to Gokul by Vasudeva. The child Krishna was brought up by the local village-head of Gokul, Nanda (that is how he got his other name, Nandlaal). Eventually Krishna lead a rebellion against the kingdom of Kansa and killed him.

The current temple complex is at the site of the prison (partly occupied by the mosque built by Aurangzeb).

However, the temple complex is not entirely undisputed birth place temple complex for Krishna. There is at least one more temple close by which claims to be the real birth place of Krishna. The local populace is quite divided about the reality.

In relatively modern time, a temple called Keshava Deo Temple was built on the spot where Krishna was born. The temple was built by Rao Veer Singh Bundela, who was a prominent Hindu nobleman at the Mughal court of Jehangir (1605-27). In late 17th century, during the reign of Aurangzeb (1618-1707), a mosque, was constructed after destroying parts of the existing Krishna temple structure. With the decline of the Mughal Empire, and by the early 19th century, the East India Company had emerged as the de facto ruler of large parts of undivided India, and exercised jurisdiction over the region.

Before India's independence, Madan Mohan Malaviya, endeavored during 1940s to build a temple over the spot where Krishna was believed to have been born. In 1953, an organization named the *Krishna Janmabhoomi Sansthan* was formed, and with the monetary assistance received from different sources, construction of a temple was commenced. The temple was opened to public in 1984.

Starting with communal tensions starting with events in Ayodhya in 1990 and 1992, the temple complex has been put under high security. The high security has taken its toll on the temple's popularity with the local worshippers.

As a result, quite a few other temples in and around the main complex have gained popularity and public support. The old Keshav Dev Temple just behind the main complex's back door.

Ram Janmabhoomi

Ram Janmabhoomi refers to a tract of land in the North Indian city of Ayodhya which is believed to be the birthplace of the Rama. The name *Ram Janmabhoomi* means "birthplace of Rama." On the morning of December 6 1992, the building which was known as "Babri Masjid" (The Mosque of Babur) by Muslims and "Ram Mandir" by Hindus on this spot was demolished by activists. A movement was launched in 1984 by the Vishwa Hindu Parishad(VHP) eventually leading to the destruction of the building which stood here. The VHP wants to erect a temple dedicated to Ram Lala (infant Ram) at this spot. Many Muslim organizations on the other hand strongly oppose the building of the temple.

According to the Hindu view, the ancient temple could have been destroyed on the orders of Mughal emperor Babur. This view is challenged by many Muslims, 'Marxist' and 'Nehruvian' Indian historians since the early 1990s. However, several contemporary archaeologists such as Prof. B.B. Lal and Western historians, such as Koenraad Elst have provided what they claim is historical evidence that lends a greater legitimacy to the Hindu claims of the Ram Janmabhoomi.

History

19th century: Hindus claim that they never lost the tradition to worship Ram on the Ramkot hill, and always returned to the site to venerate his birthplace. They were worshipping on a platform called "Ram Chabutara" during the British Rule. According to British sources, Hindus and Muslims used to worship together in the Disputed Structure in the 19th century until about 1855. P. Carnegy wrote in 1870:

"It is said that up to that time, the Hindus and Mohamedans alike used to worship in the mosquetemple. Since the British rule a railing has been put up to prevent dispute, within which, in the mosque the Mohamedans pray, while outside the fence the Hindus have raised a platform on which they make their offerings."

This platform was outside the disputed structure but within its precincts. Hindu protagonists say that they have been demanding the return of the site for centuries, and cite accounts from several western travellers to India during the Mughal rule in India (see also the sections on history and literary sources).

Sankat Mochan Hanuman Temple (Varanasi)

Sankat Mochan Hanuman Temple is one of the sacred temples of Hindu god Hanuman in the city of Varanasi, Uttar Pradesh, India. The word *Sankat Mochan* means deliverer from troubles.

In the mundir, special offerings are sold like the special "besan ke ladoo" (sweets). Also hanuman ji is offered with marigold flower garland. Outside the mundir, there are many vendors who sell pendents, rings, holy flowers for the devotees. The temple is unique in a way that both Rama and Hanumana statues facing towards each other.

On 7 March 2006, one of the three explosions hit the temple, while the aarti was in progress in which numerous worshippers and wedding attendees participated. The fearless croud helped each other in rescue operation after the explosion. These explosions did not shatter the faith of devotees as very next day a big number of devotees resumed their worship as usual. The mandir still continues to be attended by thousands of Rama and Hanuman devotees who chant Chalisa and Sundarkad (also provided in form of booklet in temple for free).

Sankat Mochan Temple was founded by Tulsidas who was the author of the *Tulsi Ramayan*, which is the Hindi version of the Hindu epic Ramayan originally written by Valmiki. Tradition promises that regular visitors to the temple will gain special favour of Hanuman. Every Tuesday and Saturday thousands of people queue up in front of temple to offer prayers to Lord Hanuman. According to Vedic Astrology, Hanuman saves human beings from the anger of the planet Saturn, and people having an ill-placed Saturn in their horoscopes especially visit this temple for astrological remedies.

This is supposed to be the most effective way for appeasement of Shani. While it is suggested that Hanuman did not hesistate in engulfing in his mouth the sun, the lord of all planets, humbling all the gods and angel, making them to worship for sun's release. Some astrologers believe that worshipping hanuman can neutralize the ill-effect of mangala (mars) ad practically any planet that ha ill effect on human life.

Someshwar Mahadev Temple

Someshwar Mahadev Temple is an ancient temple situated in the Arail area across Sangam opposite Allahabad Fort. The temple is dedicated to Lord Shankar.

Vishalakshi

The Vishalakshi Temple of Divine Mother Sati, wife of Lord Shiva stands at Meer Ghat just behind Vishwanath Temple in Varanasi, India. Devout Hindus consider this as one of the 51 Shakti Peethas mentioned in the Puranas.

13

Hindu Temples in Uttarakhand

Badrinath Temple

The Badrinath temple is the main attraction in the town. According to legend Shankara discovered a black stone image of Lord Badrinarayan made of Saligram stone in the Alaknanda River. He originally enshrined it in a cave near the Tapt Kund hot springs. In the sixteenth century, the King of Garhwal moved the murti to the present temple.

The temple has undergone several major renovations because of age and damage by avalanche. In the 17th century, the temple was expanded by the kings of Garhwal. After significant damage in the great 1803 Himalayan earthquake, it was rebuilt by the King of Jaipur.

The temple is approximately 50 ft (15 metres) tall with a small cupola on top, covered with a gold gilt roof. The facade is built of stone, with arched windows. A broad stairway leads up to a tall arched gateway, which is the main entrance. The architecture resembles a Buddhist vihara (temple), with the brightly painted facade also more typical of Buddhist temples. Just inside is the mandapa, a large pillared hall that leads to the garbha grha, or main shrine area. The walls and pillars of the mandapa are covered with intricate carvings.

History and Legend

The Badrinath area is referred to as Badari or Badarikasram in Hindu scriptures. It is a place sacred to Vishnu, particularly in Vishnu's dual form of Nara-Narayana. Thus, in the

Mahabharata, Shiva, addressing Arjuna, says, "Thou wast Nara in a former body, and, with Narayana for thy companion, didst perform dreadful austerity at Badari for many myriads of years."

One legend has it that when the goddess Ganga was requested to descend to earth to help suffering humanity, the earth was unable to withstand the force of her descent. Therefore the mighty Ganga was split into twelve holy channels, with Alaknanda one of them. It later became the abode of Lord Vishnu or Badrinath.

The mountains around Badrinath are mentioned in the Mahabharata, when the Pandavas are said to have ended their life by ascending the slopes of a peak in western Garhwal called Swargarohini-literally, the 'Ascent to Heaven'. Local legend has it that the Pandavas passed through Badrinath and the town of Mana, 4 km north of Badrinath, on their way to Swargarohini. There is also a cave in Mana where Vyas, according to legend, wrote the Mahabharata.

According to the Skanda Purana: "There are several sacred shrines in heaven, on earth, and in hell; but there is no shrine like Badrinath."

The area around Badrinath was celebrated in Padma Purana as abounding in spiritual treasures.

Badrinath has also been eulogised as Bhu Vaikunta or earthly abode of Lord Vishnu. Many religious scholars such as Ramanujacharya, Madhawacharya and Vedanta Desika visited Badrinath and wrote sacred texts, such as commentaries on Brahmasutras and other Upanishads.

Baleshwar Temple

Amidst the main city of Champawat is the historical *Baleshwar Temple*. Built by the rulers of Chand dynasty, Baleshwar Temple is a marvelous symbol of stone carving. There isn't any historical manuscript that dates the Baleshwar temple, however it is believed to be built between 10–12 century A.D.

The main Baleshwar temple is dedicated to Lord Shiva (who is also know as Baleshwar). There are two other temples in the compound of Baleshwar, one dedicated to Ratneshwar and other to Champawati Durga. The temple is built on South Indian Architecture with magnificent Stone Carving works. Close to the Baleshwar Temple is a "Naula" (freshwater resource) which has now dried up. On the day of Mahashivratri, a very crowded fair is held in the Baleshwar Temple compound.

The exteriors of Ratneshwar and Champawati Durga temples are carved with the different posters of the local deities. The stone carving work is magnificent.

Baleshwar temples at Champawat has been declared as an Indian National Heritage Monument and is looked after by Archaeological Survey of India (ASI) since 1952.

Gangotri

Gangotri is a town and a nagar panchayat in Uttarkashi district in the state of Uttarakhand, India. It is a Hindu pilgrim town on the banks of the river Bhagirathi. It is on the Greater Himalayan Range, at a height of 3,042 m.

Golu Devata

Golu Devata or Lord Golu Hindi-is the legendary mythological and historical God of the Kumaun region of Uttarakhand state of India and is their the much loved deity. He is thought to be as an incarnation of Gaur Bhairav (Shiva). Golu Devata is popularly prayed and worshipped all over the region and regarded as the dispenser of justice by the devotees with extreme faith. Golu Devata is considered as the brave son and General of Katyuri King Jhal Rai and His mother was Kalinka.

The name of His grandfather was Hal Rai and great grandfather was Hal Rai. Historically the origin of Golu Devata is accepted at Champawat. The Chand Kings of this region were His devotees. When Chand rulars annexed Almora, His temple was established at a place called Chitai situated six km from Almora.There are many temples of Golu Devata in

Kumaun. The most popular are of Chitai, Champawat, Ghorakhal. It is the popular belief that Golu Devata dispense quick justice to the devotee. Devotee in turn offers bells and Sacrifice of animals after the fulfilment of wish. Thousands of bells of every size can be seen hanging over the temple premisces. Many devotees file a lot of written petitions daily, which are received by the temple.

Jageshwar

Jageshwar is the Himalayan Hindu sacred religious pilgrim place dedicated to Lord Shiva located at the distance of 36 kms northeast from Almora town of Kumaun region of the Uttarakhand state of India and is a cluster of large and small stone temples.Jageshwar was once the centre of Lakula Shaivism Jageshwar is located at the end of lush green valley of Jataganga with enchanting dense sacred forest of Deodar or Cedar (*Cedrus deodara*) starting from Artola village on Almora–Pithoragarh highway and passses through Daneshwar temple.Two streams Nandini and Surabhi flow down the hills in the valley and meet near the sacred spot.

The altitude of this place is 1870 mts. This place is unique in having some very old specimens of *Cedrus deodara* which gives tranquil and serene atmosphere. Jageshwar is an ancient temple city, having a group of temple with 124 temples some are in the ruin.

Majority of temples are in a good preserved state and looked after by archaeological survey of India. Fairs takes place at Jageshwar during the Hindu *Shravan* month of July and August and during Shivratri festival.

Kedarnath Temple

Kedarnath temple is one of the holiest Hindu temples dedicated to Lord Shiva and is located atop the Garhwal Himalayan range near the river Mandakini in Kedarnath, Uttarakhand in India. Due to extreme weather conditions, the temple is open only between the end of April to start of November.

The temple is not directly accessible by road and has to be reached by a 13 km uphill trek from Gaurikund. The temple is believed to have been built by Adi Sankaracharya and is one of the twelve Jyothirlingas, the holiest Hindu shrines of Lord Shiva. The temple is also one of the four major sites in India's Char Dham pilgrimage.

Surkanda Devi

Surkanda Devi is a Hindu temple situated close to the small resort hamlet of Dhanaulti. It is at an altitude of about 10,000 ft, 2000 ft above Dhanaulti, which itself it at quite a height above sea level.

It is surrounded by dense forests and affords a scenic view of the surrounding region including the Himalayas to the north, and certain cities to the south (*e.g.*, Dehradun, Rishikesh) The Gange Dussera festival is celebrated every year between May and June and attracts a lot of people.

The spot is most easily reached from the southwest via Dehradun, but is a typical day-trip for visitors to Mussoorie and Landour. It is located on a hill and one has to climb a steep 2000 ft on foot after driving to Dhanaulti.

Legend has it that the head of the charred body of Goddess Sati fell here when Lord Shiva was taking her remains along with him after she give her life in the yajna started by her father.

Yamunotri Temple

The Yamunotri temple is located in Uttarkashi District Uttarakhand, India, a full day's journey from Uttaranchal's main towns—Rishikesh, Haridwar or Dehradun.

The actual temple is only accessible by a six kilometre walk from the town of Hanuman Chatti and a four kilometre walk from Janki Chatti (horses or palanquins are available for rent). The hike from Hanuman Chetty to Yamunotri is very picturesque with beautiful views of a number of water falls. The original temple was built by Maharani Gularia of Jaipur in the 19th century. The current temple is of recent origin, as past iterations have been destroyed by the weather and elements. Lodging at the temple itself is limited to a few small ashrams and guesthouses.

Ritual duties such as the making and distribution of prasad (sanctified offerings) and the supervision of pujas (ritual venerations) are performed by the Uniyal family of pujaris (priests). Unique aspects of ritual practice at the site include hot springs where raw rice is cooked and made into prasad.

14

Hindu Temples in West Bengal

Ananta Basudeba Temple

Ananta Basudeba temple is a temple of Lord Krishna in the Hangseshwari temple complex in Banshberia, in the Hooghly District in the Indian state of West Bengal. This temple is noted for the terra cotta works on its walls.

Dakshineswar Kali Temple

The Dakshineswar Kali Temple is a Hindu temple located in Dakshineswar locality, Kolkata. Situated on the eastern bank of the Hooghly River, the presiding deity of the temple is Bhavatarini, an aspect of Kali. Photography within the temple compound is prohibited.

The temple compound, apart from the nine-spired main temple, contains a large courtyard surrounding the temple, with rooms along the boundary walls. There is a bathing ghat on the Hooghly river, a bookshop, a shrine to Rani Rashmoni, a parking lot and twelve shrines dedicated to the aspects of Shiva, Kali's companion, and to Radha-Krishna. The chamber in the northwestern corner just beyond the last of the Shiva temples, is where Swami Ramakrishna Paramahamsa spent a considerable part of his life.

Ekachakra

Ekachakra is a small village, located 20 km away from the town of Rampurhat in the Birbhum District of West Bengal. Within Hindu tradition, the five Pandavas from the epic,

Mahabharata are described as staying in Ekachakra during their years in excile. It is also famous as the birthplace of Nityananda Rama (b 1474 CE), a principle religious figure in the Gaudiya Vaishnava tradition. The village extends north and south for an area of about eight miles. Other villages, namely Viracandra-pura and Virabhadrapura, are situated within the area of the village of Ekacakra. In honour of Virabhadra Goswami (the son of Nityananda), these places are renowned as Viracandra-pura and Virabhadrapura.

Hangseshwari Temple

Hangseshwari temple is a temple of goddess kali in the town of Banshberia in Hooghly District of the Indian state of West Bengal. The temple complex has another temple — Ananta Basudeba temple — besides the main temple. Also near is the Swanbhaba Kali temple built by Nrisinhadeb in 1788. The Hangseshwari temple has a distinctive architecture different from the usual pattern present in this area. The structure of the temples is the representation of "Tantrik Satchakrabhed".

Kalighat

Kalighat is a locality of Kolkata, India. One of the oldest neighbourhoods in South Kolkata, Kalighat is also densely populated and vibrant—with a rich history of cultural intermingling with the various foreign incursions into the area over time.

Kalighat Kalika

A famous temple dedicated to the goddess Kali is situated in Kalighat. This is one of the 51 Shakti Peethas. The right toe of Dakshayani is said to have fallen here. The Shakti here is known as *Kalika*, while the Bhairava is *Nakulesh*. It is a very famous place and a pilgrimage for Shakta (Shiva and Durga/Kali/Shakti worshippers) followers within the Hindu religion.

Kalika Temple

One Raja Basanta Roy, uncle of Pratapaditya and the King

of Jessore, Bangladesh built what is now known as Old Temple. This temple was situated on the banks of river Adi Ganga. The *natmandir*, a hall attached to the *sanctum sanctorum* is in the southern side while Shiva's temple is situated in the north-east. There is also a temple dedicated to Radha Krishna built in 1843 by a zamindar of Baowali. The speciality of Kali of this temple is the long protuded tongue made of gold. This is a different appearance from the other visualisations of Kali.

Kalighat temple has references in 15th century texts. The original temple was a small hut. The present temple was built by Sabarna Roy Choudhury of Barisha in 1809. They offered 595 bighas of land to the Temple deity so that worship and service could be continued smoothly. The name Calcutta was derived from Kalighata. In the early days traders halted at Kalighat to pay patronage to the goddess. The temple was initially on the banks of Hooghly.

The river over a period of time has moved away from the temple. The temple is now on the banks of a small canal called Adi Ganga, connecting to Hooghly. The present dakshina Kali idol of touchstone was created by two saints-Brahmananda Giri and Atmaram Giri. It was Padmabati Devi, the mother of Laksmikanta Roy Choudhury who discovered the fossils of Sati's finger in a lake called Kalikunda. This made Kalighat as one of the 51 Shakti Pithas. The Sabarna Roy Choudhury Family is the original owner of the temple, though at present a committee constituted by the Hon'ble Supreme Court looks after the affairs of the temple.

Ramakrishna Temple

Sri Ramakrishna Temple was consecrated in the Headquarters of the Ramakrishna Math, Belur Math on Friday, the 14th January, the Makar Sankranti Day in 1938. Swami Vivekananda, the illustrious disciple of Ramakrishna Paramahamsa, the 18th century saint of Bengal wanted that the architecture of the Temple should represent a harmony of different artistic cultures as Sri Ramakrishna had the image of harmonious blend of various religions.

15

Temples of Other States

Hindu Temples in Tripura

Chaturdasha Temple

The Chaturdasha Temple is a Hindu temple (*mandir*) situated near Old Agartala, India, and features the Bengal dome patterned after the roofs of village huts in Bengal. The dome is surmounted by a stupa-like structure which reveals traces of Buddhist influence. This temple was built in honour of fourteen Gods and Goddessess, together called the *Chaturdasha Devata*, by King Krishna Manikya Debbarma of Tripura and these deities are ceremoniously worshipped during Kharchi Puja. The Kokborok names of the fourteen deities are Lampra, Akhatra, Bikhatra, Burasa, Thumnairok, Bonirok, Sangroma, Mwtaikotor, Twima, Songram, Noksumwtai, Mailuma, Khuluma and Swkalmwtai.

Tripura Sundari Temple

It is situated in the ancient Udaipur, believed to be one of the holiest Hindu shrines in this part of the country. Popularly known as Matabari, crowns the Dhanisagar hillock and is served by the red-robed priests who traditionally, minister to the mother goddess. Considered to be one of the 51 Shakti Peethas, consists of a square type sanctum of the typical Bengali hut. It was constructed by Maharaja Dhanya Manikya Debbarma in 1501 A.D., there are two identical images of the same deity inside the temple named Chhotima, one is around 2 feet in height and the other about 5 feet in height.

Hindu Temples in Punjab

Julfa Mata Temple-Nangal

The Julfa Mata Temple is a Hindu temple in the town of Nangal in north India.

According to the story, there were demons who were harassing gods over the Himalayan Mountains. Gods decided to destroy them. Lord Vishnu was leading them. The Gods focused their strengths in a huge flame which rose from the earth. Out of the fire a young girl took birth and regarded as Adishakti (means first shakti). She grew up in the house of Prajapati Daksha. She used to be called as Parvati or Sati. Later she became wife of Lord Shiva.

Once, Prajapati Daksha insulted Lord Shiva. Parvati was unable to accept this and she killed herself. When Lord Shiva came to know about her wife's death, there were no boundaries of his extreme anger. He began stalking the three worlds while holding Sati's body. The other Gods approached Lord Vishnu for help as they were afraid of Lord Shiva's rage. Lord Vishnu fired arrows which served Sati's body into fifty one pieces. Where ever the pieces fell, the fifty one sacred Shaktipeeths came into existence. It is believed that at Julfa Mata temple, Sati's hair fell. The word 'julfa' means hair.

Lots of devotees visit the temple. The temple is situated on the hills of Nangal – Hambewal road. The temple is around five kilometres away from the Nangal township. In early days there was no road to the temple. People used to go by foot. Now there is a road and people are able to take their vehicles there.

Near the entrance of the temple, on the right hand side, there is a Shiva temple. There is a Peepal (Bo or Sacred Ficus) tree and devotees tie threads to that. The thread is known as moli. There is a belief that deity fulfils all the wishes of devotees. Inside temple there is idol of Mata. There is a priest who takes care of temple. Devotees usually bring offerings for the Devi. The offerings includes sweets (Suji halwa, laddu, barfi), kheel (sugar-coated puffed rice), narial (coconut) and flowers. In navarats and saavan days, the temple gets decorated with lights, etc.

Hindu Temples in Madhya Pradesh

Beejamandal

Beejamandal is a ruined temple in Khajuraho, that has not yet been fully excaved and explored.

Beejamandal is also the name for a ruined temple in Vidisha. 'Beejamandal' at Khajuraho not very far from the main temple-complex. In fact it is near the Chatur-bhuj temple.

In all there are supposed to be 85 temples in Khajuraho, however only 22 of them have been unearthed. Beejamandal is one of the many which are yet to be discovered. According to the local villagers this structure was under a huge mound of earth which was marked on the apex by a white stone. The villagers regularly lit the holy oil-lamp each night on this mound since time imemorial.

A visitor describes the remains:

Now we saw how the idols of Lord Shiv and goddess Parvati were slowly, carefully being scraped and dug out of the earth. The beautiful pillars, walls, etc. with intricate stone carvings emerged from underground like magic! The stone-carvings depicted human forms in various poses, along with animals and other forms of nature. We could discern some sort of Indonesian or may be some South-East Asian influence on the carvings too!

Devi Jagadambi Temple

Devi Jagadambi temple or Jagadambi temple of a group of about 25 temples at Khajuraho, Madhya Pradesh, India. Khajuraho is a World Heritage site.

The temples of Khajuraho were built by the rulers of the Chandella dynasty between the 10th and the 12th centuries.

Devi Jagadambi temple, in a group to the north, is one of most finely decorated temples at Khajuraho, with numerous erotic carvings. Three bands of carvings encircle the body of the temple. In the sanctum is an enormous image of the goddess Devi.

Kandariya Mahadeva Temple

The Kandariya Mahadeva temple is the largest and most ornate Hindu temple in the medieval temple group found at Khajuraho in Madhya Pradesh, India. It is considered one of the best examples of temples preserved from the medieval period in India. Khajuraho was once the religious capital of the Chandela Rajputs and today is one of the most popular tourist destinations in India.

The Kandariya Mahadeva temple is the largest of the Western group of temples and was built by Vidyadhara, arguably one of the greatest Chandela kings. The temple was built around 1050 on Hindu beliefs dating back to 1000 BC; The main spire or *shikhara* rises 31 m to depict Mount Meru, the holy mountain of Shiva and is surrounded by 84 miniature spires. Inside the sanctum is a marble linga representing Shiva. The Archaeological Survey of India protects the temple, which is part of the UNESCO World Heritage site at Khajuraho.

Omkareshwar

Omkareshwar is a Hindu temple in Madhya Pradesh state in India. It is on an island called Mandhata or Shivapuri in the Narmada river. It is one of the 12 revered Jyotirlinga shrines of Shiva. It is about 12 miles from Mortakka in Madhya Pradesh. The shape of the island is said to be like the Hindu Om symbol. There are two temples here, one to Omkareshwar (whose name means “OM-maker-lord”) and one to Amareshwar (whose name means “immortal lord” or “lord of the immortals”).

Omkareshwar is formed by the sacred river Narmada. This is one of the most sacred of rivers in India and is now home to one of the worlds biggest Dam projects.

Pashupatinath Temple, Mandsaur

Pashupatinath Temple in Mandsaur, India is a famous Hindu temple of Lord Pashupatinath. Situated on the banks of the Shivna River, Pashupatinath Temple is one of the prominent shrines in the city of Mandsaur in Madhya Pradesh. Lord Shiva in the form of Pashupatinath is the principal deity here. The highlight is a unique *Shiv Ling* with eight faces of

Lord Shiva. The shrine has four doors in four directions. The Shiv Ling in the temple is 2.5 x 3.2 metre and weighs 46 quintal 65 kilos and 525 grams.

It is said that the Shiv Ling emerged from the waters of the Shivna on Monday, which is considered as an auspicious day by the devotees of Lord Shiva. On Sunday, it reached the Tapeshwar Ghat of the river and was placed there. On Monday, after exactly, 21 years, 5 months and 4 days it was incarnated. The day of incarnation of the idol is celebrated as a Mela in the area surrounding the temple.

The temple built on the river is 90 feet long, 30 feet wide and 101 feet tall. On top of the temple is a 100 kilo gold plated pitcher. Every monsoon the water level in the Shivna river raises to touch the holy *Shiv Ling* of lord Shiva. This phenomenon is termed as "Jalaabhishek" which means worshipping god through water.

Hindu Temples in Jharkhand

Jagannath Temple, Ranchi

Jagannath Temple in Ranchi was built by Thakur Ani Nath Shahdeo, king of Barkagarh Jagannathpur, on 25th December 1691. About 10 km from Albert Ekka chowk (Firayalal chowk) through HEC colony, the temple is on the top of a small hillock.

Similar to the famous Jagannath Temple in Puri, Orissa, this temple is built in the same architectural style, although smaller. And similar to the Rath Yatra in Puri, an annual fair cum rath yatra is held at this temple too, attracting thousands of tribal and non-tribal devotees not only from Ranchi but also from neighbouring villages and towns.

The temple collapsed on 6th August 1990. The reconstruction was started on 8th February 1992 and is still continuing.

Vaidyanath Temple, Deoghar

Vaidyanath Jyotirlinga Temple is a famous Hindu temple dedicated to Lord Shiva and is one of the twelve Jyotirlingas, the sacred abodes of Shiva. It is located in the city of Deoghar, Jharkhand, India. It is believed that the demon king Ravana worshipped the lord here to get the boons that he later used to wreak havoc in the world.

It is also knows as Baba dham and Baidyanath dham. Held as a very holy place, more than a million pilgrims visit this shrine every year. Legend goes that the daemon king Ravana offered his 10 heads one after the another to lord shiva in a sacrifice. Pleased with this lord shiva decended to earth and cured Ravana who was injured. As he acted as a doctor, he is referred to as Vaidhya (sanskrit word for a doctor).

Legends and History

According to the Shiva Purana, it was in the Treta yuga that the demon Ravana, king of Lanka, felt that his capital would not be perfect and free from enemies unless Mahadeva stays there forever, he paid continuous meditation to Mahadeva. Ultimately Shiva got pleased and permitted him to carry his lingam with him to Lanka. Mahadeva advised him not to place or transfer this lingam to anyone. There should not be a break in his journey to Lanka. If he deposits the lingam anywhere on the earth, in the course of his journey, it would remain fixed at that place forever. Ravana was happy as he was taking his return journey to Lanka.

The gods took it ill. If Shiva went to Lanka with Ravana then Ravana would have become invincible and his evil and anti vadic deeds would have been a big threat. Therefore gods tricked Ravana. It is said that Ravana was offered water by Parvati and through this water which Ravana drank, Parvati made all the waters of three rivers (Ganga, Yamuna and Saraswati) enter into his stomach.

On his way back from Mount Kailash, Ravana felt an urgent need to urinate and as he could not do so with the holy linga in his hand, he started looking for someone who could hold it for him. At the very moment, Lord Vishnu appeared as a Brahmin in front of him. Ravana asked Vishnu to hold the linga and went to release himself. But he could not stop urinating because of the trick played on him. Vishnu, on the pretext of Ravana making it too late, kept the Linga down on earth. The moment Linga was kept down, Ravana stopped urinating!

Legend goes that Ravana needed to wash his hands after urination to make himself pious. Finding no water source around he hit the ground with his fist and a big crater was made which got filled with water.

When Ravana now tried to move the Linga, he could not. Out of anger he press the linga down with his thumb. But after restoring himself, he started to offer his prayers for the Linga.

Shravan Mela

The current shrine has many temples with major shrines of Parvati, Vishnu etc. In the month of Shravan (mid june to mid july) hundreds of thousands of pilgrims come to Baba dham. They carry water form the holy river Ganga, from Sultangunj and travel barefoot more than 100 kilometres on foot to offer to baba. Some of them cover the distance within 24 hours. They are called Dak Bam and they do not stop even once in their journey from Sultangunj to Baba Dham.

Hindu Temples in Haryana

Sannihit Sarovar

Believed to be the meeting point of seven sacred Saraswatis, the sarovar, according to popular belief, contains sacred water. Bathing in the waters of the tank on the days of Amavasyas (nights of complete darkness) or on the days of eclipse bestows blessings equivalent to performing the 'ashvamedh yajna'.

It is believed to offer peace to the wandering and unhappy souls. Prayers and 'pind daan', a memorial service for the dead, is performed here. Alongside the sarovar are small shrines dedicated to Lord Vishnu, Dhruv Narayan, Laxmi Narayan, Dhruv Bhagat, Hanuman and Goddess Durga. The Sannihit tank is believed to be the abode of Lord Vishnu.

Sthaneshwar Mahadev Temple

The ancient Sthanesvara Mahadev Temple, dedicated to Lord Shiva or Mahadev, lies in Thanesar. It was here that the Pandavas prayed to Lord Shiva and received his blessings for victory in the battle of Mahabharata. The ninth Guru, Shri

Tegh Bahadur stayed at a spot near the Sthaneshwar Tirtha that is marked by a gurdwara just besides this temple.

Legend

Legend has it that the waters of the tank adjoining the temple are holy. A few drops of water cured the King Ban of leprosy. And, no pilgrimage of Kurukshetra is believed to be entirely complete without a visit to this holy Temple. The tank and temple lie a short distance from Thanesar town, which gets its name from this temple.

The temple of Sthaneswar is the abode of Lord Shiva say the devote. It once formed an important part of the kingdom of the King Harshavardhana of the Pushyabhuti dynasty. It is also believed that Lord Shiva was first worshipped here in the form of a linga. The ancestor of the Mahabharata heroes, Kuru, performed penance on the banks of the Yamuna and Parshuram, the great warrior and sage killed many Kshatriyas (warriors) here.

Hindu Temples in Himachal Pradesh

Baba Baroh

Baba Baroh is a tehsil in Kangra, India known for a temple made of white marble to Radha Krishan and the Goddess Durga. This temple is famous for the largest amount of white marble used for any temple in Himachal Pradesh. Baba Baroh is located 23 km from Kangra. In this temple there is an idol of Goddess Durga made of metal.

Bhimakali Temple

Shri Bhima Kali Temple is a temple at Sarahan in Himachal Pradesh in India, dedicated to the mother goddess Bhimakali, presiding deity of the rulers of former Bushahr State. The temple is situated about 180 kms from Shimla and is one of 51 Shakti Peethass.

The town Sarahan is known as the gate way of Kinnaur. Down below at a distance of 7 km from Sarahan is the River Satluj. Sarahan is identified with the then Sonitpur mentioned in Puranas.

Legend about Bhimakali

According to a legend, the manifestation of the goddess is reported to the Daksha-Yajna incident when the ear of the Sati fell at this place and became a place of worship as a Pitha-Sthan.

Presently in the form of a virgin the icon of this eternal goddess is consecrated at the top storey of the new building. Below that storey the goddess as Parvati, the daughter of Himalaya is enshrined as a divine consort of Lord Shiva.

The temple complex has another three temples dedicated to Lord Raghunathji, Narsinghji and Patal Bhairva Ji (Lankra Veer)-the guardian deity.

History

Sarahan was the capital of rulers of former Bushahr State. Bushahr dynasty earlier used to controll the state from Kamroo. The capital of state later was shifted to Sonitpur. Later Raja Ram Singh made Rampur as the capital. It is believed that the country of Kinnaur was the Kailash mentioned in Puranas, the abode of Shiva. With its capital at Sonitpur this former princely state was extended up to entire area of Kinnaur where for sometimes Lord Shiva disguised himself as Kirata.

Today, the then Sonitpur is known as Sarahan. Banasura, the ardent devotee of Lord Shiva, eldest among the one hundred sons of great ablative demon King Bali and the great grandson of Vishnu votary Prahlad, during the Puranic age was the ruler of this princely state.

Hidimba Devi Temple

Hidimba Devi Temple is at Manali, a hill station in Himachal Pradesh state of north India. This is an ancient cave temple dedicated to Hidimba Devi, a character in the Hindu epic Mahabharata.

The temple is surrounded by a cedar forest at the foot of the Himalaya mountains. The sanctuary is built over a huge rock jutting out of the ground, which was worshipped as an image of the deity. The structure was built in the year 1553.

Design

The Hidimba Devi Temple has intricately carved wooden doors and a wooden shikhara or tower placed above the sanctuary. The wooden temple design is unusual. The tower is 24 metres tall, composed of three square roofs covered in timber tiles and topped by a brass cone-shaped fourth roof. The inside of the temple is occupied by the enormous rock leaving little usable space except for the ground floor. The temple base is whitewashed mud-covered stonework. The main entrance is elaborately carved of wood believed to be over 400 years old. The theme of the carvings is the earth goddess Durgha. However, only a 7.5 cm (3 inch) tall brass image represents the goddess herself. No idol is enshrined.

A rope hangs down that is said to have been used to tie sinners by the hand and swung them against the rock until they were bloody in the presence of the goddess.

Legend

According to legends Pandavas, the heroes of the Indian epic 'Mahabharat' stayed in Himachal during their exile. In Manali they were attacked by a powerful 'Rakshsa' (demon) Hadimb, in the ensuing fight Bheem, the strongest of the heroes of this epic, killed the demon. Hadimba was the sister of this demon, she married Bheem and gave birth to Ghatotkach who proved to be a great warrior in the war against Kaurvas. When Bhim returned to from exile Hadimba did not return with him, but stayed on and did Tapasya (a combination of meditation, prayer and penance) and over a period of time attained the status of Goddess.

Manikaran

Manikaran is located in a valley between two rivers, northeast of Bhuntar in the Kulu District of Himachal Pradesh. It is at an altitude of 1760 m and is located about 45 kms from Kullu.

Naina Devi

Naina Devi is a town and a municipal council in Bilaspur district in the Indian state of Himachal Pradesh.

Demographics

As of 2001 India census, Naina Devi had a population of 1161. Males constitute 63% of the population and females 37%. Naina Devi has an average literacy rate of 81%, higher than the national average of 59.5%: male literacy is 84%, and female literacy is 75%. In Naina Devi, 11% of the population is under 6 years of age.

The town is famous for the historic temple of Naina Devi.

Temple

Temple of Shri Naina Devi Ji is situated on a hill top in Bilaspur Distt. of Himachal Pradesh in India. This famous temple is connected with National Highway No. 21. The temple at the top of the hill can be reached via road (that curves round the hill up to a certain point) and concrete steps (that finally reaches the top). There is also a cable car facility that moves pilgrims from the base of the hill all the way to the top.

The hills of Naina Devi overlook the beautiful Gobind Sagar lake. The lake is huge and impressive, created by the famous Bhakra-Nangal Dam.

Hindu Temples in Bihar

Vishnupad Temple

The Vishnupada Temple is the main temple in Gaya, India. It is a Hindu temple, dedicated to Lord Vishnu. This temple is located along the Falgu River, marked by a footprint of Vishnu (according to Hinduism), or Buddha (according to Buddhism), incised into a block of basalt.

In Hinduism, this footprint marks the act of Lord Vishnu subduing Gayasur by placing his foot on Gayasur's chest. The present day temple was rebuilt by Devi Ahilya Bai Holkar, the ruler of Indore, in the 18th century.

Hindu Temples in Chhattisgarh

Kaushal

Kaushal is the temple of Kaushalya Mata, the mother of

Lord Rama. It is located at Arang, a famous temple town in Chhattisgarh 30 km from Raipur. It is stated that the region was famous as Kaushal Pradesh.

Kaushal also means Clever or Perfect or Skillful/Skilled. Its also an Indian name. Kaushal can also be a name in India *e.g.* Kaushal Karnad

"Kaushal" is also Surname for "Saraswat Brahmins" They stand Number 1 in Brahmins Category & after this Gaur, Kashmiri etc. pandits came. Very few of Indian Pandits who are Priests or Brahmin or Astrologers are still using this surname with them, they were earlier highly respected for their Knowledge in Astrology & Spiritual Healing & Ayurveda. Most of the Hindu Kings had Kaushal's as their Priests. Their origin was in North India & near the areas of Punjab & Himachal Pradesh. One of renowned Astrologer, Spiritual healer, Yoga teacher is "Pandit Rahul Kaushal" he is carrying the same traditions of his ancestors in Spiritual Healing & Predicting.

Kudargarh

Kudargarh is a famous Hindu pilgrim centre situated in Surguja District of the state of Chhattisgarh in India. It is 98 km from district headquarters of Ambikapur connected by an all weather road. The best time to visit is during Chaitra Navaratra (in the month of April).

Temple

The Maa Bagheshwari Devi Temple dedicated to Goddess Kudargarhi is perched on top of a hill and is the major attraction in Kudargarh.

The history of the temple is obscure. According to Dalton, the temple was built by Baland Kings. Balands were the original rulers of Korea state in 17th century.

Hindu Temples in Delhi

Akshardham

Akshardham is a Hindu temple complex in Delhi, India. It was inaugurated in November 2005 by the President of India,

Abdul Kalam, the Prime Minister, Manmohan Singh, and Pramukh Swami Maharaj, the spiritual leader of BAPS-the organization responsible for the creation of Akshardham. Sitting on the banks of the Yamuna River, adjacent to the proposed Commonwealth Games village, the complex features a large monument, crafted entirely of stone, permanent exhibitions on Bhagwan Swaminarayan and Hinduism, an IMAX cinema, musical fountain, and large landscaped gardens.

The Mandir

The main building at the centre of the complex is a 141ft high monument to Bhagwan Swaminarayan. Designed according to ancient Vedic texts known as the Sthapatya-Shastra, it features a blend of architecutral styles from across India. Within the monument, under the central dome, there is an 11ft high, gilded image of Bhagwan Swaminarayan. He is surrounded by the guru's of the sect.

The building itself is constructed entirely from Rajasthani pink sandstone and Italian Carrara marble, and features no steel or concrete. It's height and location on the banks of the Yamuna mean its presence is felt from afar, and its carved details of flora, fauna, dancers, musicians and deities covering its surfaces from top to bottom, leave most visitors in awe.

Hanuman Temple, Connaught Circus

This 18th century Hanuman Madir is famous Hindu situated on the Baba Kharak Singh Road (old Irwin Road) about 250m southwest of Connaught Circus in central Delhi. It was built by Maharaja Jai Singh in 1724.

Kalkaji

Kalkaji is the name of a famous Hindu *mandir*, or temple of the Hindu Goddess Kali, in the city of Delhi, India.

Situated beyond the commercial complex of Nehru Place lies Kalkaji temple dedicated to the Goddess Kalka Devi. Kalkaji mandir is very famous and has numerous devotees thronging it on many religious occasions throughout the year. Small red flags decorate the temple then, and women outnumber men among the devotees. Folklore is replete with tales of the Kalkaji temple, so much so that one does not know where legend ends and history begins.

The Kali Temple in Kalkaji boasts of an existence of 3,000 years, although the oldest surviving portion of it dates to 1764-1771 when the Marathas were in power, where perhaps even the Pandavas and Kauravas had worshipped during the reign of Yudhisthira.

The temple is situated on a hill and is dedicated to Kali. There is a very distinctive feeling there and the devotees are overwhelmed by light, which stay during the whole night. The power of Kali is ambiguous but powerful.

Devotees also try to meditate there and a spectacular aarti is held at about 7 pm. The temple is also quite near to the Baha'i Temple of India, which is just opposite on the other side of a big road.

Laxminarayan Temple

The Laxminarayan Temple, (also called the *Birla Mandir*), in Delhi, India, is a temple built in honour of the Hindu goddess of wealth, Laxmi, and of her consort, Lord Vishnu – the Preserver of the Hindu Trinity. It is a temple with many shrines, fountains, and a large garden. The temple attracts thousands of devotees on the day of Janmashtami, the birthday of Lord Krishna.

History

The temple was built in 1622 by Vir Singh Deo, and renovated by Prithvi Singh in 1793. Since 1938, funds for further renovations and support have come from the Birla family.

Temple

- The main temple houses statues of Bhagwan Vishnu and Devi Lakshmi.
- The left side temple shikhar (dome) houses Devi Durga, the Hindu goddess of Shakti, the power.
- The right side dome of the temple houses Bhagwan Shiv in meditation mode.

- The right side of the front gate houses Bhagwan Ganesh the elephant headed god of wisdom, etc..
- The left side of the fron gate houses Bhagwan Hanuman, the famous monkey bodied follower, bhakta of Lord Rama.

Nili Chatri

Nilli Chhatri Temple (nili chatri) is a Hindu temple in New Delhi dedicated to Lord Shiva. It is believed that the eldest Pandava brother, Prince Yudhisthira, established the temple and the Nigambodh Ghat adjacent to it, and conducted Aswamedha yajna from here. The temple located in the Yamuna bazar area on the banks of the Yamuna river exists even today. The temple has been mentioned only infrequently in various chronicles of Delhi.

Uttara Swami Malai Temple

Uttara Swami Malai Temple popularly known as Malai Mandir (literally, Hill Temple), is a Hindu temple complex in Delhi primarily dedicated to Lord Swaminatha (more commonly known as Lord Murugan). The main temple within the complex, formally called Sree Swaminatha Swami Temple, houses the sanctum sanctorum of Lord Swaminatha. It is situated atop a small hillock overlooking R.K. Puram and Vasant Vihar in South West Delhi. This is in keeping with the tradition of locating Murugan temples on hills.

The sign outside the main temple is written in Tamil, proclaiming Lord Swaminatha's motto, "Yaamirukka Bayamain" meaning "Why fear when I am there?". The temple is built entirely of granite, and is reminiscent of the Chola style of South Indian Temple Architecture.

Besides the main Swaminatha Swami Temple, the complex contains temples dedicated to Sree Karpaga Vinayagar (elder brother of Lord Swaminatha), Sree Sundareswarar (father of Lord Swaminatha) and Devi Meenakshi (mother of Lord Swaminatha). These subsidiary temples draw inspiration from the Pandya style of South Indian Temple Architecture, as can be seen at the historic Meenakshi Amman Temple in Madurai, Tamil Nadu.

In the Hindu religion, the peacock is considered Lord Swaminatha's mount or vahana. Accordingly, the temple has adopted a peacock as its pet. This peacock can seen and heard among the trees and foliage within the temple compound.

History

Sep 8, 1965 The foundation stone for the temple is laid by M. Bhakthavatsalam, Chief Minister of Tamil Nadu, at a function held under the presidentship of Sri Lal Bahadur Shastri, then Prime Minister of India.

Jun 7, 1973 The main temple for Lord Swaminatha-Sree Swaminatha Swami Temple—is consecrated and a Mahakumbhabhishekham performed.

Jun 13, 1990 The temples for Sree Karpaga Vinayakar, Sree Sundareswarar and Devi Meenakshi are consecrated and Mahakumbhabhishekhams performed. A Jeeranoddharana Kumbhabhishekham for the Lord Swaminatha temple is also performed on the same day.

Jul 7, 1995 The Navagraha temple (nine planets), along with a small temple for Idumban Swami, is consecrated and Kumbhabhishekham performed.

Nov 9, 1997 The Adi Sankara Hall is inaugurated.

Jun 27, 2001 The third Punaruddharana, Ashtabandhana and Swarna-Rajatha Bandhana Mahakumbhabhishekham of the temples are performed by H.H. Kanchi Kamakoti Peethadhipati Sri Jayendra Saraswati Swamigal. H.H. Sri Vijayendra Saraswati Swamigal also participates in the yagna pooja on the night of June 25, 2001.

Bibliography

Allama Wahid-uz-Zaman: *Sahih Muslim Sharif*, Oxford, Delhi, 1986.

Arthur, E. Keith : *The Veda of the Black Yajus School Entitled Taittiriya Samhita* Cambridge Ma, 1914.

Beveridge, A.S. : *Babur-Nama of Zahiruddin Babur*, N.D. Press, New Delhi, 1979.

Beveridge, H. : *Akbar-Nama of Abul Fazl,* Ahmed, New Delhi, 1993.

Biswas, T. K. Kinnara : *Chhavi 2 : Rai Krishnadasa Felicitation Volume*, Banaras, 1981.

Briggs, John : *TarIkh-i-Farishtah*, *History of the Rise of Mahomedan Power in India*, Volume III, New Delhi reprint, 1981.

Brown, W. Norman : *A Pillared Hall from a Temple at Madura, India, in the Philadelphia Museum of Art*, New Delhi, 1975.

Dhaky, Madhusudan A. : *The Vyala Figures on the Mediaeval Temples of India*, Indian Civilisation Series II, Varanasi 1965.

Dumont, P.E. : *Asvamedha. Description du Sacrifice Solenne du cheval dans la culte vedique, d'apres les Textes du Yajurveda Blanc*, Paris, 1927.

Elliot and Dowson : *History of India as Told by its Own Historians*, New Delhi 1990.

Gill, Sandrine : *Phantasmic Anatomy of the Statues of Mathura,* New Delhi. 2000.

Gillaume A. : *Sirat Rasil Allah of Ibn Ishaq* , OUP, Karachi, Eighth Impression, 1987.

Goel, Sita Ram : *Freedom of Expression : Secular Theocracy Versus Liberal Democracy*, Voice of India, New Delhi, 1998.

Goel, Sita Ram : *Hindu Temples : What Happened to Them*, Voice of India, New Delhi, 1993.

Goel, Sita Ram : *The Story of Islamic Imperialism in India* (1982), Voice of India, New Delhi, 1994.

Hamilton, Charles : *Shykh Burhanuddin Ali*, London, 1791.

Heinz , Demisch : *Die Sphinx, Geschichte ihrer Darstellung von den Anfangen bis zur Gegenwart*, Stuttgart, 1977.

Hughes, T.P. : *Dictionary of Islam* (1885), First Indian Edition (reprint), New Delhi, 1976.

Khurd, Amir : *Siyar-ul-Awliya,* New Delhi, 1984.

Lal, K.S. : *Theory and Practice of Muslim State in India*, Aditya Prakashan, New Delhi, 1999.

Lammens, H. : *Islam: Belief and Institutions*, New Impression, London, 1929.

lyer, K. Bharatha : *Animals in Indian Sculpture*, Bombay 1977.

Majumdar, R. C. : *The History and Culture of the Indian People*, The Delhi Sultanate, Bombay, 1960.

Malik, Brigadier S.K. : *The Quranic Concept of War*, Lahore, 1979, New Delhi reprint, 1986.

Margoliouth, D.S. : *Mohammed and the Rise of Islam*, Voice of India, New Delhi, 1985.

Maulana, F. M., Moh. Faruq Khan : *Quran Majid*, Sixth Impression, Rampur, U.P., 1976.

Maulana, A.H. Khan : *Sunan Ibn MAjah*, New Delhi, 1986.

Meenal, R. Kapadia, : *Semi Divine Figures in Ajanta Paintings: Gandharvas and Kinnaras, Indica*,1987.

Mode, Heinz : *Fabeltiere and Damonen in der Kunst, Die fantastische Welt der Mischwesen*, Stuttgart 1974.

Mohammad, Habib and K.A. Nizami: *A Comprehensive History of India, The Saltanat*, New Delhi, 1970.

Muhammad Arif Qandhari : *Tarikh-i-Akbari*, Delhi, 1993.

Muir, Sir William : *The Life of Mahomet*, Voice of India, 1992.

Murthy, Krishna : *K. Mythical Animals in Indian Art,* New Delhi 1986.

Nagar, Shanti Lal : *Composite Deities in Indian Art and Literature*, New Delhi 1989.

Narain, Harsh : *Myths of Composite Culture and Equality of Religions*, Voice of India, New Delhi, 1990.

Nehru, Jawaharlal : *Glimpses of World History* (1934-35), New Delhi, Fourth Impression, 1987.

Niccolo, Machiavelli, : *The Prince*, Jaico reprint, Bombay, 1957.

Pal, Pratapaditya : *Some Reflections on the Therianthropic Avatars of Visnu, Journal of the Asiatic Society of Bombay* 76, 2001.

Panchamukhi, R.S. : *Gandharvas and Kinnaras in Indian Iconography*, Dharwar 1951.

Panchamukhi, R.S. : *Proceedings of Indian History Congress*, New Delhi, 1972.

Rizvi, Saiyid Athar Abbas : *A Hisoty of Sufism in India*, New Delhi, 1978 and 1983.

Rodinson, Maxime : *Mohammad*, London, 1971

Rowlandson, M.J. : *Tuhfat-ul-Mujahideen of Shykh Zeen-ud-deen*, London, 1933.

Saiyyad Muhammad Ibrahim : *Tarikh-i-Tabari*, Volume-I, *Sirat-an-Nabi*, Karachi, New Delhi, 1982.

Sarkar, Jadunath : *History of AurangzIb*, Calcutta, 1928, New Impression, 1972.

Sarkar, Jadunath, : *Fall of the Mughal Empire*, New Delhi, 1991.

Sewell, Robert : *A Forgotten Empire*, New Delhi, 1962.

Shourie, Arun : *Eminent Historians: Their Technology, Their Line, Their Fraud*, New Delhi, 1998.

Swarup, Ram : *Hindu View of Christianity and Islam*, Voice of India, New Delhi, 1992.

Swarup, Ram : *Introduction, See Margoliouth,* Voice of India, New Delhi, 1992.

Swarup, Ram : *Understanding Islam through Hadis: Faith or Fanaticism?* Voice of India, New Delhi, 1984.

Tavakar, N.G. : *The Essays throwing New Light on the Gandharvas, the Apsarases, the Yakshas and the Kinnaras*, Bombay 1971.

Thoma, E. Donaldson . : *Hindu Temple Art of Orissa*, Leiden 1987.

Zimmer, H. : *Zimmer, H., Myth and Symbol in Indian Art and Civilisation,* Princeton, 1974.

Index

A

B

J

K

L

M

N

O

P

R

S

T

U

V

W

Y

❑❑❑